THE MAKING OF SACAGAWEA

THE MAKING
OF SACAGAWEA

A Euro-American
Legend

Donna J. Kessler

The University of Alabama Press

Tuscaloosa and London

∞

The paper on which this book is printed meets the minimum
requirements of American National Standard for Information
Science-Permanence of Paper for Printed Library Materials,
ANSI Z39.48-1984.

Library of Congress Cataloging-in-Publication Data

Kessler, Donna J.
    The making of Sacagawea : a Euro-American legend / Donna J.
Kessler.
        p.   cm.
    Includes bibliographical references (p. 221) and index.
    ISBN 0–8173–0777–X (alk. paper)
    1. Sacagawea, 1786–1884—Legends.   2. Lewis and Clark Expedition
(1804–1806)   3. Shoshoni women—Folklore. I. Title.
F592.7.S123K47   1996
917.804'2—dc20   95–12834

British Library Cataloguing-in-Publication Data available

For my mother Marian
and my daughter Katrina

CONTENTS

ILLUSTRATIONS

Tables

Figures

PREFACE

THIS TEXT, in addition to its very specific investigation of the creation and proliferation of the Sacagawea legend, explores broad implications about the status and function of the "other" in American culture. Overlaying the exploration of the causes and consequences of particular narrative traditions, including myths of native savagery, manifest destiny, and the American frontier, this work exposes some ways in which "otherness," in terms of race and gender, has been comprehended and translated on the continent.

This study also scrutinizes the possibilities and promise of cultural change. Although I ask whether or not America can begin to transform assumptions and meanings long associated with Sacagawea and other "Indian princesses," the question articulates a more sweeping concern. Can Americans begin to change how they perceive each other and comprehend their differences?

Writing a book is never a solitary pursuit, and I have many people to recognize for their aid and support. Particular thanks go to Embry-Riddle Aeronautical University's inter-library loan staff for furnishing crucial items for this study and to Roz Veltanaar for her help in creating a map of the Lewis and Clark Expedition trail. I am also indebted to Dr. John Pope who endorsed my Friday escapes from administrative duties so that I could write.

I am most grateful to Drs. Leonard Carlson, Robert Detweiller, and William Doty for their encouragement, guidance, and suggestions. Their advice and recommendations have helped me to frame the questions necessary to conduct this inquiry and to clarify my thoughts and assumptions about American mythologies and culture. The ideas and viewpoints that I advance here are my own; I accept responsibility for them.

For their patience and endurance, I thank my friends and family. I especially commend Mary Pat and Bob Whiteside and Sarah Fogle for surviving, without too much moaning or too many complaints, those seemingly never-ending conversations prompted by my research. Most important, I owe more than I can articulate to my family and friends who suffered and celebrated with me through the emotional upheavals of this long birthing process.

INTRODUCTION

SACAGAWEA, A SHOSHONE woman—child-captive of the Hidatsas, wife of a French fur trader, and purported guide to the Lewis and Clark Expedition—has become a renowned figure of the American West. Since 1805, scholarly commentaries about Sacagawea and her activities, as well as popular texts presenting her story, have proliferated throughout American culture. Writing thousands of pages of analyses about her, historians, for example, have attempted to dissect every conceivable aspect of her existence.

Unlike most of these researchers, I do not aspire to uncover any "truths" about the historical native woman. I neither support nor negate arguments that have preoccupied Sacagawea scholars and artists in the past. I forward no claims as to the "actual" spelling, meaning, or pronunciation of her name,[1] the precise level and import of her participation in the expedition, or the correct date, location, and cause of her death. This study does not analyze the "realities" of the historical woman's life in any way.

Instead, I focus on what other commentators have not contemplated. Researchers, for instance, have neglected to investigate how the Sacagawea legend initially came to be celebrated by Euro-Americans, in both popular and scholarly arenas. Neither have they explored why her story, unlike others that have eventually faded or died, has endured in the society that first endowed it with such importance. No one has examined, in any detail, the causes and consequences of the Sacagawea legend, a narrative tradition that has informed American culture from the Progressive Era to the present. As David Remley asserts in "Sacajawea of Myth and History," a causal examination of her prominence in Western American history,

along with an investigation of why artists have found her a tempting
figure for portrayal, has long been overdue.

My intent in this project is to scrutinize these very issues. The
cultural creation of an important American legend, the "making"
of Sacagawea as a legendary figure, is the concern of this study.
Rather than encompassing native issues and concerns, Sacagawea
narratives have addressed the needs of Euro-American society. In an
examination of representative texts depicting Sacagawea and her
story from the beginning of the nineteenth century to the present,
I argue that she has become the subject of legend because she has
exemplified critical elements in America's foundation myths.[2]

Not simply a single, traditional story, myth is a pattern of meaningful cultural expressions. A complex of narratives recounting a
culture's true beginnings, myths relate a society's sacred history. A
fundamental premise of this project hinges on the existence of
American foundation, or cosmogonic, myths. Some critics seem to
deny that possibility, citing the absence of supernatural beings who
materialize and act in the world during transcendent times. Others
nonetheless argue that cosmogonic myths may include more recent
stories of territorial settlements; they also assert that myths do not
require personal godly appearances.[3] As William Doty writes in *Mythography*, myths are comprised of a complex of narratives telling a
sacred history of primary, foundational events. Sacred traditions relate a time when a true and crucial reality came into existence. Accomplished through the interventions of sacred entities, these creative feats present people with models of and for beliefs and behaviors
in a society.

American culture has generated just such narratives of the
nation's true beginnings. Clusters of traditional narratives have depicted the most significant mythic patterns accepted by European
colonists in the New World, Euro-America's frontier experiences.
Embodying emotions and principles of colonial expansion, exemplifying a spirit that eventually came to be termed "manifest destiny,"
the 1804–1806 Lewis and Clark Expedition has long vivified those
frontier traditions. In concert with this narrative of America's sacred mission in the wilderness, hundreds of texts have depicted

Sacagawea as the Indian princess associated with the exploration.[4] Such works very often proclaimed her the key to its success. Since frontier myths have informed significant populations on the continent, and since Sacagawea has been intrinsically tied to that endeavor, her name and tale have sustained a high level of recognition and notoriety in America.

Another factor, in partnership with myth, also accounts for the enduring nature of Sacagawea's renown. Flexible within its mythic framework, her narrative enables those who retell it to confront diverse, and often shifting, issues that have received critical attention in America. Fulfilling an assortment of personal, regional, and/or national agendas, artists have addressed such questions as suffrage for women, social taboos against miscegenation, and modern feminism. Narratives conveying Sacagawea's story have illustrated and reinforced abiding national myths while they have simultaneously allowed a populace to test and comment on critical, timely concepts unfolding within a dynamic and diverse society.

This investigation of the Sacagawea legend, a case study of the formation of and changes in certain facets of the dominant culture, entails an examination of Euro-American myths, literature, history, and their interpenetrations. While possibly appearing to manifest only narrow knowledge and meanings, this project nonetheless points to broader issues. An examination of the Sacagawea legend, providing a concurrent analysis of text and three specific contexts, reveals a multifaceted picture of Euro-American society from 1804 to the present.

One contextual investigation reviews ideas and images pointing to the emergence and persistence of American frontier myths. Documenting these patterns of conceptualization, literary texts and historical meanings have continuously raised the same questions and offered relatively static answers to certain social realities on the continent. Works advancing the story of the native woman who accompanied Lewis's and Clark's Corps of Discovery, for instance, confirm their lasting connection to these abiding concepts and demonstrate the mythic core of the Sacagawea narrative. As indicated by the number of creators who have adopted and adapted the tale, in addition to American populations who have persistently embraced such texts, this legend testifies to the functional vitality of frontier traditions.

Overlaid on these persistent conceptions, a second context is also meaningful. As various questions have surfaced within the dynamic culture, artists have exposed and tested timely issues, subjecting them to cultural discussion and scrutinizing them for possible resolution. Again, American texts have revealed cultural pressure points, providing insights into ideological and historical movements in the nation. Works employing the Sacagawea story have divulged their affinities with such concepts, as evidenced in notable changes in narratives from one era to another. Modifications have invariably corresponded to shifts in American values and concerns. These changes prove the flexibility of the legend and perhaps account in part for its continued usefulness in popular production.

A third contextual inquiry locates connections between the personal and the cultural, illustrating how a convergence can result in particular textual production. Close reading of the novel *The Conquest* (1902), for example, confirms that Eva Emery Dye's geographical and historical lifetime intersected with ideas surrounding American myths and with critical issues facing the nation at the turn of the century. Furthermore, evidence suggests that while the novel sprang from diverse factors, it in turn influenced elements that served in its creation. Each iteration of the Sacagawea legend, consisting of a complex nexus of mythic core and individual and social goals, has documented individual and collective responses to cultural values and meanings. Produced as a result of ideas circulating within a society, these works have attempted to perpetuate, refute, and/or revise those assumptions.

Since I argue that the emergence and endurance of the Sacagawea narrative have derived from the legend's connection to a mythic core, chapter 1 begins with a review of frontier myths, ideas emerging from and serving as a charter for Euro-American culture. I then observe the ways in which the Lewis and Clark Expedition has exemplified the most important concrete event in American history embodying that colonial mission on the continent. Because frontier myths have relied on notions of savagery and civilization, I also examine dichotomous images that have defined native peoples on the continent since the seventeenth century. Noteworthy among these conceptions is the female noble savage, the Indian princess. I conclude chapter 1 by examining the continued viability of Indian princess stereotypes, images that have been continuously animated by the Pocahontas and Sacagawea legends.

Although all narratives depicting Sacagawea provide explicit, as well as implicit, commentary about frontier myths, and although one era does not suddenly give way to another, distinct themes and variations have appeared from the early nineteenth century to the 1890s, from the beginning of the Progressive period until the U.S. entry into World War I, from the 1940s to the end of the 1960s, and from 1970 to the present. In chapters 2–5 of this study, I present analyses of several representative Sacagawea works created during each period. Such texts illustrate the initial advent and various adaptations of the Sacagawea legend.

Chapter 2 examines the Lewis and Clark Expedition journals and the earliest editorial compilations of those original diaries. The first works to present Sacagawea to an American audience, these scripts document the nation's most momentous wilderness mission story and specific people's activities within that context. In addition, these journals also reveal their creators' interconnections with social "realities" informing nineteenth-century America. Displaying their immersion in culturally mandated conceptions, the diarists and editors most often employ vocabulary and images of savagism to describe Sacagawea. These men do not see nor do they create an Indian princess as they tap into American mythic needs and desires to differentiate between native savagery and Euro-American civilization. As a result, neither the expedition journals written by Lewis, Clark, or other expedition members nor the earliest editorial compilations of the diaries identify Sacagawea as a cultural heroine. The texts of the Lewis and Clark Expedition nonetheless provide the groundwork upon which the Sacagawea legend has been erected.

Chapter 3 focuses on the birth and florescence of the Sacagawea legend during the Progressive Era. Guided by enduring cultural concerns and by timely issues of their own era, novelists, sculptors, historians, painters, and playwrights expand on foundations provided by the expedition journals. Accepting the bare-bones narrative of the journey, these creators fill lapses and omissions and counter previous interpretations of this native woman. They "create" the legendary Sacagawea. During this period, she becomes an emblem of manifest destiny, her life and actions signifying the progress of civilization. Malleable enough to serve several purposes, her narrative also encompasses considerations other than frontier traditions at a time when Euro-America begins reexamining some of its most respected cultural assumptions about native peoples. During the Progressive Era, for example, creators employ the figure of Sacagawea to comment on the position and role of women in American society. An Indian princess who fulfills multiple purposes in a changing society, Sacagawea is dubbed a legendary American heroine. She is at once embraced by popular culture. No longer just a participant or even an interesting side note of the exploration, she becomes the savior of the mission, an American heroine.

In chapter 4, I survey Sacagawea works produced between the 1940s and 1969. Offering variations and elaborations of the legend, paintings, histories, novels, and films of the period continue to display an Indian princess, the guide to the expedition. Unable, for the most part, to probe contradictions between American heroism and Sacagawea, as well as the marginalization of the princess herself, these works generate many of the same questions that arise during the Progressive period. Such creators, like their predecessors, employ the character of Sacagawea to explore and question important aspects of a dynamic American culture. These texts, for example, engage in both a cultural discourse about native acculturation and an examination of American strictures against interracial relationships. From 1940 through 1969, Sacagawea continues to be a legendary figure of the American West.

Chapter 5 offers an examination of Sacagawea texts created in the past two decades. Some historians of this period attempt to correct "fictions" proliferated in Sacagawea narratives. Continuing a movement begun in the late 1960s, these scholars investigate whether Sacagawea carried out actions that have been ascribed to her. Some cast doubt on the value of Sacagawea's participation in events that led to her renown. Such historical reassessments prove that the legend has no longer sustained absolute cultural consensus on the continent. Despite these historical revisions, most popular portrayals have aspired to do the opposite. Many continue to tout Sacagawea as an American heroine, an emblem of the rectitude of manifest destiny, and they combine that purpose with other goals. A bestselling historical romance, for instance, advances traditional concepts of the Indian princess and additionally declares that Sacagawea was a woman whose character and actions anticipated twentieth-century feminist beliefs, attitudes, and ideals. Since justified frontier traditions have no longer been able to contain discontinuities of frontier traditions, however, at least one script featuring Sacagawea interrogates assumptions associated with myths of manifest destiny.

In characterizing these different periods, I do not suggest that there have been no departures from general patterns established within an era. I nevertheless assert that creators adopting the Sacagawea story have drawn their raw materials from fundamental, ideological concerns born of each period. Significant changes in characterizations have reflected and corresponded to changing needs and interests of American culture. Perhaps more important, such works also document the relative constancy of a broad cultural consensus in response to the Sacagawea legend and stories of all Indian princesses.

I review, in the concluding chapter of this study, how Sacagawea's story has struck a responsive chord in American creators and the nation's audiences for nearly two centuries. Although various critics have called for a halt in the production of works that proliferate frontier myths, especially those reproducing images of Indian princesses, Sacagawea continues to draw champions who market their texts to large Euro-American audiences. In light of such evidence, I investigate ethical implications of the rise and persistence of the Sacagawea legend. While confirming the inherent problems of uncovering or knowing anything about the historical native woman, a person whose identity has essentially constituted an invisibility replaced by mythic precepts, I examine the meanings of that arrogation. In an acknowledgment of forceful cultural realities that have

facilitated the authorship and maintenance of Indian princess legends, I then survey the possibilities of remythologizing native
women of the past and the present.

As this study indicates, Euro-American culture has revealed itself
through its fascination with the Sacagawea legend, through its presentation of the story of an enduring, yet flexible Indian princess.
Many questions associated with the project nonetheless remain un-
answered. Perhaps the most portentous is whether America can and
will someday champion other visions of native cultures and of native
women on the continent.

1

FRONTIER MYTHS AND "INDIAN" IMAGES

Essential Elements for the Making
of the Sacagawea Legend

SACAGAWEA, A WOMAN whose life and activities intersected
with the most significant continental expedition in the history
of the United States, has become the subject of a Euro-American
legend. Because of the number of statues, paintings, novels, films,
musical compositions, and histories that have featured her story, as
well as an abundance of landmarks named in her honor, scholars
from a variety of disciplines declare that she has been the most celebrated of all "American" heroines.

Although the name and story of Sacagawea are relatively well
known throughout the nation, many of the rivers, mountains, and
lakes bearing her name are located in the Upper Midwest and
Northwest, territories featured in retelling her legend. The native
woman's connection to these regions has been psychologically satisfying to wide populations. Materials portraying Sacagawea's story
and her purported likeness have also proved to be economically rewarding. This is certainly true in North Dakota.

When I returned to Bismarck in 1989 for a high school reunion,
I visited the capitol grounds to tour the North Dakota Heritage
Center, a sleek, modern building erected to replace the old, brick
museum. Suggesting a different approach to history, the title of the
new facility emphasizes interconnections with past populations
rather than a preoccupation with displays of interesting, but obso-
lete, artifacts. The Heritage Center also offers another benefit not
provided by the museum, a gift shop. When I entered the store, I

was surrounded by items bearing Sacagawea's name and her supposed image. Pictures, paintings, books, postcards, and note cards imparted her importance to the state, the region, and the nation.

According to gift shop manager Gloria Engel, Sacagawea memorabilia are among their best-selling articles. Engel adds that a postcard of a notable Sacagawea statue is particularly popular with schoolchildren, probably because it is one of the most inexpensive items depicting the legendary heroine. Arnold Doelster, representing the company that distributes the postcard, writes that this item has sold well for more than twenty years. He also states that the Heritage Center gift shop represents only one of Saks News' retail outlets. As Doelster asserts, his company has wholesaled about forty thousand cards.

Another article in the shop offers a different interpretation of the same monument. Every year, store personnel sell nearly two hundred boxes of note cards featuring a pen and ink drawing of the statue. Hometown Prints representative Eileen Linzmeyer writes that the Heritage Center gift shop began purchasing the note cards in 1981. Since then, store personnel have ordered and sold nearly two thousand boxes. As this information establishes, customers of this store alone have circulated close to thirty thousand note cards and thousands of postcards bearing the image of the cultural heroine.

Although visitors from within the state undoubtedly purchase a high percentage of Sacagawea memorabilia, Engel writes that tourists from other states and countries also buy the items. Pictures of and stories about Sacagawea have consistently provided retailers and wholesalers, at least in certain regions, with revenues because she has been hailed an American heroine. Such sales are not simply a result of Sacagawea's renown, however. They have also assured that her name remains prominent in the area, around the country, and in the world. As Sacagawea's fame is circulated by articles and pictures that pervade the culture, they subsequently beget further demand.

The Sacagawea legend has also been useful in marketing tourism in the Upper Midwest. Although North Dakota has extolled Meriwether Lewis, William Clark, and Teddy Roosevelt, the native woman reigns in North Dakota. "Sakakawea" is mentioned, for instance, more than any other person in *Discover the Spirit!*, a 1992 vacation guide to the state. In his welcoming letter to potential visitors, then Governor George Sinner refers to Sacagawea's character and actions to draw people to her "home." Reiterating these same ideas, copy writers promise that tourists coming to North Dakota can see Sacagawea's world and embark on exciting adventures similar to hers. As such anecdotal evidence confirms, Sacagawea has proved to be economically significant, as well as emotionally compelling, in areas boasting a historical connection to her.

Sacagawea's importance has not been limited to regional retail businesses and tourism industries. Long before the North Dakota Heritage Center opened and indeed continuing to the present, Sacagawea has existed in the minds and imaginations of thousands of Americans. Her animation does not speak of her as a person, nor does it confront native or tribal meanings. The Sacagawea legend instead addresses itself intimately to the needs and aspirations of the dominant culture. Her narrative has vivified Euro-American foundation myths.

In this chapter, I probe significant Euro-American cultural assumptions, past and present, in relation to culturally mandated concepts of native peoples, the land, and colonists' sacred duty on the continent. Critics from a variety of disciplines have provided textual evidence from sermons, novels, histories, paintings, statuary, and other cultural artifacts of the existence of America's most compelling myths. While allowing for creative variations and permitting modifications resulting from cultural change, the essential core of the nation's most important mythic patterns has remained unmistakable for more than two centuries. America dawned, according to these accounts, when European settlers secured areas of the continent with the help of a beneficent God. That act inspired belief in a mission to carve out a consecrated space for the erection of a new social order. Incorporating images of the land and native peoples, this compilation of stories constitutes America's cosmogonic narratives.

As colonists landed on the continent, diverse events and their social interpretations coalesced into an array of complementary doctrines and narratives that reflected and indeed crystallized America's foundation myths. These frontier traditions developed as European peoples experienced dislocations during encounters with unfamiliar, and therefore threatening, indigenous peoples and their social systems. Subsequent cultural and military clashes produced Euro-American consensus concerning native populations. Springing from these circumstances and spawning a profusion of narratives, frontier myths defined and justified the colonial enterprise. They also provided models for abiding attitudes and actions as Euro-American settlement proceeded west across the continent.

Eventually bearing the composite, streamlined designation "manifest destiny," frontier narratives have asserted American prerogatives to territorial security, Euro-Americans' geographical predestination to occupy the continent's "natural boundaries," their just claim to the soil based on perceptions of aboriginal economies, and their ordained mission to extend the area of freedom. As Albert K. Weinberg argues, manifest destiny signifies one of the most enduring and profound facets of the nation's history of ideas.[1] Weinberg accedes that these notions have formed a body of narrative justifications and rationalizations supporting American territorial expansion. He nonetheless argues that they emerged not simply from self-interested hypocrisy, but derived from unconscious need. They flourished because of their power to explain the world. Weinberg essentially outlines America's most significant mythic patterns.

As reflected in these traditional narratives, one unique circumstance profoundly influenced American culture. Each successive American "wilderness," located just west of pioneer settlements, required transformation into consecrated territory. America's primal moment thus recurred until the end of the "frontier period" in the late 1880s as trailblazers repeatedly enacted sacred stories of origin for more than two centuries. Cultural texts depicting these moments continuously revitalized America's cosmogonic myths, reinforcing principles that initially engendered those traditions. Frederick Jackson Turner, a prominent twentieth-century American historian, sums up the importance of successive wildernesses in his controversial thesis, *The Significance of the Frontier in American History*. As Turner argues, the American frontier embodied a process rather than a place. The most important factor in the New World, the frontier precipitated the development of uniquely American attitudes, identities, and institutions.

Although Turner claims that individualism, democracy, and nationalism spread as the "free land" receded, Patricia Limerick focuses on other implications of America's territorial expansion. Frontier myths, which have embraced and illustrated concepts of manifest destiny, did not just shape attitudes and actions in the past; they have continued to inform present problems in America. As Limerick argues, a key doctrine of these traditions has included an unshakable confidence in Euro-American rights to the land. Another is the persistence of certain imagery in portrayals of America's aboriginal populations. In addition to invigorating activity on the continent, successive frontiers have also helped to maintain the functional vitality of America's foundation myths. In a reciprocal relationship, myths have proliferated cultural ideologies through diverse narratives that have simultaneously illustrated, disseminated, and justified concepts of the land and native peoples.

In several analyses focusing on American mythic texts, literary critics have illuminated meanings emerging from frontier traditions. Henry Nash Smith, for example, traces mythic imagery associated with the West as presented in various American works ranging from travel brochures to popular novels. In his germinal study, *Virgin Land: The American West as Symbol and Myth,* Smith asserts that such scripts have illustrated collective attitudes about the continent. Successively portraying the West as a potential pathway to the riches of the Far East, an untamed wilderness requiring civilization's penetration and control, and a garden allowing the agrarian dream to flourish, American texts have defined the wilderness. They have also consistently embraced one cultural absolute, Euro-American primacy on the continent. Acknowledging his own immersion in cultural ideologies in a recent reassessment of his work, Smith writes, in "Symbol and Idea in *Virgin Land,*" that frontier traditions have long invigorated unexamined social realities in America.

Offering a most important study concerned with frontier ideologies, Roy Harvey Pearce concentrates on the impact of Euro-American interactions with native peoples in *Savagism and Civilization.*

Examining political pamphlets, missionary reports, literary texts, and anthropological observations produced in America between the early seventeenth and mid-nineteenth centuries, Pearce contends that these writings promulgated ideas about indigenous groups by using repeated symbols. Certain significations achieved a cultural consensus as creators employed a narrow band of persistent, socially condoned images. Collective ideas, born of symbols and imagery alike, consistently designated America's original inhabitants as "savage" while contrasting images identified Euro-American settlers as "civilized." America, according to the visions of such works, has consisted of a civilized continent, secured by pioneers who rescued it from profane contamination. Such pioneers additionally protected it, through constant vigilance, from further violation, infringement, or encroachments by savages. This dichotomy of savagism and civilization has operated as an important element of America's cosmogonic myths.

Investigating American conceptions of both the land and natives in *Regeneration through Violence,* Richard Slotkin examines American literary texts published from 1620 to the 1850s. America's cosmogonic myths, argues Slotkin, dawned only when distinctive interactions of individuals and cultures resulted in particular events in a unique place. This nexus produced collectively held ideas of the world and the "other" in narratives created by various groups encountering one another on the American continent. Although he briefly discusses native societies, Slotkin primarily focuses on myths emerging in colonial culture. He claims that as Euro-Americans encountered differing social systems, they labelled natives "savage." They also defined land outside the settlements as "wilderness."

As these and other critics point out,[2] America's most fundamental myths have been vivified by a profusion of narratives. Revealing fundamental, foundational ideas and emotions, frontier traditions have defined sacred purposes for the culture and have provided models for beliefs and behaviors of its population. Two concepts, the necessity of expanding the area of civilization and the requirement of assimilating or eliminating native cultures because of their inherent savagery, have functioned as the most important elements of these mythic patterns. Possessing the status of "reality," such ideas have informed beliefs and actions across the continent.

The Lewis and Clark Expedition of 1804–1806 explicitly illustrated, in philosophy as well as in action, the nation's foundation myths. Also known as the Corps of Discovery, the exploration signified civilization's rightful penetration into a savage wilderness. As historian Bernard DeVoto argues in *The Course of Empire*, the expedition was no mere fact-finding mission. Thomas Jefferson, who had long planned the journey, outlined its manifold purposes: discovering the North West Passage, surveying uncharted areas, asserting American authority over the huge expanse of the Louisiana Purchase, and strengthening U.S. claims to the Columbia.

DeVoto further claims that aspirations to expand America to the edge of the continent constituted only part of the expedition's purpose. Another objective was to institute trade with indigenous tribes and nations while simultaneously asserting American sovereignty over them. Functioning as ambassadors of America's "Great Father," Lewis and Clark viewed themselves as offering the benefits of an "advanced" culture to native peoples. The spirit and actuality of exploration not only represented American notions of the land but also illustrated long-standing actions and beliefs concerning aboriginal populations. Associated with dominant ideologies of continental expansion and assimilation or removal of its native inhabitants, the trek embodied American frontier myths.

Acknowledging the mythic import of the expedition, many critics have designated the endeavor as "America's national epic."[3] Helen West argues, for instance, that the expedition continues to capture the imaginations of generations because it has symbolized uniquely American perceptions of strength, courage, and justice. Demonstrating the saga's grasp on an American populace in each decade since the return of the Corps, amateur and professional researchers have generated thousands of pages of data, drawings, maps, statues, paintings, and photographs featuring the Lewis and Clark Expedition.

The Corps of Discovery has additionally exemplified another aspect of frontier traditions. As Annette Kolodny asserts in *The Lay of the Land,* American mythic texts reveal that male images of a female continent have emerged from two conflicting psychological desires. Whereas many works by southern males have reflected passive responses to absolute sensory gratification of the land as mother nurturer, texts emerging from other areas, especially those of America's successive frontiers, have illustrated men's active attempts at penetration and mastery of the wilderness.

In her later work, *The Land Before Her: Fantasy and Experience of the American Frontiers, 1630–1860,* Kolodny traces pioneer women's responses to successive wildernesses. Rather than dream about eroticized dominance of vast territorial stretches, Euro-American women visualized smaller spaces, cultivated gardens, and sanctified human communities. Although Kolodny argues that women's texts differed from those of Euro-American men and while she speculates that such imaginative constructs might have prevented much destruction of the land, she also acknowledges that American mythic traditions have virtually excluded female perceptions. Frontier myths have instead emphasized and reinforced male fantasies of penetration and mastery. Concurring with Kolodny as he describes the "superb masculinity" of the West, Stan Steiner states that American texts and culture have romanticized the conquest of the land.[4] The Lewis and Clark Expedition has symbolized that romance.

An anecdote suggests that the mythic appeal of Lewis and Clark's endeavor endures, for at least some Americans. At a 1992 deans' council luncheon at Embry-Riddle Aeronautical University, one administrator asked how my research was progressing. As I began to reply, one of the deans enthusiastically proclaimed he had walked and driven substantial segments of the Lewis and Clark Trail. Three other males in attendance soon joined in the conversation, recounting their own involvement and even identification with the captains who "opened up" America. All three stated that they had traced parts of the original journey, either through actual exploration or reading. Illustrating what Helen West calls the "irresistible" allure of the expedition journals, the first administrator then recounted how these narratives had captivated him as a boy and an adult.

Many researchers, nearly all men, have traveled large portions of the trail. Some have tackled the entire journey before submitting their own assessments of and contributions to the story of the expedition.[5] Perhaps at least viscerally aware of the journey's mythic meanings, these men and others have engaged in ritual reenactments of gallant penetration into an unknown wilderness. Their actions and words subsequently guarantee the expedition's visibility and believability as they extol its relevance to an American populace.

Although its newest enterprise was not realized, Walt Disney Company, one of the nation's most important corporate myth-makers, has recently joined others in an attempt to glorify the epic journey. Announcing its intent to create a theme park entitled "Disney America" in Virginia, Disney planned to enable visitors to relive the greatest moments in American history. A Lewis and Clark Expedition ride was to have been among the most important features of the new facility. As such evidence attests, this mission continues to resonate in American culture, evoking a positive impression of masculine action on the continent.

A participant in the most consequential continental expedition in the nation's history, Sacagawea has become an important adjunct of frontier traditions. Because hundreds of texts have connected her to this endeavor and declared her its sometime "savior," she has illustrated and validated critical facets of myths of manifest destiny. Very often featured as the sole native joining the Corps of Discovery, Sacagawea has come to signify "Indian" compliance with the mission to carve a sacred space out of the wilderness. As a result, creators have "made" her into an American cultural heroine. Texts embracing her story have initiated and propagated the Sacagawea legend, which has addressed the needs and interests of the dominant culture. Most of these works have simultaneously sustained socially constructed notions about the land, and many have reinforced stereotypes of America's indigenous peoples.

Offering meticulous examinations of nearly four centuries of characterizations, scholars argue that Euro-Americans have consistently stereotyped individual natives as well as tribal groups in all media and genres.[6] "Indian" stereotyping has provided the nation with a shared set of overly simplified notions upon which many people have based their attitudes and actions. While such images may contain certain elements of truth, the preponderance of ethnic and racial stereotyping invariably focuses on undesirable traits and assumes that all members of a group possess those characteristics. Such categorization fails to differentiate among individuals. Melding limited images with corresponding negative assessments, the term "Indian" continues to function as an intellectual classification in American culture, one that justifies prejudices and discriminatory behaviors.

Although many studies simply describe and trace specific imagery associated with native peoples, Lucille Van Keuren identifies the cultural causes of such stereotyping. As she argues, in the first few decades of the colonies, Euro-American diaries, letters, and other personal writings described natives who displayed a wide variety of behaviors and attributes. Only certain traits resonated in the dominant culture, however, and these quickly became culturally approved Indian qualities. These fixed patterns of portrayal, other researchers add, have illustrated and justified tenets of manifest destiny throughout the eighteenth, nineteenth, and into the twentieth centuries.

Lacking their own authorship as well as possessing little political power, native peoples have been unable to counter stereotypical images with any success. As Kathleen Houts and Rosemary S. Bahr write in "Stereotyping of Indians and Blacks in Magazine Cartoons," depictions of African Americans have changed considerably over the last forty years. Alterations resulted from increased power exerted by African Americans and/or their supporters after the civil rights movement gained momentum and acceptance in the mid 1960s. Corresponding revisions of "Indian" portrayals have not occurred. Indigenous peoples of the United States, claim Houts and Bahr, have never obtained a political base vital enough to exact such modifications. As a result, Euro-Americans have consistently defined indigenous peoples by collapsing tribal and individual distinctions and by delimiting them through a narrow band of unchanging traits and behaviors. Myriad texts present undifferentiated beings, stereotypes of natives repeatedly bearing messages of the innate savagery and racial inferiority of America's aboriginal populations.

Indian stereotypes were at first summarized and standardized in sermons, histories, and captivity narratives. Publishing stories of their captivity after redemption back into "civilization," colonial men and women initiated and propagated ethnocentric observations of native life. Such works as Mary Rowlandson's *A True Story of the Captivity and Restoration of Mrs. Mary Rowlandson, A Minister's Wife in New England: Wherein is Set Forth, The Cruel and Inhumane Usage she Underwent amongst the Heathens, for Eleven Weeks time: And her Deliverance from them,* published in 1632, and John Gyles's *Memoirs of Odd Adventures, Strange Deliverances, Etc., in the Captivity of John Gyles, Esq., Commander of the Garrison on St. George River, in the District of Maine,* published in 1736, defined the Indian for colonial audiences. Eventually evolving into immutable types, these patterns spread throughout Euro-American culture.

In addition to captivity narratives, eighteenth-century paintings, statues, and novels carried the central message of Indian savagery. Important contributions to the refinement and crystallization of Indian stereotypes also occurred during the nineteenth century, as travelers, ethnographers, novelists, and painters, such as George Catlin and Karl Bodmer, popularized cultural perceptions of fierce and unequivocally barbaric Plains tribes. In addition to literary and artistic analyses, researchers have examined thousands of textbooks in search of "Indian" imagery. Demonstrating a consensus, these scholars state that only occasionally has any textbook presented an accurate picture of individual natives or their tribal existence in the past or present. Even recently published textbooks offer familiar Indian stereotypes, resulting in trivialized and distorted characterizations.

Artistic and historical texts have not sufficed as the sole bearers of Indian stereotypes to the American population. Reinforcing ideas established in print, in marble, and on canvas, movies and television have also presented stereotyped Indians. American films have conflated the complexity of native existence into simplified patterns in order to explain the rectitude of the "civilizing" mission on the continent. Although a few critics believe that within the last twenty-five years film makers have begun to break down traditional stereotyping by producing pro-Indian films, others disagree.[7] While dissenters concur that recent films have incorporated certain changes in portrayals of Indians, they proclaim that even the best examples are still steeped in popular stereotypes. No other group, argue Ralph Friar and Natasha Friar, has been made to assume such a narrow and permanent fictional identity. Each medium has presented examples of a new generation's reinvention of the Indian.

While Douglas Leechman claims that Indian stereotypes have undergone eight transformations, Rayna Green outlines three distinct types in "The Only Good Indian." William W. Savage, Roger L. Nichols, Richard Brenzo, and many others nonetheless argue that two general patterns have delineated Indian stereotypes. Indians have been portrayed, according to such critics, as either noble or ignoble savages. Although these images might appear to assert contrasting conceptions, both have relentlessly outlined an inferior species. Each has proved useful to the dominant ideology in its own way.

Cruelty, barbarity, and treachery have characterized the very bad Indian, generally known as the ignoble or howling savage. These portrayals first arose from sensational accounts of Euro-American captivities by tribal groups. Written narratives of confrontations between natives and European settlers, such as those produced during the King Philip's and Pequot wars, supplemented and amplified early negative portraits. Transported to later frontiers, images of the devil's minion and fiendish torturers persisted. As Louise Barnett documents in "Nineteenth-Century Indian Hater Fiction: A Paradigm for Racism," works offering conceptions of ignoble savagery served the dominant culture well. Reinforcing myths of manifest destiny, they substantiated the inherent savagism of America's indigenous populations regardless of tribe or nation. Stories of captivity and war justified the extermination of America's indigenous peoples, notwithstanding proof of any individual's or group's actual participation in "atrocities."

Not all texts have portrayed natives as ignoble savages; others have depicted very good Indians. Characterized as virtuous, albeit primitive, children of the forest, essentially an extension of untamed nature, noble savages exuded qualities of self-sacrifice and trustworthiness. While some critics have identified the ignoble savage as the most damaging Indian stereotype, many others agree that the noble savage has comprised as negative a stereotype as that of the howling savage. Although docile behaviors did not mandate their extermination, very good Indians obstructed the progress of civilization across the continent. American texts have permitted only two alternatives for the noble savage, to assimilate into the dominant culture or to vanish. In either case, the images have explained frontier myths at the same moment that mythic traditions have justified such portraits.

While most literary and historical studies focus on stereotypes of Indian men, native women have by no means escaped narrow and fixed portrayals. Images of Indian women have also been clichéd, trivialized, and sentimentalized. As various scholars argue, Euro-American writers have always filtered characterizations of native women through their own perceptions and cultural expectations.[8] Patterns defining Indian women have melded two traditions of mythic conceptions, those qualities typifying women and those traits associated with savagery, both noble and ignoble.

As a number of studies claim, many cultures have outlined similar interpretations of woman as "other" because of supposedly innate sexual characteristics. Since maleness has been the standard measure, the point of reference for all things within these societies, womanhood has been deemed a mysterious departure from that norm, argues Teresa de Lauretis. This kind of categorization has resulted in several narrowly defined and illustrated stereotypes of women, including the wife, the mother, the siren, and the witch. Presenting an analysis of female "otherness," Sherry Ortner contends that most societies have viewed women as more closely allied with nature. Although one might assume the association would result in positive evaluations, Ortner argues that nature, in this context, has signified various ambiguous forces working outside the understandable and controlled male world of culture.

If fixed patterns have defined women as "other" based on both vague and specific notions and images, then stereotypes describing native women have assigned them to an even more marginalized position. Characteristics of the "natural" and "other" woman have combined with those of "savagery," creating a composite stereotype. Doubly removed, Indian women have become the "other others." They have been defined by their incomprehensible, savage qualities, holding no legitimate place in a civilized world.

Just as two distinct patterns have characterized Indian men, so too have they narrowly delimited native women. Fitting into classifications of ignoble and noble savagery, native women have been categorized as either squaw/drudges or Indian princesses, respectively. The squaw stereotype emerged from captivity narratives,[9] the same sources that supplied the dominant culture with concepts of the male ignoble savage. Captivities and other Euro-American texts have represented squaws as no more than slaves to their families in youth and to their husbands after marriage. Dragging and dressing meat, bearing children in the woods by themselves, and suffering the blows of men, these women have been portrayed, in some cases, as victims of a savage culture that could never comprehend the elevated treatment females deserve. Conversely, other Euro-American works have outlined squaw/drudges who behaved as savagely as their male counterparts. Seeming to combine siren and fury imagery with ignoble savage stereotypes, Indian women purportedly performed a variety of illicit and gruesome activities. Not only were they capable of lewd behaviors in an attempt to seduce "civilized" men, but they also wielded tomahawks and knives, torturing and murdering captive men, women, and children.

Although American works have generally offered only glimpses of the squaw/drudge, this stereotype nonetheless validated the message of manifest destiny by supplying proof of all Indians' inherent savagery. When the squaw, for example, has been defined as the perpetrator of heathen viciousness, her eradication, like that of the male savage, became necessary to create a safe haven for "civilization." In other cases, when texts have portrayed drudges as victims of their own societies, America simply justified its mission into the wilderness and the annihilation of all native cultures by proclaiming itself the savior of a downtrodden womanhood. Whether cast as villain or victim, the savage squaw/drudge rightfully lost her life or her culture.

While Euro-America has never canonized squaws, the opposite has been true of Indian princesses. Although traditional native groups had no concept of royalty, and thus would never have ordained any native girl or woman as a "princess," American playwrights, poets, novelists, and producers have offered sustained examinations of this truly "heroic" figure for more than two centuries. According to E. McClung Fleming in "Symbols of the United States: From Indian Queen to Uncle Sam," the Indian princess was the first figure to symbolize the promise of America, a place separated from Old World influences.

The Indian princess stereotype has actually operated as a composite portrait, a wedding of idealized womanhood and of noble savagery. Synthesizing characteristics of a sex object with those of the Virgin Mary, the archetypal ideal woman possesses and displays youth, beauty, grace, kindness, gentleness, and self-sacrifice. Echoing and amplifying such exemplary qualities, compatible traits also identify the Indian princess as a noble savage. This royal character emanates primitive virtues of childlike innocence, respect, tenderness, trust, and trustworthiness.

Despite some obvious dissimilarities in portrayals of Indian men and women, the Indian princess stereotype would not appear to function differently, within the dominant culture, from that of the noble male savage. Rayna Green nonetheless claims in "The Pocahontas Perplex" that the female image is unique. American texts have related, through portrayals of the Indian princess, a character who does not fit into the context of her own culture. Instead, she occupies an ambiguous position between savagery and civilization, both physically and mentally. Her skin, for example, is whiter than most natives, but darker than whites. More important, when the Indian princess acts, she does so to aid a white man or men, out of loyalty to his/their sacred mission into the wilderness.

The female noble savage, a character whose depiction has arisen from a mixture of racism and sexism, has been defined as good because she is receptive to and fosters the invasion of the wilderness by a superior "civilization." While her efforts have automatically separated, if not alienated, her from her own traditions and people, she becomes the heroine of the dominant culture. The Indian princess, in effect, has been evaluated in a positive light only because she reflects the needs and goals of the very society that has defined her.

In spite of her cultural status, the Indian princess could never hope for total integration into the social system she has helped to establish because she can never escape her primitive heritage.

Indian princess images possess a pervasiveness and power in America. As Raymond Stedman writes, Marlon Brando attempted to tap into positive emotions surrounding the image of Indian princesses in 1973 when he sent Sacheen Littlefeather to the Academy Awards ceremony to protest America's treatment of its native populations. Attired in stereotypical "traditional" clothes of buckskin and fringes, she symbolized the primitive nobility of all Indian princesses. Although Brando did not intend it, Littlefeather's appearance and verbal message projected complex, contradictory meanings. Ironically, at the same instant Littlefeather verbally criticized U.S. political policies, she symbolized the rectitude of the nation's mission on the continent. Despite her words, as the Indian princess, Littlefeather physically projected mythic images and cultural ideologies that helped to establish the very policies she denounced. Whether the traditional interpretation of this image, as reinforced by Littlefeather's physical appearance, fortified, countered, or cancelled Brando's political intentions remains unknown.

In *Custer Died for Your Sins,* Vine Deloria, a prominent writer and attorney of Lakota heritage, also relates an anecdote highlighting the pervasiveness of Indian princess stereotyping. When Deloria was the executive director of the National Congress of American Indians in the 1960s, thousands of people visited his office each year. They proudly proclaimed their Indian heritage as handed down by grandmothers. Each maternal ancestor was invariably, and miraculously, a princess of her tribe. No tourist ever mentioned his/her relationship to a native man. As Deloria argues and other critics have illustrated, this phenomenon occurs because Euro-American culture has applauded its Indian princesses.

An additional factor helps to explain why Indian grandmothers are eagerly acknowledged. By maintaining at least one generational remove from savagery, anyone asserting such a relationship essentially certifies his/her assimilation into American culture and civilization. In spite of the Indian princess's inability to escape a native birthright, her innate understanding of justice spurred her to help in the conquest of the wilderness. Although she occupied a marginal space between savagery and civilization, her progeny have easily integrated. They, in effect, offer physical proof of the virtues of manifest destiny and the synergism of American democracy. By declaring an Indian princess grandmother, American men and women have maintained their positions within the dominant culture. They simultaneously avow their connection to, and inheritance of, the nobility that helped to create it.

Extensive literary and historical research, in addition to this anecdotal testimony, confirms that the Indian princess has been one of the most significant images produced by Euro-American culture. In spite of their usefulness in reinforcing frontier myths, few Indian princesses have attained long-standing, nationwide acclaim. An apparent reason for their dearth relates to Doty's discussion in "Silent Myths Singing in the Blood: The Sites of Production and Consumption of Myths in a 'Mythless' Society." As Doty argues, until recently American society has venerated the non-mythic, has insisted on its own mythlessness, and has denied the intersection of those two classifications. Although Doty asserts that images and stories of myth have been, and continue to be, as important in America as in any other culture, the nation seems to have demanded a prerequisite of its cultural heroines. Their narratives must be grounded in the semblance of historical fact. Whereas Indian princess legends have purportedly arisen from historical fact, their cultural prominence ironically has sprung from mythic appeal and meaning. Such a relationship belies the myth/history dichotomy that America has certified, an association that these legends themselves have seemed to verify.

Pocahontas and Sacagawea have achieved the status of American cultural heroines, both women passing the two-pronged test of historicity and mythic appeal. Several literary and history researchers proclaim Pocahontas as the most renowned of all native women ever having lived in the United States.[10] Frances Mossiker carefully outlines the historical facts of Pocahontas's life. He also supplies speculative recreations of related events based on his knowledge of native and colonial cultures. The most important features of Pocahontas's narrative, argues Mossiker, have been her royal status as the prized daughter of the chieftain Powhatan and her rescue of Captain John Smith of the Jamestown colony. Because of her inherently superior nature, Pocahontas supposedly demonstrated her willingness to sacrifice her own royal life in Smith's place.

Numerous scholarly disputes have arisen over the historical accuracy of details associated with the supposed rescue of Smith and other aspects of the Pocahontas story, including her subsequent conversion to Christianity, her marriage to John Rolfe, the birth of a son, a trip to England, and her death. As Philip Young writes in "The Mother of Us All: Pocahontas Reconsidered," what actually happened makes no difference. Of importance is the way the legend has captured America's imagination, the way that Pocahontas has permeated the dominant culture as a figure in paintings and sculpture, the heroine of poetry, drama, and fiction, and the focus of biographies and essays.

Mossiker also traces the proliferation of the Pocahontas legend, asserting that important aspects of her narrative have coalesced, begetting the female noble savage stereotype. Serving as the model for all subsequent noble Indian women, the Pocahontas narrative has supplied physical and mental traits later standardized as typical of all Indian princesses. A young, beautiful woman, innately aware of the superiority of colonial culture, Pocahontas risked her life to save the only man capable of safeguarding Euro-American lives in the New World. By rescuing Smith, Pocahontas preserved the civilization she later embraced. Although Rayna Green asserts in "The Pocahontas Perplex" that Pocahontas has symbolized an integration of disparate cultures, the synthesis does not entail a blending of equal parts. The Pocahontas narrative confirms that a painless fusion of colonial and native worlds produces no synergistic social systems, but reproduces the dominant culture. As Euro-American society has reinforced conceptions of its own superiority, the Pocahontas legend has operated as a constituent of national mythologies.

Mossiker claims that no native woman has ever seized American culture so profoundly as Pocahontas, but Sacagawea is a premier Indian princess as well. Her narrative has also manifested the basic qualities of a Euro-American cultural heroine: historicity and mythic appeal. Providing the historical foundation, expedition journals document her existence. They also capture her activities, which have been easily tied to frontier traditions. In spite of, or perhaps because of, significant omissions in these primary sources, others have subsequently built upon this infrastructure. Myriad American texts have created the legendary Sacagawea. Appearing as the sometime savior of the Lewis and Clark Expedition, she is that most astute primitive who alone can realize that white settlement endows natives with blessings of contact with a more advanced civilization. Her story points out that people who might be construed as potential victims of the national enterprise instead become benefactors of its enactment.

In an examination of social studies texts and biographies written for children, Carol Haupt argues that Indian princesses are beginning to lose their hold over the American imagination. Basing her conclusions on scaled scores of characters' activity levels, illustrations accompanying the written text, and evaluative terms employed in descriptive passages, Haupt writes that this stereotypical pattern has nearly disappeared.

A closer look at some of Haupt's premises produces doubt about her conclusions, however. First, Haupt admits that in the twelve social studies texts she evaluates, Pocahontas and Sacagawea receive nearly universal attention and emphasis. The same works most often offer negligible or no information about other native women. Secondly, although she identifies seven prominent historical Indian women for her research, Haupt can locate only one biography about each person, except for those works concerned with Pocahontas and Sacagawea. Ten works focus on each of these two renowned Indian princesses, and they are the only biographies of native women available in most libraries. Pocahontas and Sacagawea, attaining legendary status because of their purported roles in helping "civilization" to achieve its goals, thus continue to be featured in textbooks and biographies, most often to the exclusion of other historical native women.

In addition to the number of children's biographies featuring premiere Indian princesses, many publishers persist in assigning Pocahontas and Sacagawea prominent space in social studies textbooks. Because publishers have recently begun to consider gender and ethnicity as they allocate space in texts, they have proliferated, rather than undermined, Indian princess stereotyping through their editorial choices. Because they have responded to the demands and expectations of a market economy, as well as the constructs of cultural myths, biographers, editors of textbooks, and publishers have conjoined in reiterating the importance of Indian princesses and maintaining the traditional meanings of their existence.

Despite Haupt's assertions, America's most prominent Indian princesses, Pocahontas and Sacagawea, receive nearly exclusive attention in children's textbooks and biographies. The language used to assess them has not changed significantly either. In her research, Haupt designates certain adjectives, including "helpful," "determined," "courageous," "friendly," and "brave," as "positive" characteristics. Indeed, writers have implied their approval of Sacagawea when describing her as "helpful." What Haupt and many other writers, publishers, and readers have not explored, nonetheless, is that these socially approved evaluations have eliminated the possibility of conflicting interpretations.

Although not part of North American legend, an important Mexican myth has offered just such alternate meanings, confirming that different understandings of a prominent native woman are possible. Precluding "positive" interpretations of a native woman who aids a white man, repudiating Indian princess imagery, folklore about Cortez's native mistress has defined her as the symbol of native capitulation to Spanish conquest. Even more pointedly, the Aztec noble woman Malinche, also known as Malintzin or Marina, has become the embodiment of female treachery. She is a traitor to native men and her own heritage. Many versions of the Malinche tradition have contended that her parents offered her to Cortez in exchange for their son's advancement. The circumstances of her becoming Cortez's concubine, the mother of illegitimate children, and the conquistador's adviser have not absolved her. According to Mexican narratives, she was guilty of sexual betrayal and genocide. As several recent studies assert, the Malinche legend has pervaded Mexican culture, engendering, disseminating, and maintaining negative interpretations of Chicana women.[11]

If Malinche folklore has related a plot not significantly different from narratives of Sacagawea and Pocahontas, how can cultural meanings of the Mexican legend contrast so sharply with those of Indian princesses of North America? Perhaps numerous understandings of all three native women have been enunciated by varying populations, but only those serving particular ideological purposes have survived. If such a process has transpired, another question arises. How and why has one culture disseminated meanings so profoundly different from another?

The answer could lie in differences between Catholicism and Anglo-Saxon Protestantism and/or disparities between conquistadors and colonists. Different interpretations of the legends, in addition, might have stemmed from dissimilar missions in the New World. While conquistadors came to explore, conquer, and plunder, colonists arrived on the North American continent determined to make it their permanent home. Since then, Euro-Americans have prevailed as the dominant culture in the United States, a society that has dedicated itself to its separation from, and superiority to, native groups on the continent. Created by the dominant culture, the Sacagawea legend has reflected that ideology. The construction of Mexican "realities" undoubtedly underwent similar processes. The Malinche legend, however, has been interpreted by Mestizo males, the group whom Malinche purportedly betrayed. For each narrative, interpretation of the native woman and her actions has depended upon who has shared an "interest" in the story and who has "owned" the rights to determine meanings.

Suppression of alternate interpretations inevitably occurs when culturally condoned understandings become fortified and enriched. Such has been the case with the legendary Sacagawea, at least until recently. Since Euro-America has assumed ownership of the Sacagawea narrative, almost no text embracing her story has pondered a number of compelling questions. Could credible alternate motivations, for example, have spurred her actions? Might Sacagawea have hurt others by helping the explorers to reach the Pacific? Would some readers interpret her behaviors as other than helpful? Rather than address these issues, most Euro-American writers and artists have applied "positive" words and meanings to Sacagawea. They have sustained the viability of the Indian princess stereotype as they have silenced other representations.

Certain critics argue that it is time for Euro-Americans to ask those perplexing questions, time to confront their ignorance of native populations, time to see that what has previously been thought does not approach reality. But what these exhortations seem to ignore are the power and pervasiveness of culturally created realities. Although I concur with the spirit of these admonitions and recognize that stereotypical images of Indians tell very little about the peoples they appear to describe, I believe that an investigation of such notions reveals important truths. An analysis of those portraits can relate much about the culture from which they have sprung. Produced over nearly two centuries, texts embracing the Sacagawea story illustrate the birth, growth, and changes in Euro-American conceptions of one of the nation's most important Indian princesses. These works also demonstrate the power of cultural ideas and imagery.

2

ORIGINAL EXPEDITION JOURNALS AND EARLIEST EDITIONS
Raw Materials of Legend

NARRATIVES OF INDIAN princesses have long elicited a positive response in Euro-American culture, an emotion first tapped by Captain John Smith's portrayal of Pocahontas. Nearly two centuries later, several members of the Lewis and Clark Expedition record daily observations of their trek into America's newest wilderness. In doing so, they supply materials from which yet another Indian princess legend eventually arises. Although these journals detail instances of Sacagawea's cooperation and helpfulness during the journey, the nation did not immediately embrace her as a cultural heroine. Expedition members may have been subconsciously aware of the symbolic importance of the native woman's apparently enthusiastic participation in the mission, but they do not point to Sacagawea as a unique contributor to the expedition.

The men provide considerable commentary about Sacagawea, but such material is negligible in comparison to descriptions of the territory and its peoples, as well as narratives of events occurring during the trip. Typically focusing on their own activities and concerns, the journal keepers include accounts of the native woman only when her actions intersect with theirs. While the writers commend Sacagawea because of special contributions to the success of the mission, they hardly single her out for higher praise than they confer on other members of the Corps of Discovery. Basing their judgments on the number and types of comments these writers advance, readers of the original journals would not automatically dub Sacagawea a "heroine."

If these texts appear to deny Sacagawea's heroism, the earliest compilations of the journals, which reached the American public decades before the original scripts were published, portray Sacagawea as an even more peripheral character. Thomas Jefferson, who ordered members of the Corps to keep daily logs, never intended that the originals would be published because of their lack of polish, their bulk, and the costs of printing. Although Jefferson urged the captains to edit their scripts as quickly as possible to familiarize the public with western frontiers and to prove the feasibility of establishing American settlements there, a variety of complications arose, preventing their immediate publication.

Nicholas Biddle and later Paul Allen eventually edited Lewis's and Clark's journals, producing *History of the Expedition under the Command of Captains Lewis and Clark to the Sources of the Missouri, Thence Across the Rocky Mountains and Down the Columbia River to the Pacific Ocean. Performed During the Years 1804–5–6. By Order of the Government of the United States* in 1814. This two-volume text, popularly known as the Biddle edition, is an exceedingly condensed work. After completing his editing duties, Biddle insisted that expedition manuscripts be deposited in the Archives of the American Philosophical Society of Philadelphia to assure their safety. As a result, general readers had access to only edited, condensed versions of the journey for nearly a century.[1]

Biddle and Allen include most of the major incidents relating to Sacagawea's activities and some of the captains' evaluations of her. But other elements of the condensed logs impede the spread of Sacagawea's name into popular culture. The editors, for instance, omit many specific details of Sacagawea's actions. More important, the text collapses Lewis's and Clark's individual entries into a single, composite narrative of each day's most important events. As they present the journey through a single lens of a collective "we," Biddle and Allen deny the existence of two individual voices. Instead, they posit the notion that the captains saw the same things and felt identically about them. Some readers might prefer the simplicity and directness of the Biddle edition, but this homogeneous representation of the expedition and its people essentially suppresses the polyvocality of the original journals. While Lewis and Clark express some markedly differing opinions about Sacagawea, the composite commentary of the Biddle edition projects a flatter character, one that would never be viewed as the key to the sacred mission into the wilderness.

Neither the original journals, which few people examined, nor the earliest editorial compilations, which enjoyed only moderate readership,[2] point to Sacagawea as a unique contributor to the expedition. The original expedition journals of Lewis, Clark, Whitehouse, and Ordway, the Gass log as edited by Patrick M'Keehan, and the Biddle edition nonetheless require analysis in conjunction with the Sacagawea legend for two reasons. First, these scripts are cultural artifacts, disclosing interconnections with certain intersubjective, socially constructed values and ideals associated with frontier mythic traditions. In this chapter, I consider how seminal works of the Sacagawea legend connect to patterns of collective conceptualization, including notions of mission, the land, and native savagery.

The expedition journals and early editions have, in addition, served as a fountainhead to the Sacagawea legend. If American culture has required that narratives of legendary figures derive from historical fact, such texts testify to Sacagawea's "real" existence. They also advance the first depictions of Sacagawea. Reflecting common frontier ideologies, the men of the Corps of Discovery most often define Sacagawea as a savage squaw, but at certain points in their narratives, these writers depart from collective constructions. In several places, they characterize Sacagawea in ways that appear to repudiate her inclusion in the category of savagery. Although they stop short of announcing her heroism, the original journals present a complex portrait of an ambiguous woman.

The original journals and earliest editorial publications of the Lewis and Clark Expedition thus provide vital data concerning the Sacagawea legend. They testify to her historical existence and supply initial portraits of her. Such works also record correlations, lapses, and discontinuities in common cultural meanings that intersect with descriptions of this native woman. In the remainder of this chapter, I discuss the initial portrayals of Sacagawea and identify questions that emerge from those texts.

A significant organizing principle of certain beliefs and values in

America, frontier myths have motivated actions and influenced interpretations of events on the continent over a long period. These narratives maintained unique potency from the earliest colonial period until the turn of the nineteenth century. One component of these traditions is the notion that God mandated a Euro-American mission to sanctify the wilderness by usurping savagery.

According to Segal and Stineback, as well as Leitch Wright, colonists watched European diseases annihilate more than half of indigenous populations during the seventeenth century. Believing that God sent these epidemics to chastise heathens for wickedness and to vacate the land for Euro-American use, settlers additionally declared that native lands were *vacuum domicilium.* As they voiced and enacted such collective beliefs, colonists furthermore claimed that "empty" or "wasted" territories would be "sanctified" through agriculture.[3] Eventually engaging in open conflicts with indigenous peoples, Euro-Americans typified their actions as "just wars," religious enterprises to rebuke natives for capturing colonists and for threatening civilization.

Throughout the eighteenth century, as colonists encroached on other native territories, further hostilities broke out along the western line of America's frontiers. These wars also illustrated and reinforced collective conceptions of mission, land, and native savagery in the New World. Colonial perspectives have been inscribed in the titles and imagery associated with two of the most important conflicts of this period.

In 1756–63, colonists participated in the French and Indian War. Not the European Seven Years' War, this conflict, according to its Euro-American designation, distinctly identified the double enemy of the civilized New World, heathen savages and heretical Frenchmen. Captivity narratives, histories, and sermons, the most important written texts of this period, disseminated images of colonists as being surrounded by savages. As these sources testified, heathens abducted Protestant New Englanders and subjected them to the perils of the untamed wilderness. Native allies of the French then delivered these innocent victims to Canada for conversion to Catholicism, an eventuality that would condemn their eternal souls. As colonists engaged in and defined the French and Indian War, they conceived of themselves as staving off native and French enemies who jointly threatened consecrated ground and the religious foundations of American civilization.

Almost immediately after the French signed the Treaty of Paris in 1763, an act marking their abandonment of former native allies, Pontiac organized the Ottawas and other indigenous groups of the Great Lakes region to resist encroachments on their lands. Although frontier mythic traditions had, for some time, projected the conception that all aboriginal peoples belonged within the single category of savagery and that they shared the desire and potential to destroy America's mission by overrunning "civilized" land, Pontiac's Uprising marked the first time that natives united to stop further Euro-American settlement. This incursion thus provided concrete evidence verifying collective understandings of savagery. Terming this episode an "Uprising" or a "Rebellion" rather than a "War," American historians have legitimated the concept that the savage enemy unjustly attempted a violent, but limited, insurrection against appropriately established, civilized settlements.

After the American Revolution, the young republic initiated several key strategies to deal with indigenous populations within its borders. These policies also reflected culturally condoned images of the nation's sacred mission and native savagery. As Francis Paul Prucha asserts, U.S. officials sought to protect natives and their sovereign rights through the Trade and Intercourse Acts of the 1780s. Although he states that the Acts imposed numerous restrictions upon Euro-American settlers, Prucha also concedes that government officials failed to enforce aboriginal land rights.

In *Expansion and American Indian Policy: 1783–1812*, Reginald Horsman contends that these policies sanctioned the desire for expansion during the last decades of the eighteenth century and into the nineteenth century. As a result, natives lost huge tracts east of the Mississippi through land cessions, an integral element of treaty making with the American government. Such actions were possible because Americans held individual and collective convictions about their prerogative, if not obligation, to convert wilderness into agricultural lands. U.S. policies, the most profound means of converting frontier territories into civilized settlements, manifested an inherent interconnection with frontier myths.

Just as historic events and their interpretations intersected with narrative traditions from the earliest colonial period, a variety of cultural texts from this era also reflected and reinforced collective constructions of a sacred mission on the continent and of native savagery. One American literary genre performed this task exceptionally well. Published as early as the 1680s, captivity narratives maintained great popular appeal throughout the eighteenth and the nineteenth and into the twentieth centuries. Mary Rowlandson's captivity, *A True Story of the Captivity and Restoration of Mrs. Mary Rowlandson, A Minister's Wife in New England: Wherein is Set Forth, The Cruel and Inhumane Usage she Underwent amongst the Heathens, for Eleven Weeks time: And her Deliverance from them*, appeared in at least thirty printings. Rowlandson's narrative and another captivity were among the eight best-sellers of the century, according to Louise Barnett (*Ignoble Savage* 15). Soon after 1700, John Williams's narrative, *The Redeemed Captive Returning to Zion or the Captivity and Deliverance of Rev. John Williams of Deerfield*, sold one thousand copies in a single week (Slotkin, *Regeneration* 96).

Religious approval of captivities possibly accounted for the genre's popularity, since these scripts were not considered frivolous fictions. Mythic considerations also helped to explain their devoted readership. The most influential of all early American texts, captivities illustrated commonly held beliefs, and they helped to frame, reiterate, and justify conceptions of mission, the land, and aboriginals. Portraying native savagery and a frontier that languished under the horrors of barbarism, indeed characterizing a land that yearned for civilization, captivity narratives possessed a power that inspired a nation. They were among the most important texts serving to project and compel a belief in native savagery and the mission to convert the frontier into civilization.

Nearly all captivity narratives define indigenous peoples as ignoble savages, heathens in open conflict with people charged to fulfill the mission of extending the sacred space. Puritan captivity writers characterize natives and their culture as entirely "other." When Rowlandson confronts the "savageness and brutishness of the barbarous Enemy," for example, she describes the natives as "a company of hell-hounds, roaring, singing, ranting and insulting," ready "to devour" her and her child (2). In contrast to civilized peoples, "black creatures" dance in the night, creating a scene that is "a lively resemblance of hell" (3). In this text and others, Puritan readers encounter the paramount enemy, beasts who will, at any moment, eat Christians. Even worse, such savages will tempt colonists to adopt heathenish ways.

Ironic tensions arise in Rowlandson's captivity, however, as some of her comments conflict with proclamations about her captors' savagery. Although she offers no praise of the natives, Rowlandson survives her ordeal because of the treatment she receives from them. When she becomes tired during a march, for instance, one native gives her a horse; another furnishes a Bible. They always provide food (4, 7, 13). Characterizing these specific acts of kindness as manifestations of God's mercy, Rowlandson continues to profess that her captors are cruel and savage. By displacing the agency of benevolence from natives and ascribing it to God, Rowlandson avoids the ambiguity of presenting a complex enemy. These captors cannot be both "savage" and "civilized."

Rowlandson is the first American captivity writer to illustrate and reinforce precepts of native savagery, but as David Beer writes, "The captivity story followed the frontier as it crept westward, and was always handy as 'evidence' that the natives of the land were savage beasts" (215). John Williams's 1795 narrative also presents these images. He describes "cruel and bloodthirsty" heathens who murder innocent settlers (14, 16, 19). Although Williams eventually admits that natives carry him and other captives in their arms to the village, he claims that this phenomenon occurs because "their savage cruel tempers were so overruled by God" (29). Like Rowlandson, Williams and narrators of later captivities proliferate the model of a dehumanized enemy, the savage "other."

In captivities, war narratives, and histories, writers verify the savagery of native culture by illustrating the harsh treatment of native females. In *Memoirs of Odd Adventures, Strange Deliverances, Etc., in the Captivity of John Gyles, Esq., Commander of the Garrison on St. George River, in the District of Maine,* New Englander John Gyles describes the "drudgery" of "squaws" (89). Further proving the severity of native women's subordination, Gyles writes that although male slaves eat the evening meal with the other men of the tribe, native women are permitted to retrieve and to eat leftovers only after the males have eaten their fill (99). Elizabeth Hanson's as-told-to captivity,[4] *An Account of the Captivity of Elizabeth Hanson, Now or Late of Kachecky, in New England: Who, with Four of her Children and Servant-Maid, was taken captive by the Indians, and carried into Canada,* concurs with other representations of the mistreatment of indigenous women. Although an aboriginal mother and grown daughter attempt to help Hanson and her children, the native women state that they can do nothing because they must resign themselves to male authority (Bownas 13).

Captivity narratives also reinforced the idea of mission on the continent. Although the earliest captivities defined the frontier as a threat to Euro-American society, by the mid-eighteenth century, these scripts began to extol the virtues of expanding civilization. As Phillips Carleton argues in "The Indian Captivity," this uniquely American genre helped to create frontier myths by depicting the "line of the fluid frontiers receding into the West, [changing] the colonists into a new people" (180). Other texts of the period, such as sermons, histories, and travel literature, also transformed images of a threatening wilderness. As the growing population's attraction to fertile western lands increased, the frontier no longer signified a place where God's chosen would degenerate into heathenish ways; the wilderness instead became a potential garden. New portraits of the frontier reinforced belief in the continental destiny of America.

By the turn of the nineteenth century, historical events and their interpretations, as well as captivity narratives and other cultural texts, exemplified and proliferated a constellation of common ideas that compelled strong emotion on the continent. America's frontier myths, according to Francis Jennings, have possessed immense power because the very words used to express thought gave them shape and direction and symbolic substance.

The nation in effect codified the idea that all aboriginal cultures were essentially alike and that civilization had an obligation to tame the land. By identifying natives as "others" and their actions as "invasions," "raids," and "incursions," collective concepts typified indigenous peoples as savages with no right to land or voice. The dominant culture also precluded speculation on the legitimacy of the pioneer settlements in other ways. By their very existence, Euro-American communities stood as proof that the mission to transform wilderness into civilization was just. In a simplified bifurcation of savagery and civilization, natives and their traditions justified expansion. "Less developed" cultures and customs had to yield to more "advanced" societies. By 1800, myths of manifest destiny, depicting the wilderness as the line separating savagery from civilization with pioneers as its vanguard, made the issue of progress irrefutable in America.

The Lewis and Clark Expedition, born of Thomas Jefferson's dreams and aspirations for America, embodied the idea of progress on the continent. Concerned about dense eastern populations and convinced of the need to keep natives behind the line of civilization, Jefferson hoped that abundant western lands would assure Americans the simplicity and virtue of an agrarian life for centuries. Their consensus spanning more than 150 years, nearly every source discussing the Lewis and Clark Expedition has argued that this journey constituted America's most important achievement because it "opened up" land for settlement and inspired Americans' pioneering spirit.[5] Explicitly expressing tenets of manifest destiny in his 1905 work, Frederick Young claims that this mission extended "the realm of enlightenment, science, and the arts, and the securing of a grander home for the institutions of liberty and equality" in a land whose history underscored "the central and enduring process of progress in civilization" (2, 12).

In *The Journals of Lewis and Clark*, Bernard DeVoto enlarges upon Young's arguments, maintaining that documents produced during the journey also proliferated conceptions of manifest destiny. While DeVoto claims that the expedition "gave the entire West to the American people as something with which the mind could deal," he further asserts that the original journals projected America's future. These texts simultaneously created and satisfied the westering desire in the American people (lii). As evidenced by specific references to their wilderness mission and to the peoples they encountered, journal keepers of the Lewis and Clark Expedition illustrated their relationship to certain principles of frontier mythic tradition. Not merely aware of such values and beliefs, Captains Lewis and Clark and their men also enacted and illustrated them for westering Americans.

Most sources concerned with written materials emerging from the expedition focus exclusively on Meriwether Lewis and William Clark and their journals. Some scholars nonetheless discuss texts produced by other members of the Corps of Discovery, including those of Sergeant Patrick Gass, Private Joseph Whitehouse, and Sergeant John Ordway. A few researchers also comment on these men's lives. According to Ernest Osgood, this "band of intrepid voyagers" had previously been hunters, trappers, and traders in America's "wilderness" (xiii). Although many researchers merely offer generalizations about the rank and file of the expedition, some critics also comment on individual members.

In *The Journals of Captain Meriwether Lewis and Sergeant John Ordway,* Milo Quaife asserts that little information exists concerning Ordway's life before or after the expedition. Arguing that he was second in command to the captains and therefore the most valuable of the men, Quaife adds that Ordway "continued to the end to play a man's part in the development of America's great inland empire" (28). James Hosmer does not directly counter such declarations, in the introduction to Gass's *Journal of the Lewis and Clark Expedition.*[6] He nevertheless asserts that Gass, a frontiersman raised on the "utmost limit of the frontier" as a soldier and "Indian-fighter," deserved the highest recognition for his contributions to the mission (xiv–xvi).

Despite slight differences in critical estimations of the men's individual worth, scholars concur on the value of Ordway's, Whitehouse's and Gass's journals. In addition to manifesting certain personal information, these scripts, produced by those who enlisted during America's epic journey into the wilderness, relate that Sergeant Ordway, Private Whitehouse, and Sergeant Gass embraced values and ideas inscribed by myths of manifest destiny. Although a sense of mission to convert wilderness into civilization is an important tenet of such narrative patterns, these men do not write directly about the fundamental goals of the enterprise. That phenomenon, in all likelihood, stems from the fact that the rank and file of the expedition had little, if any, role in conceiving the mission or formulating plans to achieve it.

Clark's journal plainly states this fact. When the captains decide not to dispatch a small party back to St. Louis, for example, Clark writes that the change in plans should create no problems because "We have never hinted to any one of the party that we had such a scheem in contemplation, and all appear perfectly to have made up their minds to Succeed in the expedition or perish in the attempt. . . . no one shows anything but the greatest devotion" (Thwaites 2: 175–76).[7] The first portion of this entry essentially substantiates the idea that the men have not participated in planning and executing the mission. The rest of Clark's commentary points out another consideration, one that Lewis also addresses. As Lewis writes, everyone is "zealously attached to the enterprise, and anxious to proceed" (1: 284–85). Although the men do not themselves write about the mission, such comments suggest that they know their duty, that they are devoted to it, and that they are willing to die in the effort to succeed in its execution.

If rarely offering philosophical commentary, these journalists compensate in their documentation of everyday details of the journey. Concentrating on their own lives and activities, the expedition men are particularly prolix, for example, in their descriptions of illnesses. Within entries relating commonplace events, Gass, Ordway, and Whitehouse also illustrate their interconnections with frontier mythic traditions, divulged particularly through their assertions about indigenous peoples. Sometimes referring to aboriginals as "natives" or by tribal designation, each writer most often employs the label "savages." The men thus codify at least two culturally significant principles. First, although native groups were separated by hundreds of miles and despite their remarkably varied customs and traditions, the rank and file of the expedition collapse all local distinctions. Such notations imply that, in the minds of these men,

similarities far outweigh differences. Second, insofar as they view
natives as basically alike, Gass, Whitehouse, and Ordway essentially
categorize all indigenous peoples as "other" and juxtapose them and
their societies with those of "civilization." Not merely neutral designations, "savage" and "savagery" bear implicit cultural judgments.

Specific entries from the men's journals document those estimations. One common characteristic of savagery, according to their
entries, is avarice and thievery. As Whitehouse writes, the men of
the Corps had to bury their boats in different places "So that if the
Savages Should find one perhaps they would not find the other &
we would have Some left Still" (7: 98). Ordway concurs that savages
go to extreme lengths to steal goods, describing how one native
plotted to kill another for an ordinary blanket (Quaife 321).

Thievery is not the sole mark of savage existence, however. As
Gass writes of the Mandans, "Their superstitious credulity is so
great, that they believe by using the head well, the living buffaloe
will come, and that they will get a supply of meat" (66). Gass perceives the ritual feeding of a buffalo skull to assure abundance for
the next season as mere superstition. He thus separates himself and
his culture from natives to show their savagery. Also commenting
on indigenous customs, Ordway observes, "then all the Savages men
women and children of any size danced forming a circle round a fire
& jumping up" (348). Although the expedition men eventually join
in the dancing, they do so only as short-term participants of savage occupations. Echoing images and interpretations offered in
Rowlandson's captivity narrative, Ordway writes about two distinct
peoples, men who will one day return to civilization, and natives
who will forever remain savage.

Like captivity writers, these diarists accept the tenet that the level
of any culture's "civilization" corresponds to behavior and treatment of its females. Ordway, for example, points out the "drudgery"
native women are forced to endure while the men take their ease
(348). In a commentary about native women, Gass highlights another element of savagery when he claims that "chastity is not very
highly esteemed and the severe and loathsome effects of *certain
French principles* are not uncommon among them" (original emphasis,
70). Associating venereal disease with native women's lewd behav-

iors, Gass also attributes the source of the scourge to the Old World. He excludes Americans from sharing in responsibility for its spread. Reflecting and reinforcing cultural interpretations of his time, Gass concretizes the ideas that truly civilized women should be, above all else, pure and that native women remain outside that definition.[8] By extending this reasoning, all indigenous peoples, because of their traditions and behaviors, define savagery. Recounting qualities of savagery in their entries, the rank and file of America's epic journey into the wilderness illustrate their immersion in America's mythic tradition.

If scholars have failed to discover details about the expedition's enlisted men's lives, they have neglected no facet of Lewis's and Clark's existence. Every edition of the journals and several biographies probe the captains' early and later experiences. Although researchers do not agree on all points, such as whether Lewis was murdered or committed suicide not long after the expedition, they generally concur that certain early seasoning helped the captains to become uniquely qualified leaders of the mission. Both had been frontiersmen who hunted and blazed trails; both were soldiers who participated in protecting pioneer settlements from "incursions" by native groups. Though neither obtained extensive formal education, Lewis and Clark received a far superior form of instruction for their task. The wilderness tested them.

Reflecting attitudes and beliefs undoubtedly reaped from such experiences, Lewis and Clark display their immersion in frontier mythic traditions in their journals. Although the enlisted men do not directly address the issue of mission and its importance to America, both captains express themselves on the topic. The pragmatic Clark writes that the valley of the Columbia River will be able to support forty to fifty thousand people "if properly cultivated" (4: 220). In this entry, Clark underscores two important ideas. First, he connects their journey to a future goal inscribed by myth. By examining the terrain, members of the Corps of Discovery blaze a trail into the wilderness and prepare the way for pioneers to settle the valley and extend civilization. Secondly, in his use of the words "properly cultivated," Clark demonstrates his acceptance of distinctions between savagery and civilization. Since indigenous economies in this region were primarily based on hunting and gathering, Clark observes their subsistence strategies and evaluates them through Euro-American conceptualizations. Essentially declaring the territory *vacuum domicilium,* he projects a future when the land will no longer be empty or wasted. Rather, it will be put to appropriate agricultural use, according to God's decree.

Clark's remarks about the mission focus on pragmatic matters, but Lewis's are more philosophical. When they leave the Mandans, Lewis writes, "This little fleet altho' not quite so rispectable as those of Columbus or Capt. Cook, were still viewed by us with as much pleasure as those deservedly famed adventurers ever beheld theirs . . . we were now about to penetrate a country at least two thousand miles in width, on which the foot of civilized man had never trodden" (1: 284–85). Here Lewis documents how important it is to open territories to civilization. Although he points out the simplicity of his boats in comparison to those of Columbus and Cook, Lewis equates the challenge and significance of his mission to theirs. This journey, in his perception, will have as great an impact on America's future as Columbus's had on the world.

In another evaluation of the mission, offered on the evening of his thirty-first birthday, Lewis comments, "I reflected that I had as yet done but little, very little, indeed, to further the hapiness of the human race, or to advance the information of the succeeding generation. [I] . . . resolved in future, to redouble my exertions and at least indeavour to promote those two primary objects of human existence . . . to live *for mankind,* as I have heretofore lived *for myself*" (original emphasis, 2: 368). Although most critics cite this portion of the log as evidence of Lewis's melancholy or of his tendency toward introspection, such remarks also record the author's attitudes about humankind and its future. As far as Lewis is concerned, this mission, the necessary precursor to the establishment of pioneer settlements, is his offering to "mankind." If he succeeds, he may then have adequately contributed to humanity. Such comments essentially explicate Lewis's devotion to America's mission and his participation in frontier traditions.

Another issue suggested in this entry remains clouded, nevertheless. What peoples, in Lewis's mind, form the "human race" and "mankind?" Does he believe that his endeavor will benefit indigenous populations, or does he even consider them? Although the entry does not clarify these points, other observations in Lewis's and Clark's logs document certain shared perceptions about native peoples, concepts arising from mythic traditions.

A chart prepared for Congress, for example, provides evidence that Lewis and Clark might not have wholly joined in the practice of conflating all natives into a single category since they differentiate native societies by name, population, territories, and other distinguishing characteristics (7: 80–120). As James Ronda argues in *Lewis and Clark among the Indians,* the captains desired to be accurate in their ethnographic assessments, but they maintained no sense of impartiality whatsoever. He writes, "Disinterested observation was the farthest thing from their minds. Because the captains were confident of their own cultural superiority, they never doubted the wisdom of judging Indians by white standards" (114). When commenting on potential trade, Lewis and Clark state that the Tetons are "the vilest miscreants of the savage race" (7: 98). Although they differentiate between the Tetons and other natives, this comment subsumes differences, placing indigenous peoples into a universal classification. Tetons, as all natives, are savages. Still other commentaries suggest that natives have no conception of land possession, they lack agriculture, and they wander throughout their territories. While reporting actual patterns of native life, the captains interpret cultural systems through frontier mythic meanings.

Specific journal entries submitted by both Lewis and Clark also demonstrate such evaluations. The leaders refer to individual natives and their nations as "savages" or as "uncivilized" throughout the logs (2: 363, 355; 3: 152, 362). Lewis writes of his distress that the mission's success depends on the "caprice of a few savages who are ever as fickle as the wind" (2: 258). Seemingly less judgmental, Clark notes, "Their Laws like those of all uncivilized Indians consist of a Set of customs which has grown out of their local Situations" (3: 361). In spite of his acknowledgment of native laws and his awareness of the relationship between customs and "local situations," Clark exhibits his acceptance of essential differences between "civilized" and "uncivilized" peoples.

If Clark maintains a mental model strictly differentiating the two classifications, Lewis expresses open disgust when he witnesses Shoshones eating a deer: "they dismounted and ran in tumbling over each other like a parcel of famished dogs each seizing and tearing away a part of the intestens . . . some were eating the kidnies the melt and liver and the blood runing from the corners of their mouths. . . . I really did not untill now think that human nature ever presented itself in a shape so nearly allyed to the brute creation" (2: 355). This behavior, in Lewis's estimation, signifies more than local customs or mere differences in food ways. By first presenting a simile that compares natives to "famished dogs," he begins to define a line separating human beings from animals. As he asserts, Shoshones are closer to the latter. Lewis then illustrates that natives eat animal parts he considers unfit for human consumption as they devour the entire animal raw, an act not permissible for civilized beings, even if driven by the extremes of hunger. Positioning himself offstage from the bloody scene, an obviously superior observer from a clearly advanced culture, Lewis does not necessarily deny the Shoshones' humanity. He nonetheless places such "savages" on a level far below that which defines "civilization."

Lewis's and Clark's diaries, in addition to the Biddle edition, verify that savagery implies the mistreatment of women. As Clark remarks in his field notes, Teton and Arikara women do all the drudgery and are slaves to their men (Osgood 149, 159), and Lewis provides the same observations about the Shoshones (3: 10). Relating similar descriptions, a chapter headnote of the Biddle edition states with ringing irony, "the treatment of women is the standard by which the virtues of an Indian may be known" (526). Like their men, the captains also employ arguments about women's chastity as indications of savagery, often citing a combination of female drudgery and promiscuity to validate their conclusions (2: 371; 3: 239).

When Lewis observes Clatsop, Chinnook, and Killamuck societies, he states that native men force their wives and daughters to perform drudgery. They also prostitute them for mere trifles (3: 315). In another entry, Lewis seems to distinguish Columbia River groups from others. But his attending phrase "in common with other savage nations," documents his inability to conceive of social or cultural distinctions among tribes. As Lewis proclaims, "our women" are "indebted to civilization for their ease and comfort" (3: 316). According to this observation, only civilization, the savior of Euro-American females, can overcome savage conditions enslaving all womanhood. That argument alone substantiates the need to spread the sacred space of freedom.

Although these entries expose the captains' evaluations of native life, others point to a more serious equation, one which signifies that all indigenous peoples are innately and permanently savage. Both Lewis and Clark concur with their men that theft is a quality of savage life (4: 258–330), but Lewis extends the argument by writing that "the treachery of the aborigenes of America" constitutes a "trait in their character" (4: 90). Again conflating all natives, Lewis hints that theft is naturally associated with the savage condition.

What he only implies in the previous entry, Lewis expresses explicitly in commentary concerned with native women. When a Shoshone woman stops to have a baby and then catches up with the group on the move, Lewis states, "It appears to me that the facility and ease with which the women of the aborigines of North America bring fourth their children is rather a gift of nature. . . . and it is a rare occurence for any of them to experience difficulty in child-birth" (3: 40–41). The Biddle editors rework Lewis's words but maintain his meaning by stating, "easy delivery of the Indian woman is wholly constitutional" (364–65). In spite of the congratulatory tone of these proclamations, they imply no real admiration of native women. Instead, phrases like "a gift of nature" and "wholly constitutional" certify that native women are intrinsically different from civilized women. These comments affirm that aboriginal peoples are distinct from Euro-Americans not only because of social variations but also because of their genetic inheritance. However long it might take, native convention could eventually be superseded by Euro-American custom, but innate savagery cannot. Such thinking in effect precludes "savages" from ever becoming "civilized."[9]

Journals written by various members of the Lewis and Clark Expedition and the earliest editions of such scripts thus display their creators' immersion in particular intersubjective realities of frontier traditions. Not simply reflecting patterns of Euro-American thought, these works also prescribe socially mandated interpretations about the land, the natives who occupied it, and America's transformation of wilderness into civilization. Through illustration and validation, they project the virtues of such mythic conceptions to an accepting populace, authorizing individual and collective beliefs and actions in America.

The original journals and subsequent editions, moreover, present raw materials from which the Sacagawea legend has sprung. As G. S. Snyder asserts, nothing should cloud readers' knowledge of the "real" Sacagawea since she is "clearly on record" in the daily diaries (36). In some sense, Snyder is correct. The men testify to Sacagawea's presence during the mission, and they concur on the order of events and most often about Sacagawea's role in them. Careful reading of these texts, however, shows that they do not represent a single voice. Arising from disparate viewpoints born of the complex nexus of event, context, and observer/creator, the original logs document the interplay of personal observation and cultural interpretation. The diarists, in fact, provide diverse opinions and offer sometimes different Sacagaweas, personae from which subsequent writers and creators have chosen and upon which they have expanded. In the remainder of this chapter, I examine how these various texts depict Sacagawea.

Although every journal keeper acknowledges Sacagawea's presence during the mission, disparities in their perceptions of her are apparent. One difference in their projections, for example, is partly attested to by the number of times they write about her. Captains Meriwether Lewis and William Clark, for instance, mention her frequently in the nearly two years they are in contact with her. Clark comments on Sacagawea most often, offering more than forty-eight observations, while Lewis totals more than thirty-eight notations. Sergeant Ordway and Privates Gass and Whitehouse describe her activities also, but far less often, with nineteen, nine, and eight references, respectively. Table 1 presents data of the expedition men's and subsequent editors' most significant commentaries about Sacagawea.

The difference between the number of times the captains and their men comment on Sacagawea might be explained in part by

Table 1. Important Expedition Incidents Involving Sacagawea[1]

Date	Event	Expend. Jour. 1804–6					Early Ed. 1814–93		Later Ed. 1904–64				Total
		L	C	W	G[2]	O	B[3]	CO[4]	T[5]	Q[6]	D[7]	BK[8]	
11/04	Appears at Fort	x		x			x	x	x	2	2		9
1/05	Pregnant	x					x						2
2/05	Baptiste Born	x		x			x	x	x	x		x	7
4/05	Personnel List	x	x	x	x		x	x	x	2	x		10
pass.	Gathers/Fixes Food	5	8	x	2		2	2					20
5/05	Squall	2	x	x			x	x			x		7
5/05	River Named for S.	x					x	x					3
6/05	Illness/Recovery	8	9	3	4		2	2				x	29
6/05	Storm/Flash Flood	x	x	x	x		x	x	x		x		8
pass.	Walks on Shore	3	2	2	x		2				x		11
pass.	Recognizes Country	2		x	x		2	x	x			2	10
7/05	At Abduction Site	2	x	x	x	2	x	x			x		10
8/05	Beaten by Husband	x	x										2
8/05	Meets Shoshones	x	x	x	x		x	x	x	x			8
pass.	Interpreter	3	4	x	x		2	2			x		14
8/05	Averts Treachery	x					x	x	x		x		5
10/05	Peace Sign		2				x	x					4
11/05	Belt/Otter Robe		4	x			x	x					7
11/05	Gives C. Bread		2				x				x		4
12/05	Gives C. Present		2				x						3
1/06	Sees the Whale	x	x				x	x			x		5
7/06	Points out Pass	x		x									2
7/06	Serves as "Pilot"		2				2	2			x		7
8/06	Left at Fort	x		x			x	x	x	x			6
1804–6 Totals		33	46	8	8	19	25	25	6	11	7	7	193

[1] An x indicates that expedition members noted these events in their journals, that early editors published those edited entries, and that later editors offered additional commentary as they related such incidents. Numbers indicate multiple entries.

[2] In 1811, David M'Keehan edited and published Gass's journal (G).

[3] In 1814, Nicholas Biddle and Paul Allen (B) published and edited portions of Lewis's and Clark's journals.

[4] In 1893, Elliot Coues (CO) edited Lewis's and Clark's journals and provided commentary.

[5] In 1904–6, Reuben Thwaites (T) first published the original journals of Lewis (L), Clark (C), and Whitehouse (W).

[6] In 1916, Milo Quaife (Q) published Ordway's original journal (O).

[7] In 1953, Bernard DeVoto (D) published the original journals and the Biddle edition and provided commentary.

[8] In 1964, John Bakeless (BK) published portions of Lewis's and Clark's journals and provided commentary.

their functions within the expedition. Many remarks, whether offered by the captains or their men, focus on her daily activities, such as gathering and/or preparing foods, walking on shore, or identifying landmarks. Occupied by hunting and scouting, the enlisted men were often separated from the larger group. Lewis and Clark, on the other hand, generally stayed within easy range of the main body of the Corps, unless one or the other undertook a secondary exploration. Like the captains, Sacagawea nearly always traveled with the principal party. Even when gathering various foods, she sought them along the main route. Sacagawea, therefore, probably spent more time near the captains than the other diarists.

An additional factor helps to explain the difference in the number of comments submitted about Sacagawea. Although all of them interacted with her nearly every day, Sacagawea also proved useful to Lewis and Clark during official events that the enlisted men might not have witnessed. Clark, for instance, mentions that she functioned as their translator on four occasions, and Lewis comments on that role three times. Whitehouse, Gass, and Ordway, combined, note her translating efforts only twice. Clark, moreover, is the only member of the expedition who reports on Sacagawea's importance as a peace sign among various native groups while Lewis is the sole writer who mentions her role in averting treachery among the Shoshones. Probably not even aware of these situations, the other men do not comment on them. More consistent physical proximity, combined with Sacagawea's specific usefulness to the captains, likely accounts for some difference in the number of entries highlighting Sacagawea.

Although the number of commentaries about Sacagawea might hint at the men's individual estimation of her significance, the content of the entries points out more accurately how they perceive her. Some of the captains' remarks seem more obviously evaluative than those offered by their men, but even apparently descriptive commentaries provide glimpses of observers' judgments and their relationship to common cultural conceptions. All of the diarists, for example, most frequently term Sacagawea "the squar" or "the Indian woman" or "our interpreter's wife." Whitehouse never mentions her by any designation other than the last. From the first moment they become aware of her until they leave her nearly two years later, only rarely do any of the diarists use her name. Claiming that "Sacagawea" was too difficult to pronounce, much less spell, several critics assert that the writers are forced to use other means of identification. This argument, however, does not withstand scrutiny as the diarists often cite the names of other natives, always men and usually leaders of their peoples.

Because the writers prove their ability to tackle native names when they deem it important, their use of various titles to identify Sacagawea suggests that certain cultural conceptions might have informed their choices. By employing the designation "our interpreter's wife," the men describe a doubly removed type, a being acknowledged only in relation to an implicitly more important person, one whose higher status is based on gender and function. Other ways of referring to Sacagawea are perhaps even more telling because they combine cultural ideas about women with mythic notions about native women. Titles such as "the squar," or "the Indian woman," not only define Sacagawea as a type but also subsume her under the general classification of ignoble savagery.

While reflecting and reinforcing collective notions about females in general and about native women in particular, these designations concurrently generate important tensions in the expedition texts. How can the men of the Corps, if they remain immersed in conceptions about savage peoples, explain their attachment to and admiration for Sacagawea when their portrayals seem to claim that she possesses no unique qualities? Manifesting no awareness of these tensions in their writings, the diarists offer no answers to such inquiries.

A few journal entries, nevertheless, document the diarists' inability to contain Sacagawea within that reductive category. Because classification of native peoples as "savages" has been based on a set of arbitrary characteristics and has hinged on an observer's ability to subsume important differences, to ignore contradictory evidence, and to disregard the individuality of particular natives, it is not surprising that expedition writers cannot sustain such a portrait of Sacagawea. In constant contact with her for a long period, they see her in various circumstances. They learn about her as a person and discover portions of her past. Considering these factors, the wonder of these journals is not that the writers sometimes depict Sacagawea as an individual but that usually they do not. Many passages of these scripts testify to the power of mythic constructions.

In spite of such declarations, occasional comments conflict with collective conceptions of frontier traditions. Although myths attempt to integrate all cultural meanings, cultural conceptualization can never achieve complete unity, resulting in omissions and lapses in totalizing reasoning. These writers essentially present a native woman who is simultaneously inside and outside a classification and meaning. They create an ambiguous character whose contradictions they never acknowledge, much less justify.[10]

The best means of observing these varied and sometimes conflicting portrayals of Sacagawea is a concurrent analysis of expedition documents as they outline a chronology of events involving her. To visualize the expedition route and the general location of significant events involving Sacagawea, refer to the map presented in Figure 1. Although an examination of the journals often leads to questions rather than conclusions concerning the men's observations of Sacagawea, these very questions isolate and interrogate critical points in the narratives. Here cultural notions confront an individual native woman and her life. These texts document that encounter.

Ordway and Clark note Sacagawea's first appearance at the expedition campsite among the Mandans, in early November 1805. As Ordway writes, "a frenchmans Squaw came to our camp who belong to the Snake nation She came with our Intreperters wife & brought with them 4 buffalow Robes and Gave them to our officers" (164). In distinguishing between the two native women, Ordway intimates that a "wife" holds a legitimated position and a "squaw" remains an inferior. By noting that difference, he displays more than his ignorance of Mandan marriage tradition. He outlines a hierarchical vision informed by Euro-American cultural conceptions. Although he essentially concurs with Ordway, Clark writes that both women are Charbonneau's wives, but his comment also bears judgments concerning savage acceptance of polygamy (1: 219). While they note Sacagawea's arrival, neither observer supplies names, physical descrip-

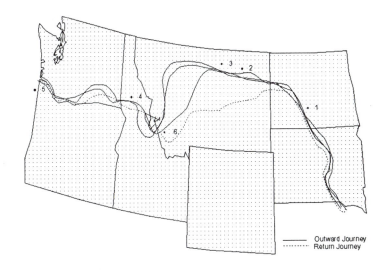

Figure 1. The Lewis and Clark Expedition Trail October 1804–1806[1]

Featured Events Involving Sacagawea

Date	Place	Event
Oct. 1804	1	Arrival at Ft. Mandan
Feb. 1805	1	Birth of Sacagawea's baby
Apr. 1805	1	Departure from Ft. Mandan
May 1805	2	Squall Incident
June 1805	3	Sacagawea's illness
Aug. 1805	4	Among the Shoshones
Jan. 1806	5	Whale incident
July 1806	6	Sacagawea's guidance of Clark
Aug. 1806	1	Leave-taking at Ft. Mandan

[1] Although state and country borders did not exist during this period, I supply them in order to visualize the geography of the trail more readily.

tions, or any other details about the two women. These writers appear to take more notice of the buffalo robes they receive as gifts than of the people presenting them. Remaining undifferentiated squaws, the women initially draw no more attention than any other native visitors.

On February 11, 1805, Sacagawea gives birth to a son, an event evoking comments from two other expedition men, Gass and Lewis. Although Gass's entry simply states that their interpreter's wife has added to their number (68), Lewis's account is quite long. As he writes,

> about five Oclock this evening one of the wives of Charbono was delivered of a fine boy. it is worthy of remark that this was the first child which this woman had boarn, and as is common in such cases her labour was tedious and the pain violent; Mr. Jessome informed me that he had frequently administered a small portion of the rattle of the rattle-snake, which he assured me had never failed to produce the desired effect, that of hastening the birth of the child . . . I was informed that she had not taken it more than ten minutes before she brought forth. (1: 257–58)

Such lengthy remarks might seem to suggest a special interest in Sacagawea and her child. They could possibly point to Lewis's acknowledgment of unique characteristics that somehow separate Sacagawea from other savages. Details of this entry negate that speculation, however, by demonstrating that although he is present during her long and difficult labor, Lewis does not remain with her through the delivery. "Informed" that she has "brought forth," Lewis shows no real concern for Sacagawea. As this and several subsequent entries indicate, he is instead keenly interested in testing the effectiveness of traditional native medicines and cures, since they might benefit "civilization."

Another issue in this commentary merits examination as well. Lewis writes that Sacagawea's labor is "tedious" and that her pain is "violent." Although not particularly personal in tone, such observations are significant as they appear to contradict Lewis's later assertions that all native women "enjoy" easy deliveries. Has he simply forgotten about Sacagawea's difficulties when he provides generalizations about native births months after her delivery? Or is Sacagawea, in Lewis's estimation, unlike other native women? Is she somehow less "savage" as evidenced by her labor and perhaps other factors he does not mention? Might he believe that she experiences unusual pains because the father of her child is French rather than native? Lewis displays no awareness of such contradictions in his narrative, nor does he acknowledge what they might imply about Sacagawea or about native women.

When leaving the Mandans in early April, Gass and the captains note that Sacagawea is with the company. While Gass simply terms her "a woman" who is going "up the river" with them (73), Lewis lists her as an expedition member in his journal and in a letter to Jefferson (1: 284; 7: 319). Not merely including Sacagawea on the Corps of Discovery roll, Clark also claims she holds an official position. He writes that Charbonneau and his "*Indian Squar*" will act as "Interpreter and interpretress for the snake [Shoshone] Indians" (original emphasis, 1: 278). Clark's field notes additionally mention that she is an interpreter as early as November of the previous year (Osgood 174, 185). While this discrepancy might seem minor, editors of the Biddle edition are forced to choose one version. They list Sacagawea as a member of the Corps, but one without purpose. Here expedition texts begin to document three versions of Sacagawea's function.

Is she merely a woman tagging along, a member of the Corps with no specified role, or an official interpreter? If the captains plan that she will interpret, as Clark states in his writings on three occasions, why does Lewis not acknowledge her assignment as well? Does Clark simply afford Sacagawea more responsibility and dignity than her actual position warrants, or does he hold her in higher regard than does Lewis? Could the omission of a designated role imply Lewis's and the Biddle editors' refusal to legitimate a function for a woman, much less a native?

On May 14, when a near-disaster threatens the lives of several expedition members, including Sacagawea, Lewis supplies a detailed account of the incident. He writes that while Charbonneau is at the helm, a puff of wind pushes one boat onto its side. It quickly fills with water, and a panicking Charbonneau retains control of the

rudder only when another of the men threatens to shoot him. As
Lewis notes, "there were two other men beside Charbono on board
who could not swim, and who of course must also have perished
had the perogue gone down to the bottom" (2: 35). Presenting the
same basic details, Clark claims that "the articles which floated out
was nearly all caught by the Squar who was in the rear" (2: 37). Again
the captains tell different stories about Sacagawea.

Lewis's oversight could relate several meanings. First, he might
not have been aware of Sacagawea's presence on the boat or her
actions. Belying that premise, Lewis's submission two days later
praises her response during the crisis. He ascribes to her "equal fortitude and resolution, with any person onboard at the time of the
accedent" (2: 39). Though Lewis qualifies his commendation, he offers high tribute to the woman whose presence in the craft he has
not even mentioned two days before. Second, since Lewis lists only
those who cannot swim, his earlier omission might suggest knowledge of Sacagawea's abilities. In another portion of the original entry, however, Lewis claims that although he is a strong swimmer,
he realizes he would die in an attempt to rescue the boat because
of the treacherous rapids. He cannot believe that Sacagawea would
survive.

Considering these factors, why then does he not mention Sacagawea? Is it simply a matter of perspective? Is Lewis's attention di-
verted to details different from those which Clark sees? Does he
simply forget, when he writes his initial comments, that she is on
board? Or are the implications more pointed? Does Lewis not consider Sacagawea's potential death as worthy of concern? Would her
death, in his opinion, spell no significant loss to the mission? Although Lewis later commends Sacagawea and even writes in a subsequent entry that they name a river after her (2: 52), his original
omission seems to document a persistent tone and meaning. He responds to a savage woman of no particular individuality or worth.

During the entire trip, nothing concerning Sacagawea elicits
more notations from the men than her illness. In the first six days
of her infirmity, she becomes progressively worse, and all of the diarists except Gass write about the extremity of her case.[11] Ordway,
for example, notes on three occasions that she is "verry Sick" (229,

230, 231). In the same period, Clark describes her condition seven times while Lewis comments only twice. This occurrence seems a continuation of the captains' previous responses toward Sacagawea since Clark appears more solicitous of her because he mentions her illness so often.

As Clark and Lewis testify, however, Lewis's notations are limited because of his absence from the main party during a portion of that time. Although this fact may reinforce the impression that Lewis views Sacagawea as insignificant, because he knows about her illness before he leaves, another interpretation is possible. Lewis might not have realized the seriousness of the case, inasmuch as the logs are littered with thousands of declarations of severe illnesses. Supporting that interpretation, both captains report that, upon his return, Lewis takes over her care and writes about her condition daily. Clark, at that same point, drops the subject.

The numbers of entries submitted about Sacagawea's illness, therefore, point out less than might first seem evident. The content of specific comments proves more revealing. When Sacagawea will take no medicine from him but cooperates with Charbonneau, Clark writes, "if she dies it will be the fault of her husband as I am now convinced" (2: 165). Bound to culturally mandated images of women, Clark's observations imply that Charbonneau is entirely responsible for Sacagawea, not because of her illness, but because she is his wife. Her status as a "squaw" moreover compounds the depth of her husband's obligation because, as a savage, Sacagawea possesses no sense of what is necessary for her recovery.

Although Lewis's entries largely center on treatment, one comment discloses an estimate of Sacagawea. At a time when both captains remain doubtful about her chances of recovery, Lewis writes, "this gave me some concern as well for the poor object herself, then with a young child in her arms, as from the consideration of her being our only dependence for a friendly negociation with the Snake Indians on whom we depend for horses to assist us in our portage from the Missouri to the columbia river" (2: 162–63). The worry, even sympathy, that Lewis expresses for Sacagawea and for her nursing baby, who would starve if she were to die, seems at first to counter certain comments he has previously submitted. This impression is immediately abrogated, however, as Lewis proves that his largest anxiety is the possibility of losing someone who might prove useful in the mission. Complementing his references to their dependence on Sacagawea, Lewis's phrase "poor object" reflects his conception of her as a tool. Ironically enough, these comments do not just register his objectification of Sacagawea; they simultaneously acknowledge her unique worth. No longer contained within an undifferentiated category of savagism, Lewis's Sacagawea occupies an ambiguous position. She is savage, but she is also useful because of particular knowledge and skills.

The Biddle edition presents another vision of Sacagawea's illness. On days corresponding to diarists' notations of her infirmity, Biddle includes nothing about Sacagawea. Instead, a later entry explains that she has been ill, remarking that she is now recovering as a result of the treatment Lewis provides (236). By delaying the commentary, the editors redirect the focus of the entire incident. Not at all consequential, Sacagawea becomes the vehicle to highlight Lewis's heroism. Biddle and Allen echo the same sentiment when they subsequently glorify Clark's heroic efforts to save Sacagawea and the baby during a flash flood. Projecting mythic models of understanding, these notations and many others illustrate the knowledge and goodness of both captains. America's best, they represent "civilization's" guardianship over "savagery."

The expedition men write many commentaries about the coincidence of their camping on the site of Sacagawea's previous capture. Although Clark remains silent on the issue and while the rank and file restrict their notations to few details, Lewis writes,

> Our present camp is precisely on the spot that the Snake Indians were encamped at the time the Minnetares of the Knife R. first came in sight of them five years since. from hence they retreated about three miles up Jeffersons river and concealed themselves in the woods, the Minnetares pursued, attacked them, killed 4 men 4 women and number of boys, *Sah-cah-gar-we-ah* o[u]r Indian woman was one of the female prisoners taken at that time. (original emphasis, 2: 283)

Lewis's use of Sacagawea's name might seem to imply a change in perception, an attempt at individuation rather than conflation. His next comments negate the effect. As he proclaims, "I cannot discover that she shews any immotion of sorrow in recollecting this event, or of joy in being again restored to her native country; if she has enough to eat and a few trinkets to wear I beleive she would be perfectly content anywhere" (2: 283). When Sacagawea tells the story of her capture, Lewis translates her calm into evaluations consistent with mythic meanings.

Assuming a tone similar to that employed in the entry describing the Shoshone's eating deer meat, Lewis is a removed and obviously superior interpreter. Excluding her from natural emotions of "civilized" women, as documented by centuries of captivity narratives, Lewis essentially denies that Sacagawea possesses the capacity to feel. Instead he describes a creature who remains contented as long as its simplest needs are met. Living in the present and responding solely to immediate sensory input, this Sacagawea cannot reflect. She feels no pain from her past, nor can she anticipate the future with hope or desire. This impassive creature embodies concepts of ignoble savagery.

Not long after this appraisal, Sacagawea is reunited with her people, and the logs describe a seemingly different woman, one who can no longer be contained by reductive judgments. After Lewis and a few men split from the main party to search for the Shoshones, Clark relates the moment that his group catches up with Lewis and the natives. He notes that Sacagawea "danced for the joyful sight, and She made signs to me that they were her nation" (2: 265). In his analysis of Sacagawea's subsequent arrival at the Shoshone campsite, Lewis adds that "the meeting of those people was really affecting, particularly between Sah-cah-gar-we-ah and an Indian woman, who had been taken prisoner at the same time with her" (2: 361). Offering more detail about a later council meeting than either captain supplies, the Biddle edition states that she "came into the tent, sat down, and was beginning to interpret, when in the person of Cameahwait she recognised her brother: she instantly jumped up, and ran and embraced him, throwing over him her blanket and weeping profusely; the chief was himself moved, though not in the same degree" (334).[12] Biddle then adds that even after Sacagawea recovers her composure, she is so overcome by emotion and a profusion of tears that the captains postpone the meeting (335).

Is this the same woman Lewis describes not more than two weeks earlier? How do such characterizations correspond with previous assessments? Reports of this suddenly dancing and joyful woman who greets her childhood friend with "affecting" warmth and who loses control at her reunion with her brother substantiate that Sacagawea possesses strong emotions and is capable of remembering and reflecting upon her past. They also imply that she responds to the present through the context of that past as well as the future. These portrayals display evidence that contradicts common cultural notions about unemotional, irrational squaws. Although not claiming that Sacagawea is civilized, they do nonetheless distinguish her from undifferentiated "savagery."

During their stay with the Shoshones and the long trip to the coast, the men mention Sacagawea numerous times. Most often focusing on tasks she performs, the entries domesticate the native woman and her actions. Lewis, for example, notes that she mends moccasins and boils tallow from elk shank bones. The commentaries do not address her feelings or motivations, and rarely do they exhibit the men's responses to her activities. Clark's writings from late November through late December exemplify this tendency. In three entries, Clark describes Lewis's and his own efforts to barter for a robe made of sea otter skins. As he claims, they finally "precured it for a belt of blue beed which the Squar-wife of our interpreter Shabono wore around her waste" (3: 238, cf. 237, 239). Nowhere does Clark state how they secure the belt from Sacagawea; nor does he address her feelings about the transaction. Do they simply take it from her, an action codifying their disregard for her property and her opinions? Or does she surrender it willingly, a gesture nullifying Lewis's comments that equate her contentment with trinkets?

A little more than a week later, Clark describes another interaction with Sacagawea in the same way. As he states, "The squar gave me a piece of bread made of flour which She had reserved for her child and carefully Kept untill this time, which has unfortunately got wet, and a little sour. this bread I eate with great satisfaction, it being the only mouthfull I had tasted for Several months past" (3: 259–60). Although Clark expresses his gratitude for the bread, despite its faults, he does not verbalize appreciation for his benefactor.

He is not alone in his methods of discussing her activities; all the men describe what Sacagawea accomplishes without communicating real regard for her during that winter on the coast. Since the men, for the most part, include her within the category of savagery, do they simply accept her labors as natural to her condition? Has she become the group's squaw, expected to fulfill tasks they would not assume a white woman could or would discharge?

Their universal silence hints at several possibilities. In their minds, Sacagawea may possess no emotions, as Lewis previously claims. Even if they do not deny her capacity to feel, the men may still perceive no obligation to understand, or at least to write about, those emotions. In either case, Sacagawea clearly remains in the background, a person whose existence is defined by her functionality within the context of their mission. As expressed in Lewis's passage during her illness, Sacagawea is a tool.

According to these entries, Lewis and Clark and the other men portray Sacagawea as unobtrusive and cooperative in a variety of ways throughout the journey. They acknowledge that she even anticipates individual and group needs and tries to fulfill them. In one case, however, both captains document that Sacagawea makes a request. When the captains do not initially include Sacagawea in a side trip, Lewis writes, "the Indian woman was very impo[r]tunate to be permited to go, and was therefore indulged; she observed that she had travelled a long way with us to see the great waters, and that now that monstrous fish was also to be seen, she thought it very hard she could not be permitted to see either (she had never yet been to the Ocean)" (3: 315). Clark's entry mimes this passage nearly word for word. Because the captains occasionally shared each other's notations to fulfill their obligation to keep a daily record, there is no way of knowing which one originated the commentary. Whichever captain wrote the entry, it supplies a picture of a superior male. This captain condescends, "indulging" a subordinate woman's desires.

The diarist also submits one of the most important evaluations concerning Sacagawea. Not simply responding to sensory impulses, not denied the capacity to feel, Sacagawea vehemently argues for her rights. She demonstrates that she has needs beyond those which food or trinkets can fulfill. This woman, in addition, not only persists in her argument but also uses the logic of past accomplishments to justify her demands. Although neither Lewis nor Clark shows awareness of these conflicting meanings, their remarks present significant slippages from cultural conceptions of the savage squaw.

During the return trip, after the expedition has split into two groups, Ordway and Clark write that Sacagawea points out a passage through the mountains (347; 5: 250), and a week later, Clark describes Sacagawea as "The indian woman who has been of great service to me as a pilot through this country" (5: 260). Although scholars have vehemently argued over the meaning and import of these notations, such entries are not inconsistent with the bulk of the portrayals offered about Sacagawea. She remains the "Indian woman" or "Interpreter's wife" in each reference, a type whose familiarity with the territory, whose kinship with nature, supplements rather than contradicts notions of savagery.

This pattern of response is abruptly reversed in Clark's last notation about Sacagawea. After having paid Charbonneau his earnings, Clark remarks that they have taken leave of the "interpreter and interprete[s]s" (5: 344). Although continuing to acknowledge an official role during the trip, Clark does not expound upon his perceptions of Sacagawea until two days later when he pens a letter to Charbonneau. Among other things, Clark asserts that "your woman who accompanied you that long dangerous and fatigueing rout to the Pacific Ocean and back diserved a greater award for her attention and Services on that rout than we had in our power to give at the Mandans" (7: 329). Echoing Clark's sentiments, the Biddle edition notes that Sacagawea was "particularly useful among the Shoshones. Indeed she has borne with a patience truly admirable, the fatigues of so long a route, uncumbered with the charge of an infant, who is even now only 19 months old" (780). These last two passages mark a significant departure from many previous assessments of Sacagawea.

Rather than simply codifying their expectations, Clark and the editors note the atypicality of her service. Although still described in terms of her utility to the mission, this unique woman compels praise. She is a figure of strength and even nobility. How can such appraisals be understood in comparison to the preponderance of evidence that all of the men assign her to the undifferentiated ranks of savagery? Is Clark merely voicing sentiment he does not feel, or has Sacagawea in those eighteen months demonstrated her individual, if not civilized, character?

The men of the Lewis and Clark Expedition, writers that illustrate their immersion in mythic conceptions throughout their journals, offer what may be the only written materials documenting Sacagawea's existence. Although he discusses the dilemma of depicting Pocahontas, Leitch Wright could be writing about Sacagawea when he notes that "it is not possible to guess her thoughts accurately," because there exists "not a single line revealing her innermost feelings, forcing us to rely on the perceptions" of white men (71). Offering no physical descriptions nor attempting to probe her motivations, diarists of the Corps of Discovery and their editors reveal a great deal about themselves and their mythic traditions as they almost always delimit Sacagawea through American conceptions of savagery. They portray her as a woman who, for the most part, requires no acknowledgment. She fulfills many tasks but deserves little recognition.

As seen in a few incidents of the expedition, some of the original documents also provide glimpses of an occasional breakdown in such totalizing perceptions. Never proclaiming her as part of civilization, these sporadic notations nonetheless allow Sacagawea certain unique qualities, a denial that she is indistinguishable from other savages. Although not an Indian princess or an emblem of the rectitude of manifest destiny, neither is this Sacagawea completely ignoble. In spite of these slippages, the men who originally interpret Sacagawea for the world, both the journals writers and the earliest editors, seem to note her efforts without clearly interpreting them as extraordinary, much less heroic.

Scholars and writers of later eras, such as Eva Emery Dye and Grace Raymond Hebard, decry the delay in Sacagawea's renown. That lag, however, was probably unavoidable. Early nineteenth-century America was not yet ready for a heroine from among the savage aboriginals of the western frontier, especially since those were the groups that were resisting the spread of Euro-American settlements at that time. Moreover, the only version of the story available to the public, the Biddle edition, inhibited Sacagawea's emergence as a legendary heroine as it omitted details and resolved ambiguities in her portrayals.

No one, therefore, publicly recognizes Sacagawea's cultural importance until near the turn of the twentieth century, when editors and writers return to the polyvocal originals. Such texts revisit the complex and sometimes conflicting interpretations of the journey, of the writers' actions, and of the people they encounter. Only then do Elliott Coues and Eva Emery Dye and others display an awareness of Sacagawea's connection to concepts of manifest destiny and her usefulness in illustrating its merit. Only then is Sacagawea propelled into legend.

From that period to the present, Sacagawea's character and actions, as initially related by the original texts, have offered challenges to later interpreters. She could not become an American heroine if she remained primarily savage. The original texts nevertheless enumerate the many times that Sacagawea helps the men and the expedition, in large ways and small. At times they also seem to question her status as an ignoble savage, allowing enough room for subsequent writers to interpret Sacagawea as the noble Indian princess.

3

THE BIRTH AND PROLIFERATION OF THE SACAGAWEA LEGEND

The Progressive Era

IN 1804–6, the diarists of the Lewis and Clark Expedition—Meriwether Lewis, William Clark, Joseph Whitehouse, John Ordway, and Patrick Gass—relate their stories of America's epic journey into the wilderness. Within their journals, the men offer generalizations and details about the sole native woman accompanying the Corps of Discovery. Predominantly interpreting her essence and behaviors in terms of ignoble savagery, as informed by a nexus of historical, cultural, and mythic realities, expedition writers place Sacagawea in the background of their tales. Because detailed portraits of a "squaw" were not necessary, at that time, to solidify collective understandings of the expedition, early editors of expedition manuscripts follow the example of the original writers in their depictions of Sacagawea. Her name, therefore, remained relatively unknown for nearly a century.

By the early twentieth century, researchers and artists (including Grace Raymond Hebard, Maria Edge, and L. T. Scott) report their regret that such an important "American" heroine was "neglected" for so long. Original expedition journals offer vague and open-ended portraits of the woman participating in the trip, so subsequent creators redefine Sacagawea's character and reinterpret the meanings of her actions. During the Progressive Era, writers, painters, and sculptors transform Sacagawea from a savage squaw into an American heroine. They do so by turning to another image made available through frontier myths. Inverting previous interpretations of Sacagawea, sloughing off assessments of her ignoble savagery, they define her as the noble helper of white men in the wilderness.

Rather than presenting a "squar" whose efforts are of little significance during the expedition, several historians of this period highlight Sacagawea's helpfulness and cooperation. Based on these activities, Sacagawea becomes a heroic figure of the American West. Others expand on these initial assertions by declaring that Sacagawea was an Indian princess. Fulfilling her purpose as the noble savage of frontier traditions, she displays her innate wisdom and knowledge by enthusiastically escorting civilization into America's western wildernesses. In speeches and scholarly articles, in fiction and in bronze, Progressive period creators depict Sacagawea as the Indian princess of the trans-Mississippi West. A symbol of the rectitude of manifest destiny, Sacagawea helps to explain Euro-American exploration of western frontiers and to justify the subsequent transformation of the wilderness into civilization. Progressive Era texts usher her into legend.

While embracing mythic images of the Indian princess in their works, certain writers also employ Sacagawea for an additional purpose during this period. Engaged in a reexamination of women's roles in American society and immersed in the effort to win suffrage, some writers and speakers characterize Sacagawea as a prototype for the emancipated woman. Susan B. Anthony, Anna Howard Shaw, Eva Emery Dye, and others invoke Sacagawea's name and story to inspire American women to brave the "wilderness." Rather than blazing trails through actual mountains, such women are exhorted to venture into social and political arenas and to take their rightful places in American culture.

Beginning in the 1890s, new editions of the Lewis and Clark journals, historical novels, scholarly and popular articles, speeches, and public statues transform Sacagawea from the savage squaw into an Indian princess and an American heroine. In this chapter, I analyze three Progressive period texts that reinterpret Sacagawea and her contributions to the expedition. The first to declare Sacagawea an American heroine, Elliott Coues published *History of the Expedition under the Command of Lewis and Clark, To the Sources of the Missouri River, thence across the Rocky Mountains and down the*

Columbia River to the Pacific Ocean, performed during the Years 1804–5–6, by Order of the Government of the United States in 1893. In this edition of the Lewis and Clark journals, Coues highlights Sacagawea's unique qualities and contributions in chapter and page headings and in footnotes.

Eva Emery Dye produced *The Conquest: The True Story of Lewis and Clark* in 1902 after she read extant versions of the expedition manuscripts, including the original Lewis and Clark logs and the Coues edition of the journals. Penning the most significant written work concerned with Sacagawea during the period, Dye promotes suffrage, with Sacagawea becoming a model for independent American women. Dye, in addition, illustrates the correlation between this Indian princess's life and actions and the glorious settlement of America's western lands.

After the publication of *The Conquest,* a variety of texts reiterate the Sacagawea story. They include Leonard Crunelle's *Bird Woman,* a statue dedicated in North Dakota in 1910. Continuously occupying a prominent place near the Bismarck capitol since its unveiling, Crunelle's work has been one of the few sculptures on the grounds until the late 1980s. Typical of other Sacagawea texts of the period, this larger-than-life bronze projects Sacagawea as a heroine based on her support of America's mission.

These Progressive Era texts and others introduce new and culturally useful perceptions of the native woman who accompanies the Lewis and Clark Expedition to the Pacific Ocean and back. In doing so, they not only establish an enduring pattern of portrayal but also initiate and disseminate the Sacagawea legend. Because these works reflect collective conceptions of savagery and civilization and the mission on the continent, especially as such ideas have intersected with images of Indian princesses, I first examine changes and continuities that unfold in frontier traditions from the early nineteenth century until America entered World War I.

According to Berger and Luckmann, myths legitimate socially constructed realities, passing cultural knowledge and collective understandings to new generations. Although this model seems to imply a complete transference of information, Doty in *Mythography* and Eliade in *Myth and Reality* concur that the transmittal of such meanings is not perfect. While primary and implicit myths demarcate the only natural way of perceiving the world, adjustments in such understandings can occur as meaningful personal visions become important to the corporate body or as social changes and/or historical events make new meanings possible. When disruptions in cultural consensus occur and when myths no longer maintain cogency, secondary legitimations often arise to preserve previous conceptions of the world.

During the seventeenth and eighteenth centuries, primary and implicit frontier myths required little more than illustration and reiteration among Euro-Americans. From the earliest colonial period into the beginning of the nineteenth century, captivity and war narratives, sermons, and histories projected images that reflected and reinforced America's frontier myths. From the mid-nineteenth through the early twentieth centuries, however, the totalizing logic of frontier traditions no longer sustained such implicit belief. Americans faced conflicting cultural realities, including the Civil War and the urbanization of large portions of the East.

In "Examination of Stereotyping," Ward Churchill, Mary Anne Hill, and Norbert Hill assert that "as the empire began to stretch its legs for the long haul of consolidation . . . the history of conquest needed popular revision if it were to be utilized as a matter of national pride" (37). Describing how America reconciled its history with the story of the sacred mission and the triumph of civilization over savagery, these critics outline the process by which cultural texts legitimated frontier myths during this period.

From the early 1800s until World War I, an array of American works reflected and reinforced images associated with frontier traditions. In *Savagism and Civilization,* Roy Harvey Pearce traces how novels, speeches, travel journals, and sculptures systematized notions of savagism after 1825. By the late 1800s, for example, Buffalo Bill's Wild West Show and other popular texts presented conflated images drawn from Plains groups' clothing, headdresses, and behaviors. All confirmed traditional belief systems concerning savagery and mission. As Frederick Hoxie and Robert Trennert claim in their respective studies, the 1876 Century of Progress Exposition at Philadelphia and the 1893 Columbian Exhibition at Chicago also projected collective conceptions about native savagery. These popular texts and others did not question past actions and motivations on the continent.[1] Instead they stressed and rehearsed the inevitability of the removal or obliteration of native populations to clear the wilderness for civilized settlement. Through these means, Americans received reassurances of the legitimacy of frontier traditions during this period.

As in earlier centuries, captivity narratives were important cultural texts during the nineteenth century and into the early twentieth century. Appealing to a wide audience, these works documented the "reality" of Euro-American frontier experiences. In addition, they defended the mission to convert the wilderness and depicted native savagery. Three representative captivity narratives of this period, Abbie Gardiner-Sharp's *History of the Spirit Lake Massacre and Captivity of Miss Abbie Gardiner,* Fanny Kelly's *My Captivity Among the Sioux Indians,* and F. M. Buckelew's *Buckelew: The Indian Captive or The Life Story of F. M. Buckelew While a Captive among the Lipan Indians in the Western Wilds of Frontier Texas, as Related by Himself,* published in the as-told-to format by S. E. Banta, vividly illustrated and substantiated collective frontier conceptions.

Since novelists began to use captivity plots by this time, most nineteenth-century captivity narratives employ various means to validate their stories, to assure American audiences of the "reality" of their experiences. In his introduction to the Buckelew captivity, for example, S. E. Banta asserts that the tale is "simple and absolutely true," not a blend of fact and fiction (6). Captivity writers of this era also append affidavits of authenticity to their narratives to eliminate skepticism about the truths they relate. Abbie Gardiner-Sharp provides testimonials from such distinguished people as B. R. Sherman and C. C. Carpenter, both past governors of Iowa (367–72). Fifteen pages of affidavits from army officers attest to Fanny Kelly's account (270–85).

While confirming the "realities" of Euro-American captive experiences in the wilderness, nineteenth-century captivities also verify certain frontier conceptions. According to such stories, settlers would fulfill America's destiny on the frontier. Offering no reasonable explanation for gratuitous attacks on innocent Euro-American populations, captivities depict pioneers defending the land against natives who threaten to return it to a primitive state. Banta proclaims in the preface to the Buckelew captivity that "No danger was too great, no war-path too bloody, no savage ambush too dangerous, no call to duty so hazardous, and no task so insurmountable as to check their [Texas pioneers'] magnificent strides of national development" (1). Other passages justify the transformation of the frontier. The narratives testify, for instance, that the land reaps benefits from the arrival of civilized occupants. As Banta asserts, Texas pioneers had secured "much of the fertile portion of the State, then undeveloped and waiting for the hand of industry" (2, 7). Essentially echoing *vacuum domicilium,* Banta verifies that the frontier languished before civilized pioneers allowed it to flower.

Of the "realities" recounted in nineteenth-century captivity narratives, native savagism is possibly the most important and definitely the most often reinforced concept. As Buckelew states, an old Lipan squaw whips him and then forces him to run the gauntlet (67). Moments later, according to his story, another old woman "began leisurely to draw the knife back and forth across my throat" (69). Fanny Kelly not only relates the savagery of the Sioux ambush of her wagon train but also provides ghoulish, graphic details of the subsequent murder of most of the travelers. Although she is spared from the slaughter, Kelly is beaten, starved, and tortured whenever the whim strikes her savage captors (110, 124, 203). A witness to the murder of Mrs. Fletcher, Kelly further relates how native men first drown the victim and then shoot her full of holes. They literally empty their guns into the body (117). Summoning pity for pioneer victims and hatred for their oppressors, nineteenth-century captivities illustrate native savagery.

Although Abbie Gardiner-Sharp's Oglala captors do not torture her, she refers to their savagism many times. When describing the return of a raiding party, for instance, Gardiner-Sharp notes the absurdity of the squaws' struggles to put on dresses taken from pioneer homes. She claims that such women could not possibly fit into "civilized" clothes. As the captive asserts, "they were too broad-shouldered, and brawny, to get the waist into position, or fasten it.

. . . They were altogether too much the shape of a barrel, to wear the dresses of white women" (149–50). Through such observations, Gardiner-Sharp declares that squaws are not civilized. More important, she indicates that they could never become civilized since savagery is an inborn characteristic. Although one could suppose that "squaws" might be trained to put on a "proper" dress, their bodies preclude that possibility. Civilization remains closed to them forever because their physical characteristics certify their innate savagism.

Captivity narratives and a profusion of other American works produced during the nineteenth century thus reflect and legitimate essential elements of frontier mythic traditions. Proclaiming the rectitude of the mission to convert the wilderness, maintaining the bifurcation of savagery and civilization, and attesting to the "truth" of frontier experiences, these texts confirm that Euro-American settlers rightfully supplanted natives on the frontier. As Reginald Horsman argues in "Scientific Racism and the American Indian in the Mid-Nineteenth Century," scientific theories developed in the 1840s conjoined with cultural texts to explain savagism and to justify territorial expansion. Concurring with Horsman, Bernard W. Sheehan asserts that these concepts were translated into federal policy and government action. The removal of indigenous peoples to territories west of the Mississippi, rapid continental expansion, wars against Plains natives, and the formulation and enactment of the Dawes Act were among the most important events reflecting mythic traditions during this period.

Beginning in the 1820s, significant numbers of Euro-American pioneers intruded on native territories in the Old Northwest and the South. As tensions increased in these "wilderness" areas, important U.S. policies centered on moving indigenous groups, including the Sauks, Foxes, Cherokees, Seminoles, and other tribal nations, to areas west of the Mississippi. Removals guaranteed that aboriginal peoples would no longer hinder American "progress." Former native lands would be open to civilized agriculture. Because indigenous peoples of the Old Northwest survived on mixed economies that featured hunting and because they also actively resisted Euro-American encroachments, U.S. expropriation of tribal lands created little public commentary or controversy. Mythic projections of the conversion of wilderness into civilization, in effect, explained the battles, treaties, and land cessions of the Old Northwest.

Subsequent removals of specific southern nations, on the contrary, created considerable public dissension in some regions. As Cherokee leaders resisted removal, for instance, Americans learned through newspapers and magazines that southern aboriginal economies, including those of the Cherokee, Choctaw, Chickasaw, Seminole, and Creek nations, relied on agriculture. They also discovered that Cherokees, in an effort to maintain their homelands, had begun to adopt certain components of Euro-American lifestyles. Melding traditional native customs with strategies employed by pioneers, Cherokees cultivated various grains, raised livestock, and lived in cabins like those of Euro-American settlers. These images and "realities" conflicted with declarations that such peoples were "savage."

Furthermore, as a result of a lawsuit filed by Cherokee leaders, Chief Justice John Marshall declared, in 1832, that Cherokee sovereignty could not be exterminated nor could their lands be confiscated. President Andrew Jackson, whose reputation had been established as an "Indian fighter" in previous wars against native groups, refused to enforce the ruling. Verbalizing the primacy of civilization over savagery throughout the removal controversy, Jackson spoke directly to the Cherokees in 1835. As he stated, "Circumstances . . . render it impossible that you can flourish in the midst of a civilized community" (Nash et al. 440). Tapping into the "metaphysics of civilization" (Takaki 107), Jackson protected America's moral character while simultaneously justifying pioneer claims to aboriginal lands. Although many American citizens grappled privately and publicly with conflicting realities that arose from the removals, the invocation of frontier myths nonetheless retained power to motivate and vindicate such actions on a national scale.

Even before the removals ended in 1842, vanguards of Euro-American pioneers proceeded across the Mississippi, proving that government policies had not satisfied settlers' desire for land. As American territorial sovereignty expanded rapidly in the West, John L. O'Sullivan coined the phrase "Manifest Destiny."[2] The expression explained that since America was divinely ordained, the nation had the right to secure the entire continent. No longer would the sacred territory be limited to east of the Mississippi, for God presented Americans with the obligation to expand the consecrated area. By employing such reasoning and rhetoric, political leaders rationalized U.S. claims to western territories and justified the wars, diplomacy, and treaties that America embraced and enacted from the 1840s through the 1860s.

Euro-American farmers, ranchers, and miners began migrating to the Great Plains during this period. Despite a relatively peaceful pattern of early settlement, hostilities erupted in the 1860s. For nearly thirty years, U.S. troops sought to quell Plains native uprisings and to restrict the Dakota, Lakota, Cheyenne, Arapahoes, Modocs, Nez Perces, Apaches, and other aboriginal nations to reservations. Unlike the southern removals, U.S. policies toward these essentially nomadic natives created little, if any, public discord. Instead, Euro-American reports of frontier atrocities, perpetrated by savages, reinforced mythic concepts of their continuing threat to civilization. These stories also augmented the contention that the continent must be secured.

Construed as contemporary reenactments of colonial beginnings, vivid descriptions of armed hostilities produced intense emotional response among populations on the frontiers and in the East. Newspapers throughout the country, for example, declared that General George Armstrong Custer was a hero after he led his troops to slaughter against confederated Plains groups in 1876. Perhaps ignorant of Custer's imprudent plans and their reckless execution, reporters and novelists based their interpretations of the event on a common belief in the mission to convert the wilderness and in the unequivocal heroism of those who attempted to achieve that goal. Events at Wounded Knee provide another illustration of such evaluations. After a detachment of the U.S. Army massacred more than two hundred unarmed Lakota men, women, and children in 1890, reporters and historians described this occurrence as an unfortunate "incident." As writers claimed, the Lakota posed a threat to civilization by persisting in the savage Ghost Dance, and the army was justified in its actions.

During the same period that the U.S. Army pursued the last Plains natives and placed them on reservations, Eastern progressivism sprang up in response to profound social and economic changes in America. According to several studies, urban growth, the birth of corporations, expanded transportation systems, an unprecedented influx of immigrants from southern and eastern Europe, and many other concerns confronted the nation in the 1880s.[3] Tapping into the energy and commitment generated from the abolitionist campaign, various reform groups tackled these new problems. Although some researchers have typified such groups as radical, Hofstadter claims that reformers shared common cultural understandings and attempted "to realize familiar and traditional ideals under novel circumstances" (213).

Among the most important reformers, Euro-Americans concerned with native populations and U.S. Indian policy coalesced into a unified group during the Progressive period. Meeting at Lake Mohonk, New York, in 1883 and each year thereafter for several decades, members of the Women's National Indian Association, the Indian Rights Association, the Board of Indian Commissioners, and other organizations attempted to resolve the "Indian problem." Like other reformers of the period, this group embraced frontier traditions. They sought to transform natives into Americans and to convert reservations, which they saw as enclaves of savagism, into agrarian models of civilization. Philanthropists, anthropologists, and politicians achieved nearly complete consensus in formulating plans to raise "primitives" to a level at which they could assimilate into the general population.

Indian reformers' most critical program was the Dawes Act of 1887.[4] Also known as the General Allotment Act, this piece of legislation was to serve as a panacea to the problem of savagery. After reservations had been divided into individual farm allotments, tribal members could no longer rely on communal forms that had held them back from "civilized" life. According to this plan, individual ownership would infuse aboriginals with a sense of industry and propel them toward a goal of accumulation, necessary first steps toward becoming American citizens.

Not only validating concepts of savagery and civilization, the

Dawes Act also reflected mythic notions of mission as it legalized the opening of "surplus" tribal lands to Euro-American homesteaders and land speculators. It also enabled Euro-Americans to purchase allotments from natives as soon as they had received patents. Compatible with essential ideas of frontier mythic traditions, the Dawes Act and its lease policies legitimated long-term goals of transforming savages into civilized farmers. It concurrently enacted short-term aims of hastening the confiscation of millions of acres of indigenous land.

During the nineteenth and into the early twentieth centuries, as indicated by events occurring on the continent, policies embraced by the U.S. government, and images and ideas embodied in cultural texts, frontier traditions sustained belief and conviction in Euro-American populations. Some studies, however, suggest that such myths did not maintain compelling persuasiveness during this period. As Harold P. Simonson writes in his introduction to Frederick Jackson Turner's *The Significance of the Frontier in American History*, by the beginning of the twentieth century, wide populations had begun to question assumptions and meanings that had previously defined America. As they read such works as Lincoln Steffen's *The Shame of the Cities* and Upton Sinclair's *The Jungle* (14–15), certain audiences interrogated the bases of American "civilization."

Other texts countered such questions. Frederick Jackson Turner, for instance, embraced and legitimated frontier mythic traditions. In *The Frontier in American History*, a work based on previous essays that had received considerable acclaim and acceptance by the turn of the twentieth century, Turner asserts that "free land" of frontiers and the pioneering experience shaped American ideology, institutions, and history. He claims that these same factors also produced America's unique greatness. Although frontier myths might not have been uniformly compelling nor comprehensively convincing to all Americans from the turn of the nineteenth century until World War I, such traditions informed wide and varied populations.

During this period, many historians also proclaimed that the Lewis and Clark Expedition was America's most important exploration of the wilderness. New editions of the expedition journals provided the best means of retelling that mythic experience and recounting the progress accomplished on the frontier. Combining an interest in natural history with his travels to expedition sites, army surgeon Elliott Coues published an annotated edition of the journals in 1892–93. The most important version of those scripts to that point, Coues's text is essentially an aggregate of the Biddle edition and the original texts. Like editors Biddle and Allen, Coues collapses the polyvocal original journals into the collective "we." In footnotes and appendixes, however, Coues incorporates selected quotations from the original scripts. He also provides supplementary scientific data and his own evaluations of various people who are portrayed in expedition texts.

Like Lewis and Clark and the Indian reformers of his own period, Coues reflects important frontier concepts in his work. Although the dedication, "To the People of the Great West," might not imply a reductive approach to the composition of such "People" or the constitution of the "Great West," Coues does not obscure his meaning for long. Immediately following the general dedication, Coues writes: "Jefferson gave you the country. Lewis and Clark showed you the way. The rest is your own course of empire. Honor the statesman who foresaw your West. Honor the brave men who first saw your West. May the memory of their glorious achievement be your precious heritage! Accept from my heart this undying record of the beginning of all your greatness" (n.p.). Not the least ambiguous in these lines, Coues cajoles the "you" and "your" of the passage, obviously Euro-American pioneers, to fulfill the destiny that Jefferson and the captains made possible. Coues embraces the concept of mission and attests to the previous "emptiness" of the land. Seemingly unaware of any other peoples who might have had a "precious heritage" in the West, Coues is also oblivious to endings that might have accompanied "the beginning of all your greatness." He depicts the West as a vacuum that welcomes civilized settlement.

In spite of the lack of commentary about native peoples in the dedication, Coues carefully presents the names of indigenous groups and describes their characteristics in footnotes and appendixes throughout his text. Coues, nonetheless, also validates ideas of savagism. In an appendix entitled, "Essay on an Indian Policy," for example, Coues states that for too long aboriginals have "wage[d] war on the defenseless inhabitants of the frontier" (3: 1220). He adds that the only means of civilizing such savages is to force them to understand the benefits of agriculture (3: 1236–67). Undoubtedly referring to the Dawes Act, Coues then suggests that a certain plan was about to consummate "philanthropic views toward those wretched people of America, as well as to secure to the citizens of the United States all those advantages which ought of right exclusively to accrue to them" (3: 1239–41). Through such commentary, Coues reveals his acceptance of the savagery/civilization dichotomy and his devotion to the conquest of the continent.

Coues also offers considerable commentary on Sacagawea. Although he calls her "the wife of Charbonneau," the "squaw," and "our interpreter's wife," as the original journalists have done previously, Coues consistently accompanies such references with her name in brackets. Unlike the original texts, Coues personalizes Sacagawea throughout his work. No longer is she an undifferentiated, savage squaw or a being whose existence is understood solely by virtue of her relationship to another person. Sacagawea has a name. Coues furthermore declares that Sacagawea was a heroic contributor to America's epic journey. He asserts, for example, that "Excepting Lewis, Clark, Gass, and Shannon, we know next to nothing more than the names of the men and woman [Sacajawea] who accomplished an immortal purpose" (1: 253; original interpolation). As seen in this passage and others, Coues focuses attention on Sacagawea. He does so throughout the work by featuring her in chapter and page headings and by stressing her actions in several footnotes.

Coues first mentions Sacagawea by comparing her to her husband. Describing Toussaint Charbonneau's initial appearance at Fort Mandan just after the arrival of the Corps, Coues writes that he was "of no particular merit . . . in comparison with his wife Sacajawea, the wonderful 'Bird-woman,' who contributed a full man's share to the success of the expedition, besides taking care of her baby" (1: 190). Sacagawea has not yet arrived at the expedition campsite, nor has she met the captains or performed any services for them. Coues nonetheless uses the occasion of Charbonneau's appearance to praise Sacagawea. Asserting that she "contributed a full man's share" during the trip, he essentially argues that Sacagawea was equal to the expedition men, except perhaps the captains. By stressing the additional burden of the baby, Coues in some ways portrays a woman who surpasses all of the men around her. Even before she appears in the narrative, Coues establishes that Sacagawea is a woman and a mother, proclaims that she is "wonderful," and affirms that assessment based on services she renders. By summing her up in such a positive way, he invites readers to follow Sacagawea's story as it unfolds in conjunction with the tale of the journey.

Coues features Sacagawea next when he details the events of February 11, 1806. Although he paraphrases Lewis's entry, Coues offers his own feelings as well. In a departure from Lewis's text, Coues refers to Sacagawea as "brave" when she endures a difficult labor. To direct attention to Sacagawea in this entry, Coues employs the page heading, "Birth of Sacajawea's Infant." Coues additionally argues in an accompanying footnote, "This little volunteer recruit joined the Expedition, and was brought back safe from the Pacific coast by one of the best of mothers" (1: 232). Although both the page heading and footnote imply that Baptiste is the locus of the event, Coues emphasizes Sacagawea and her actions. He does so in the first instance by employing Sacagawea's name while merely referring to her progeny as "infant." In the second case, although the baby is deemed a "little volunteer," Coues makes it clear, through the passive voice, that "the best of mothers" performed the important action. Sacagawea, not her child, is the significant "recruit" of the Lewis and Clark Expedition.

Coues again employs Lewis's journal to narrate the incident of the squall that nearly overturns an expedition boat. Like Lewis, he reports Charbonneau's poor steersmanship but does not allude to Sacagawea's role in the incident. In a sense, Coues recreates Lewis's seeming disregard for Sacagawea since the editor does not appear to consider her potential death significant enough to mention. In a footnote to that entry, nonetheless, Coues immediately provides a portion of Lewis's later notation about the squall. He juxtaposes the omission of Sacagawea's presence with commendations for Sacagawea's "fortitude" and "resolution" in rescuing critical articles during the crisis. Coues thus mediates the impression of his indifference to her. He furthermore argues in an adjoining footnote that "Sacajawea's conduct on this occasion is to be admired in itself, as well as by contrast with that of her craven French apology for a male" (1: 311). Coues additionally fortifies the sense of his respect for Sacagawea in the page heading, "The Hero and the Heroine." While obviously employing sarcasm in reference to Charbonneau, Coues assesses Sacagawea's heroism with real admiration.

As he compares Sacagawea with her husband on this and other occasions, Coues embraces a combination of national, racial, and gender issues. For example, he dwells on the fact that Charbonneau is French and sets up a causal relationship between nationality and behavior. As far as Coues is concerned, this Frenchman, because he is French, is a laggard and a coward. Charbonneau, according to such thinking, serves the captains badly because the French are not real men and because they could not truly support a mission that would eventually undermine their country's power in the region.[5]

Charbonneau serves as a foil to Sacagawea. Her reported bravery contrasts sharply with her husband's cowardice. By emphasizing Sacagawea's sex and motherhood, moreover, Coues also illustrates that her deeds are unexpected and, thus, even more impressive. By virtue of such courageous service, Sacagawea proves her devotion to the cause. She is entitled to be declared an American heroine.

In several other instances, Coues offers page and chapter headings that draw special attention to Sacagawea. Such examples include "Sacajawea Ill—Sulphur Spring" (2: 377), "Affecting interview of Sacajawea with her long-lost brother, whom she recognizes in the Shoshone chief Cameahwait" (2: 508), and "Sacajawea Recognizes Cameahwait" (2: 509). In each case, Coues emphasizes that Sacagawea is an important person. In other instances, however, Coues does more than identify Sacagawea as an individual worthy of special attention; he also offers examples of her wisdom and helpfulness. Recounting Sacagawea's instructions to Clark to take a southerly gap in the mountains on the return trip, Coues writes in a footnote that Clark is very sensible to follow the course "of the remarkable little woman, who never failed to rise to the occasion, even when it was mountains high." In the next footnote, Coues adds that "Sacajawea's knowledge was certainly extensive and accurate" (3: 1132). Not the least reticent to credit Sacagawea with meaningful expertise, Coues illustrates her usefulness to the mission and praises her accomplishments. He augments his claims of Sacagawea's heroism.

Coues's last commentary about Sacagawea describes the Corps' leave-taking at Fort Mandan. In a footnote, Coues expresses dismay that although the captains compensate Charbonneau, they fail to remunerate Sacagawea. As he asserts, "It could hardly have occurred to anyone, in 1806, that Chaboneau's wife had earned *her* wages too" (3: 1184–85, original emphasis). In this commentary, the only time he does so in the entire text, Coues fails to refer to Sacagawea by name. Only here is she just a "wife." Adopting the original scripts' reductive, relational reference while also employing an emphatic "her," Coues, in effect, underscores the irony of this injustice. Moreover, as he conjoins this footnote with the page heading, "The Debt to Sacajawea Not Discharged," Coues further accentuates the error. Although he excuses Lewis and Clark for their oversight, based on the apparent universal ignorance of their times, Coues registers his disappointment that America failed to recognize or compensate Sacagawea's contributions.

Elliott Coues offers America another edition of the expedition journals. In doing so, he illustrates and justifies frontier traditions and is the first person who strives to "discharge" the "debt" to this American heroine. As he combines such goals, however, certain tensions arise in this text. Coues's comparisons between Sacagawea and Charbonneau, for example, create a number of questions. If Charbonneau is despicable because of his nationality, how can Sacagawea, a Shoshone, be admired as an "American?" If her husband is abhorrent because of his cowardice, does she "prove" her citizenship through bravery? Other contradictions arise throughout Coues's work. Although he never eliminates commentaries from the original journals that imply Sacagawea's savagery, Coues always confirms evaluations that suggest her heroism. He reproduces, and in many ways magnifies, dissonances observed in the original texts. Is this native woman an undifferentiated squaw, illustrative of savagery, or is she an individual whose life essentially denies such conflation? Does Sacagawea occupy some ground in between?

Although he proclaims that Sacagawea was an American heroine, Coues never resolves the essential incompatibility of Sacagawea's savagery and her heroic actions during the expedition. In spite of such contradictions, Coues's declarations serve as the first step in the creation of the Sacagawea legend. Less than fifteen years after the publication of this text, writers, painters, and sculptors tout Sacagawea as the "key" to the success of the mission. Before that is possible, nonetheless, before Sacagawea can become a legendary heroine of the American West, conflicting claims concerning Sacagawea's savagery and her heroism have to be mediated.

At the turn of the twentieth century, as progressivism spawned reform groups that attempted to deal with a variety of cultural problems, Eva Emery Dye sought to extinguish ambiguities surrounding Sacagawea. In *History of Oregon Literature,* Alfred Powers writes that after this Oberlin graduate moved to Oregon with her husband and children in 1890, Dye ran a household and raised four children. She also conducted intensive research into the history of the territory and produced several novels, as well as poetry, songs, and histories. Convinced by her publishers to relate the Lewis and Clark Expedition story just before the mission's centennial year, Dye scoured the Biddle and Coues texts and the original expedition journals before publishing her most acclaimed and most popular work, *The Conquest: The True Story of Lewis and Clark,* in 1902 (404–6).

Not satisfied with retelling a narrative of male heroes, Dye highlights Sacagawea in *The Conquest.* An activist in the woman suffrage movement, Dye struggles to find a heroine that American women can admire and emulate. As she writes in her journal, "Out of a few dry bones I found in the old tales of the trip, I created Sacajawea and made her a living entity. For months I dug and scraped for accurate information about this wonderful Indian Maid" (qtd. in A. Powers 93). Dye presents a woman whose existence and actions are to serve as a template from which other women can model their lives. Through her portrayal of Sacagawea, Dye urges the American public to visualize beyond that single, heroic example. If given suffrage and other opportunities, American women across the continent could also display their heroism.

Adopting the chronology of the original journals, Dye weaves a tale of a young woman whose life and actions determine the fate of the expedition. Dye writes, for example, that the captains are eager for Sacagawea's recovery after the difficult delivery of her child because she can translate among the Shoshones. As Dye asserts, "Poor little Sacajawea! She was really very ill. If she died who would unlock the Gates of the Mountains?" (197). Unlike the native woman of Lewis's or Biddle's accounts, Dye's Sacagawea does not merely accompany the explorers. Neither is she simply an interpreter, as Clark first records. Less tentative even than Coues, Dye declares that Sacagawea is the key to the success of the mission.

Like all previous texts recounting the events of the Lewis and Clark Expedition, Dye provides many examples of Sacagawea's helpfulness during the journey. Ever industrious as she carries her baby on her back, this native woman identifies landmarks (215, 224), translates among various indigenous groups (228, 232), and assures the safety of the men (236–37). When Dye describes the squall incident, moreover, she writes that "Cruzatte alone is calm, and Sacajawea, who, with her baby and herself to save, still manages to catch and preserve most of the light articles that were floating overboard" (213). In recounting this incident, Dye departs from previous scripts that neglect to mention Sacagawea at all or report her efforts in a footnote. Instead she features Sacagawea. She declares that if Sacagawea had not managed to rescue these important materials, the explorers would have had to turn back.

Notations of Sacagawea's cooperation and helpfulness do not preclude questions and tensions generated by earlier assertions of Sacagawea's savagery, however. To overcome these dissonances, Dye seeks to prove that Sacagawea was not a typical native. Unlike Lewis, Clark, Biddle and Allen, and Coues, Dye attempts to deny that Sacagawea was a savage. Only once does she term Sacagawea a "squaw." Since that occurs when she writes of Sacagawea's initial arrival at Fort Mandan, Dye documents the impossibility of recognizing nobility from a glimpse at any native woman. After that brief moment, Sacagawea's essence becomes apparent, and Dye never calls her a "squaw" again. Thereafter throughout the novel, Dye contrasts the beautiful, young Bird Woman with those "leathery dames" who were wrinkled and old at thirty (188, 193).

Such comparisons, by themselves, do not suffice in separating Sacagawea from the savage masses, nevertheless, because the Bird Woman too will eventually age. Dye instead relies on an important facet of frontier mythic traditions to illustrate Sacagawea's unique status. When expedition members discover that her brother is a Shoshone chief, Dye writes that Sacagawea is "a Princess, come home now to her Mountain Kingdom" (228). Sacagawea becomes an Indian princess. Her nobility stems from her "royal" heritage, proving her innate superiority. Combining declarations of royalty with other signs of Sacagawea's exceptional character, such as industry, devotion to the cause, and courage, Dye introduces a unique American heroine.

Expounding on this characterization, Dye describes Sacagawea as the quintessence of nineteenth-century "true womanhood." Although she stresses the baby's presence at every point, Dye never implies that the child is too great a burden. Never does Baptiste prevent his attentive and devoted mother from achieving impressive goals. In addition to emphasizing Sacagawea's motherhood, Dye highlights Sacagawea's domesticity throughout the novel. Not only does she care for a baby in the dangerous wilderness, but she also finds and prepares foods for the entire group (209, 245) and nurses the men when they are ill (241). Describing an evening at the group's winter quarters near the Pacific Ocean, Dye writes: "All day the firelight flickered on Sacajawea's hair, as she sat making moccasins, crooning a song . . . with the baby Touissant [Baptiste] toddling around her on the puncheon floor. . . . The modest Shoshone princess never dreamed how the presence of her child and herself gave a touch of domesticity to that Oregon winter" (245). This Sacagawea exemplifies a life of "true womanhood." Just as the baby represents each expedition member's son/brother, Sacagawea becomes that man's modest and pure mother/sister/wife. As Dye illustrates, popular nineteenth-century notions of purity, domesticity, and motherhood reveal a woman's moral superiority.[6]

In conjunction with such declarations, nonetheless, Dye never loses sight of her goal to depict a powerful and authoritative heroine. During that same winter, according to Dye, Charbonneau tells Sacagawea that the captains will not allow her to see the whale because the journey of a few miles might be too arduous. Aware of the ridiculousness of such reasoning, since she has just completed a trek across half a continent with a baby on her back, Sacagawea is angry. Dye writes, "This was a staggering blow to Sacajawea, but her woman's determination had been aroused and she took the rostrum, so to speak" (250). Unswayed by convention, Sacagawea thrusts the baby at her husband Charbonneau and argues her own case before Lewis and Clark. Apprised of the capriciousness of the previous decision and humbled by this "brave little woman" (250), Clark agrees to let Sacagawea see the ocean. In this passage, Dye abandons all previous interpretations of the incident. While Lewis and Clark note that Sacagawea cites past accomplishments to achieve her goal, neither of their diaries implies that the force of her arguments or the authority of her person has the least effect on them. Instead, they declare that Clark merely indulges Sacagawea's whim. Rather than being acted upon, Dye's Sacagawea initiates action and demands a response. She does not rest until she has achieved the desired outcome.

Dye offers the culminating portrait of Sacagawea's authority in descriptions of the return trip. A member of Clark's party near the Continental Divide, Sacagawea "led the way into the labrynthine Rockies" (283). Pointing the way, she cries, " 'Onward!' . . . 'the gap there leads to your canoes!' " (284). Later, when a network of peaks bewilders the men, Sacagawea again indicates the route, and Clark merely follows (285). Elaborating beyond Clark's casual notation or Coues's commentary, Dye projects a powerful woman. This heroine not only ventures into the wilderness with men, but at times she supersedes them in knowledge and motivation.

The explorers' departure from Fort Mandan provides Dye with the best opportunity to sum up this native woman, "Sacajawea, modest princess of the Shoshones, heroine of the expedition, stood with her babe in her arms and smiled upon them [the expedition men] from the shore. So had she stood in the Rocky Mountains pointing out the gates" (290). No savage squaw, Dye's Sacagawea is an Indian princess; a devoted and tender mother; a model of purity, modesty, and domesticity; an American heroine by virtue of her courageous service to the mission.

According to Jane Tompkins in *Sensational Designs,* writers like Dye attempt to redefine certain aspects of the social order by articulating and proposing solutions to problems of a particular historical moment (xi).[7] As she presents a heroine in *The Conquest,* Dye seeks to provide society "with a means of thinking about itself" by defining certain aspects of a shared social reality and by "dramatizing its conflicts, and recommending solutions" (Tompkins 200). Devoted to the woman's movement, fighting for suffrage, tempering potentially threatening images of Sacagawea's female power and authority with assertions of her modesty and domesticity, Dye proposes that women can be liberated and yet retain qualities of true womanhood. As contemporary American women incorporated new social constructions into culturally approved models of behavior, they would benefit not only themselves and their families but also their entire society.

Thousands of readers embraced the first fictional Sacagawea, as illustrated by the fact that Dye's publisher, McClurg, offered three printings of *The Conquest* between November 1902 and January 1903. Commenting on this response in her journal, Dye remarks, "The beauty of that faithful Indian woman with her baby on her back, leading those stalwart mountaineers and explorers through the strange land appealed to the world" (qtd. in Clark and Edmonds 94). Was this characterization of Sacagawea the only aspect of the novel that attracted such an audience? Surely, as Dye declares, some women were in search of a heroine, but that search cannot entirely account for the popular appeal of *The Conquest.* Coterminous with the tale of a heroine, many notations glorify the exploration and subsequent settlement of the West. Such commentaries also explain the novel's widespread acceptance.

In this historical romance, Dye depicts a tale of notable people's lives in a particular place and at a specific time. Not simply relating a story of heroism, she additionally shows how historical figures illuminate past meanings in terms of present conditions. Dye essentially taps into national consciousness and collective understandings of frontier traditions and connects them to her own time. As she offers a sentimental look at the expedition, she celebrates the conquest of the wilderness and reaffirms American frontier traditions.

Alfred Powers claims that Dye, like many Oregonians of that

time, maintained a frontier perspective. The conquest of the wilderness, argues Powers, was in her memory and on her tongue (408). Dye reflects such a perspective throughout *The Conquest,* but no more explicitly than in the following passage:

> The Indian? He fought and was vanquished. How we are beginning to love our Indians, now that we fear them no longer! . . . We might have tamed him but we had not time. The movement was too swift, the pressure behind made the white man drivers as the Indian had driven before. Civilisation demands repose, safety. And until repose and safety came we could do no effective work for the Indian. We of today have lived the longest lives, for we have seen a continent transformed. . . . We have forgotten . . . that the Indian beleaguered our wooden castle. (442)

As she explains how and why natives had to be subdued and as she reiterates the benefits Euro-American culture reaped in that process, Dye explicates significant components of manifest destiny.

Asserting several times that the savage "Indian" resisted civilization, Dye does not simply conflate all aboriginals into one type. She reduces them to a single unit and subsequently identifies this lone savage as male. In doing so, Dye invokes images long associated with the ignoble native man: captivity of innocent pioneer women, threatening sexuality, potential torture.[8] As she further argues, this solitary male constitutes the antithesis of the "we" who rightfully occupy the frontier. Not just identifying her audience, Dye counts herself as one of these pioneers. In addition, by stressing that a profusion of settlers needed the land of that lone savage, Dye tacitly points out that her people, because they are civilized and by virtue of their numbers, justly took possession of the continent.

As she embraces the dichotomy of savagery and civilization, Dye also reflects other frontier conceptions. She implies, for instance, that some powerful, unstoppable force compelled the mission on the continent. Although Dye claims that the Indian "fought," she does not name the recipient of such action. Employing the passive voice, she states that this Indian "was vanquished" in the next phrase, intimating that the action occurred without agency. In other words, whom the Indian fought and who vanquished him remains unidentified. Later proclaiming that the "movement was too swift," Dye suggests that a power, one that was not to be denied or controlled, initiated the rush of settlement. As she names that source of energy in the next sentence, Dye asserts that civilization demanded "safety" and "repose." Civilization itself commanded the "transformation" of the frontier.

Certain about the mission on the continent, confident of her audience's concurrence, Dye does nothing to specify material, social, or cultural conditions before or after the transformation of the continent. Nor does she enumerate the costs or benefits of the change for either savages or civilized settlers. Such omissions indicate that Dye is persuaded that the transformation was manifestly positive. Although the process itself might have proved painful to the contesting sides, both are obvious beneficiaries. No further details, explanations, or illuminations are necessary.

Dye does not totally dismiss settlers' behaviors, however. Claiming that pioneers became "drivers" during the "movement," she reports that "we might have tamed" the savage. Although she acknowledges a certain level of failure on the part of settlers, Dye also absolves them of responsibility as she claims that "the Indian had driven before." Preceding white men in the act of conquest, the savage was simply a previous participant in the appropriate cycle of acquisition. Since the "Indian's" former action essentially attested to the validity of a successive possession of frontier territories, "he" is forced to acquiesce to more numerous, more powerful, and more advanced Euro-American pioneers.

Throughout the passage, Dye inscribes a sense of the inevitability of these past events. "We" held no dominion until civilization justifiably drove the savage out of his wilderness. Until civilization overcame obstacles in its path, "we" could initiate no other action. Such claims verify that civilization had an obligation to accomplish its goal. Even as she asserts that "we" could begin to help the "Indian," Dye reminds the reader that this benevolence was possible only because the savage no longer posed a threat to civilization. Only when "the castle," the locus of that civilization, was in safe repose, could settlers begin to love the "Indian."

In attempting to accomplish one kind of cultural work, which

Jane Tompkins describes, Dye also embraces another objective. As Philip Fisher discusses in *Hard Facts: Setting and Form in the American Novel*, popular literature often retraces the past in an effort to perform valuable service for the present. By stabilizing, simplifying, and justifying past events and by repeating their culturally mandated meanings, these works install "habits of moral perception." Such cultural texts furthermore facilitate the "forgetting" of the strenuous process that helped to convert learned meanings into collective understandings. As Fisher writes, many nineteenth-century works performed these tasks in America as they rehearsed the conflation of native groups, the inevitability of the expulsion of natives from their territories, and the progress of civilization on the continent (3–5).

Therefore, as Dye models a female character to be admired and emulated, a prototype from which other women might build their lives, she simultaneously justifies American frontier traditions. Although these goals harmonize in many ways, the joining of such concerns also creates dissonances as they converge with the meanings of Sacagawea's character. By differentiating between savagery and civilization, for example, Dye defines two mutually exclusive categories. Although she consciously excludes Sacagawea from the ranks of savagery, neither does Dye portray Sacagawea as civilized. Sacagawea's ambiguous situation is evident throughout *The Conquest*.

When introducing Sacagawea's husband Charbonneau, for example, Dye asserts that "The worst white man was better than an Indian husband" (197). Here Dye clearly distinguishes between the behaviors of a savage, as opposed to a civilized, husband and states that Sacagawea benefits from the better spouse. Dye also shows, nonetheless, that Charbonneau is among the worst of civilized men. Like Coues, Dye bases such assessments, at least in part, on Charbonneau's purported cowardice during the mission. She also stresses that Charbonneau is the prototypical French trader. A despicable "squawman," Charbonneau is a "civilized" male who succumbs to the seduction of the wilderness as he adopts savage ways and marries native women.

In spite of the implications of these comments, Dye never protests that her heroine, her wonderful Indian princess, is married to

Charbonneau. In fact, Dye implies that although Charbonneau is obviously diminished by his marriage and lifestyle, he remains civilized. Sacagawea, who is raised by the match, cannot be included within that category. Even as Dye illustrates that behavior and environment influence the degree of a person's savagery or civilization, she essentially contends that placement within those classifications is determined by birthright.

Dye establishes Sacagawea's marginal status in other passages as well. As she details the scene in which the expedition men prepare to leave Fort Mandan, Dye summarizes Sacagawea: "Madonna of her race, she had led the way to a new time. . . . Across North America a Shoshone Indian Princess touched hands with Jefferson, opening her country" (290). Pure in both body and spirit, Princess Sacagawea not only assures the success of the mission but also has "led the way" to the future. As a result of the magnificent service she renders, she "touches hands with Jefferson." Despite such metaphoric flourishes, Dye still proclaims that Sacagawea is a Shoshone and a member of "her race." This Indian princess cannot supersede her savage heritage even if she is superior to other natives.

Dye reinforces the concept of innate savagery as she describes Sacagawea's thoughts. Watching the men leave Fort Mandan, Sacagawea "looked wistfully. She, too, would like to visit the white man's country" (289). Despite her service and her nobility, Sacagawea does not belong among civilized peoples. Nor does she deserve the best that civilization has to offer. Even in her own mind, Sacagawea knows that such a place is "white man's country," not hers. Confined to a marginal position, the celebrated Indian princess articulates a profound irony. Because of her "royal" birth, her experiences on the arduous journey, and her contact with the men of the Corps, Sacagawea possesses an acute awareness of civilization's promise and gifts. That comprehension, rather than enriching her life, compounds the incongruity of her exclusion from civilization. In spite of Dye's admiration for this "American" heroine, *The Conquest* reflects the idea that civilization remains closed to all native peoples, even those who purportedly espouse principles of manifest destiny.

As Ronald Taber argues in "Sacagawea and the Suffragettes: An Interpretation of a Myth," Sacagawea became a focal point of western women's groups after the publication of *The Conquest.* The Women's Club of Portland, for example, employed Sacagawea's name and story to advance their cause. They organized the Sacajawea Statue Association and commissioned a statue of Sacagawea for the 1905 Lewis and Clark Expedition centennial celebration in Portland. This bronze work, designed and executed by Alice Cooper, was funded through contributions from Federated Women's Clubs across the country. According to Millard McClung, reference librarian of the Oregon Historical Society, the statue was moved to its present location in Portland's Washington Park in 1906.

Despite the connections that he documents, Taber neglects to mention that not all works featuring Sacagawea during this period were created by suffragists. Although he carefully traces the history and significance of the Portland piece, for instance, Taber does not discuss a statue dedicated to Sacagawea during the 1904 Louisiana Purchase Exposition in St. Louis. Mrs. Fred C. Harrington, librarian of the Missouri Historical Society during the 1960s, notes that this monument was created by Bruno Zimm and paid for by the Louisiana Exposition Corporation.[9] Zimm's work is only one example of no fewer than thirty-three texts highlighting Sacagawea within fifteen years of the publication of *The Conquest.* Of these histories, novels, articles, news stories, speeches, poems, and plays, suffragists produced fewer than half.

Taber also fails to recognize that Sacagawea became a legendary figure during this period because her story was an integral part of America's celebration of the western conquest. Although Taber and Ella Clark and Margot Edmonds in *Sacagawea of the Lewis and Clark Expedition* link certain Sacagawea texts to the suffrage movement, they do not acknowledge that all of the works featuring her during this era celebrate manifest destiny. Promotional campaign materials and the dedication ceremony for Leonard Crunelle's *Bird Woman,* as well as the statue itself, display the connection between Sacagawea and frontier myths.

The superintendent of Federated Women's Clubs of eastern North Dakota, Mrs. Mattie M. Davis, began a statewide campaign in 1905 to erect a statue in honor of Sacagawea, according to Bertha Palmer. Palmer, art division chair of the federation, also writes that club women adopted a two-pronged strategy to accomplish their goal. They raised funds while simultaneously circulating promotional materials about Sacagawea.

Club members, together with public school children, collected over $3,500 to pay for the statue. Children contributed $555.78 in pennies, and club women donated $1.00 each ("Statue Unveiling" 6). Unwilling to ask for public monies, women raised additional funds by offering entertainments, festivals, concerts, suppers, and bridge lessons. They also sold flowers, paintings, postcards, and Christmas stamps (8). No one wrote of the irony that this exclusively Euro-American crusade to honor a historical native woman occurred in a state populated by indigenous peoples who remained isolated on reservations. Natives took no part in the monument drive.

Such ironies apparently went unrecognized as club women inaugurated a campaign to promote Sacagawea's fame across North Dakota. As the *Tribune* story relates, 20,000 copies of *Sakakawea (Bird Woman) Statue Notes* were given away or sold between 1906 and 1910 (8).[10] Created to inform the public about this American heroine, the brochure lists reasons a statue should be dedicated to Sacagawea. It claims, for example, that she provided a variety of essential services during the journey. Citing another proof of Sacagawea's virtue and heroism, *Statue Notes* states that Sacagawea was the first Indian west of the Missouri River to convert to Christianity (n.p.). Proposing as fact an event not even hinted at in the journals nor verified in any other historical materials, the brochure is the first to incorporate another facet of the Pocahontas story as part of the Sacagawea narrative. Like her East Coast counterpart, Sacagawea helped white men in the wilderness, saved their lives, and adopted their religion.[11]

Not only touting her accomplishments, the brochure also asserts that Sacagawea was not a typical savage, but "more erect, more slenderly built . . . a princess of uncommon grace of mind and of person" (2). She is not a stooped and barrel-shaped squaw, not the type of savage that Gardiner-Sharp witnesses attempting to put on civilized clothing. Instead, Sacagawea is a unique native, the assumption at least partly based on the shape of her body. Such purported distinctiveness not only displays her physical superiority but also points to her mental and emotional preeminence. She is a princess by birth and worthy of that title, according to her actions. The ideal Indian princess, Sacagawea is an American heroine because she "welcomed with intelligent appreciation the civilization of the white race" (n.p.). Motivated by an uncommon devotion to manifest destiny, Sacagawea is heroic because she has the sagacity to understand and support the mission into the wilderness. As promotional materials for the campaign explicitly connect Sacagawea to frontier myths, Euro-American men, women, and children from across North Dakota honored her.

This crusade culminated as North Dakota Federated Women's Clubs members and others gathered in Bismarck on October 13, 1910, to dedicate Crunelle's statue of Sacagawea. Demonstrating the significance of this event, editors of the *Bismarck Tribune* devoted the entire front page and three inside pages of the next day's edition to stories about the ceremony. Gathering on the capitol lawn to hear presentations and to see the unveiling of *Bird Woman* as the "autumn sun" sank "in the west" (1), approximately five thousand people witnessed the unmistakable bond between Sacagawea and America's glorious conquest of the West.

During the ceremony, club women and state historical society officers spoke about the project and about Sacagawea. In each case, presenters espoused frontier concepts and linked Sacagawea to that tradition. Chair of the "Sakakawea Committee," Mrs. C. F. Amidon said, "The True pioneer spirit has passed along from the first pioneer, she whose statue is being dedicated here, to the western women of today" (6, original capitalization). Judge B. F. Spalding, accepting the statue on behalf of the state, stated that Sacagawea deserved grateful remembrance because of the selfless and faithful services she performed in "the land of promise and of plenty, which she helped save to this great nation" (1). Like the scripts promoting the statue, dedication speeches embraced and reiterated frontier myths. Sacagawea was an integral part of these traditions.

As in other Progressive Era texts, the dedication ceremony also showed that Sacagawea's actions had benefited America's native peoples. Secretary of the North Dakota State Historical Society, Dr. O. G. Libby stated in his speech that Sacagawea's efforts had assured that "our good friends" were now able to receive education in government schools (6). The *Tribune* underscores that idea in a sidebar about natives who attended the unveiling. Focusing on specific Shoshones, Hidatsas, Mandans, Arikaras, and Sioux, the story highlights information that rationalized manifest destiny.

According to the *Tribune*, Gros Ventre James Holding Eagle, a graduate of Santee Nebraska government school, influenced his parents to "farm and make a home for themselves" (6). Shoshone Mattie Johnson, a graduate of Haskell in Kansas and "a clever lady in every way," was employed in the Bismarck Indian school as instructor in the laundry department (6). Arikara James Beauchamp, also a graduate of a government school, was "one of the successful Indian farmers and stock raisers on the Berthold reservation and one who is doing much for the betterment of his brother in the way of getting better acquainted with better methods both in farming and living" (1). Never having heard of Sacagawea before the monument drive began, according to the news article, such native peoples did not signify traditional ties between themselves and this "American" heroine. Instead they illustrated the benefits that all aboriginals had realized since the closing of the frontier.

Speaking English, embracing "civilized" pursuits, reflecting the virtues of assimilation, they stood as evidence that native peoples could accomplish something in America. These images of purported assimilation also reveal overt signals of separation. As Hoxie asserts in *A Final Promise,* American policies after 1900 created a segregated educational system for native peoples. Unconvinced that innate savagism could be eradicated, framers of such programs halted their efforts to integrate indigenous peoples into American culture. Instead they shifted to a policy of training natives to become marginally productive wards at the bottom of America's social structure.

In reflection of these principles, native students, for example, were not integrated into Bismarck High School, but were shunted to the school south of town. Attending segregated schools in this state capital and throughout the country, such pupils also learned a vastly different curriculum. Trained to become laundresses, farm hands, and ranchers, rather than educated to become doctors, lawyers, and teachers, these students might have seemed more civilized as they adopted language, clothing, and haircuts of the dominant culture, but they would remain peripheral to civilized America.

In addition to the speeches of the day and the presence of "assimilated" natives, the unveiling of Crunelle's statue provided the most conspicuous correlations between Sacagawea and manifest destiny. According to the *Tribune* story, the 14th U.S. Infantry Band played "The Star Spangled Banner" as the ribbon was cut to "release the folds of the National Flag that veiled the bronze features of Sakakawea" (1). The flag fell away, and "people cheered, and murmurs of appreciation and wonderment fell from the lips of those who gazed upon the beautiful figure" (6). Although *Bird Woman* was bathed in a national anthem that was not hers, no one wrote of that irony. Nor did anyone note that those who performed the song to honor Sacagawea were military men, similar to those who had expropriated native peoples' lands across the West. Quite literally wrapped in the national flag, Sacagawea became one of the most recognizable emblems of America's mission into the wilderness.

While written materials promoting the statue became unimportant after the campaign met its goals and although the dedication speeches and ceremony lasted only a few hours, the statue itself establishes and permanently reinforces the connection between Sacagawea and frontier myths. Figure 2, a photograph of *Bird Woman*, illustrates some of these correlations.

The twelve-foot work is set on a block of rough granite. Seemingly emerging from that rock, an imposing woman stands erect, head and chin tilted slightly upward. Her strong, bronze features show signs of neither sorrow nor pleasure, but seem to reflect a sense of concentration or determination. Dressed in traditional garb of fringed buckskin and blankets, this native mother raises her right hand to her shoulder, assuring the security of the sleeping baby on her back. As her right foot is placed only slightly in front of the left, she seems to walk at an unhurried, but purposeful, pace. In all these ways, *Bird Woman* appears to signify and thus to honor any traditional indigenous woman.

Although the statue might not at first seem to represent a specific person or display a definite ideology, *Bird Woman* identifies the singular subject of its image and establishes the connection between

Figure 2. Leonard Crunelle's *Bird Woman* (Photo courtesy of the Picture Collection of the North Dakota State Historical Society)

this "American" heroine and manifest destiny. Relating the identity of the figure, the inscription on the statue base reads, "Sakakawea— the Shoshone Indian 'Bird Woman,' who in 1805, guided the Lewis and Clark expedition from the Missouri River to the Yellowstone." Not a text representing the grandeur or heroism of a universal, aboriginal female, the monument honors a single historical woman. Furthermore, it freezes her essence at a particular moment. Although both the statue and the plaque stress Sacagawea's native origins, she is not honored for that reason. Instead, Sacagawea is commemorated because of her actions during the expedition. Because she is an "Indian," moreover, her heroism is cause for greater attention and celebration as she signifies that the best natives might also recognize the rectitude of America's mission on the continent.

Symbolically expounding upon Sacagawea's unique heroism, the statue faces directly west. This purposeful placement converges with the meanings of all other physical signs of the work. Her intense gaze becomes an indication of her devotion to the expedition and her desire to serve. A "True pioneer," as Amidon declares her, Sacagawea scans the western horizon to envision America's future. Her stance represents the long journey she has endured on foot, an accomplishment that is more impressive because she bore her baby on her back. That stride, however, also signifies the perseverance of American pioneers as they moved westward across the frontier. Reflecting Annette Kolodny's assertions in *The Lay of the Land,* the statue *Bird Woman* seemingly arises from the raw materials of the land. Compliant and supportive, this unique native woman symbolizes the willingness of the continent to receive civilized settlement.

Working for five years to fund and dedicate a statue, North Dakota Federated Women's Clubs assured that Sacagawea would be recognized as North Dakota's most celebrated "daughter." So too did sculptor Leonard Crunelle. As the promotional materials, the dedication ceremony, and the statue itself offered a heroine to the state and to America, each text linked her story to celebrations of manifest destiny.

Although Sacagawea's name remained obscure in America for nearly one hundred years, Coues's edition of the journals, Dye's *The*

Conquest, and Crunelle's *Bird Woman,* in addition to a considerable number of other texts, initiate and proliferate the Sacagawea legend. Transforming her into an American heroine during the Progressive period, writers and other artists characterize Sacagawea as a singular native woman. Most declare that she was an Indian princess. Unique by birth, an American heroine by virtue of her actions and attitudes, Sacagawea explicates and justifies America's frontier traditions during this period.

In spite of their efforts to yoke Indian princess imagery with affirmations of manifest destiny, Sacagawea's Progressive Era proponents generate significant questions. When suffragists, for example, claim Sacagawea as a symbol of modern American womanhood, they attempt ambitious cultural change. Perhaps blinded by their own aims to rectify one kind of injustice, such women seem unaware of other discriminations they inscribe. How can Sacagawea signify a melding of "American" women's past and future if she were not an American? How can she represent the emancipated American woman when she could never be ranked among them?

Although suffragists and others aspire to exclude Sacagawea from the category of ignoble savagery, they nonetheless bar her from civilization because of her race. If Sacagawea occupies such an ambiguous position, neither savage nor civilized, how can she symbolize the "civilization" that has spurned her? How can she stand as an argument for a society that has rejected one of its most important champions? Portrayed within all of these works is the ambiguous Indian princess, the noble but innately savage woman whose existence symbolizes the very civilization from which she is set apart.

Perhaps because American culture was unconcerned with such questions at that time, the legend of Sacagawea proliferates after the publication of *The Conquest.* As Table 2 illustrates, once Dye declares that Sacagawea was not only an American heroine but also an Indian princess, other works follow her example. During the Progressive period, Sacagawea is transformed from a savage squaw, as she is predominantly defined in original texts of the expedition and early editions of the journals. Instead, she becomes the Indian princess, the royal guide, the essential helper in the penetration and conquest of the West.

Table 2. Sacagawea's Transformation from a Savage into an Indian Princess[1]

Date	Author	Genre	Savage	Princess	Guide	Key	Am. Heroine
1804–6	Lewis	Journal	x				
1804–6	Clark	Journal	x		x		
1804–6	Whitehouse	Journal	x				
1804–6	Gass	Journal	x				
1804–6	Ordway	Journal	x				
1814	Biddle	Journal Ed	x		x		
1893	Coues	Journal Ed	x		x		x
1902	Hosmer	History	x		x		
1902	Dye	Novel	x	x	x	x	
1903	Hosmer	History		x	x	x	x
1905	Cooper[2]	Statue		x	x	x	x
1905	Fletcher	Article		x	x		x
1905	Chandler	Elem Reader			x	x	x
1907	Hebard	Article		x	x	x	x
1910	Crunelle[2]	Statue		x	x	x	x
1910	Preston	Poem		x	x	x	x
1915	Scott	History		x	x	x	x
1916	Hough	Novel		x	x	x	x
1918	Schultz	Novel		x	x	x	x
1918	Wolfrom	Play		x	x	x	x

[1] An x indicates that Sacagawea is defined as a "savage," a "key" to the mission, and so forth.

[2] Although the Cooper and Crunelle statues do not verbalize that Sacagawea was a princess, ceremonies and promotional materials emphasize that designation.

4

VARIATION AND ELABORATION
The Sacagawea Legend from the 1940s
through the 1960s

DURING THE Progressive Era, historians, novelists, sculptors, and other artists offer reinterpretations of original Lewis and Clark Expedition scripts. Such people transform Sacagawea from the helpful, yet savage, squaw into an Indian princess and an important American heroine. Citing her cooperation during the trip, her devotion to the mission, her "royal" heritage, and in some cases her womanly power and independence, these portrayers initiate the Sacagawea legend. Because of these works, the once obscure native woman becomes an important symbol of American frontier traditions.

Certain discontinuities emerge in those same texts, however, as framers meld images of the Indian princess with rhetoric of manifest destiny. Although they assert that Sacagawea is helpful during the trip because of her devotion to expedition goals and her belief in manifest destiny, such portrayals do not sufficiently probe Sacagawea's motivations. Never do they ask a variety of questions that might have accompanied explanations of her behaviors. Convinced that manifest destiny was the primary motivator for anyone capable of realizing its merits, Progressive Era creators do not question assumptions that Sacagawea was spurred to action for that reason. Texts produced from the 1940s through the 1960s nonetheless explore other possible motivations for her behaviors, some advancing significant narrative changes. Many of these revisions emerge from a text published in 1932.

As Raymond Stedman notes, the period between the two world wars was a "light one" for Indian princesses (68). The Sacagawea legend reflects this trend, as American creators of the era apparently turn their attentions from portrayals of the frontier past. Between 1920 and 1939, for instance, writers produce fewer than one-third the number of works concerned with Sacagawea as had been generated in the two previous decades. Although she evidently becomes a more inviting subject in the 1940s, 1950s, and 1960s, the lowest level of production during that time occurs while America was still engaged in World War II. Nevertheless, between 1917 and 1939 a few "interim" texts embrace the Sacagawea story. Accepting and disseminating interpretations initiated during the Progressive Era, they designate that Sacagawea was an Indian princess, the guide to the Lewis and Clark Expedition, and the key to its success.

One interim researcher introduces important additions to the Sacagawea legend. A suffragist who became interested in Sacagawea during the campaigns of the early 1900s,[1] Grace Raymond Hebard wrote "Pilot of First White Men to Cross the American Continent" in 1907. In that article, Hebard simply restates familiar assertions about Sacagawea. Dissatisfied with such repetitions, this professor of political economy at the University of Wyoming focused her research activities almost exclusively on Sacagawea for the next three decades. Since Hebard was also unwilling to limit her investigations to the Sacagawea story as it intersects with the Lewis and Clark Expedition, she searched for information about the later life of America's western heroine.

Hebard's efforts came to fruition in 1932 when she published *Sacajawea: A guide and interpreter of the Lewis and Clark expedition, with an account of the travels of Toussaint Charbonneau and of Jean Baptiste, the expedition papoose.* Citing Coues (85, 95) and acknowledging her special indebtedness to Eva Emery Dye (115, passim), Hebard emphasizes, in the early pages of this work, that Sacagawea guides the explorers and aides them in innumerable ways. She also extrapolates beyond the narrative about the mission, arguing that Sacagawea did not die in her early twenties. Basing her conclusions on oral testimonies of F. G. Burnett, James Irwin, and James I. Patten, Euro-American agents and traders among the Shoshones during the late nineteenth century, Hebard asserts that Sacagawea died when she was nearly one hundred years old.[2]

After visiting St. Louis and then living among the southwestern

Apaches, Hebard's subject purportedly returns to the Shoshones to convince them to accept a treaty with the U.S. government and to settle on the Wind River Reservation in Wyoming (151–68). Hebard writes that "Sacajawea proved of the greatest value to the whites through her influence with her own people. She was able to understand the white man's point of view and to present this to the Indians" (169). The elderly native woman, described as slight of stature, beautiful despite her age, with skin as light as a half breed's, also allegedly urges the Shoshones to adopt agriculture. Tutoring her people to raise various grains, Sacagawea informs them that they must accept "white man's ways" to survive (184).

With Hebard's emendations and additions, the Sacagawea legend suddenly expands, and so too does the cultural work it entails. Although original expedition texts offer no information about Sacagawea's appearance, Hebard's informants supply physical details that coincide with mythic images of Indian princesses. These witnesses confirm her genetic superiority as they testify that her physical characteristics match those of the prototypical Indian princess.[3] Not a common savage, more closely akin to Euro-American females, Sacagawea is a singular native woman.

More important, this text also broadens the basis of Sacagawea's heroism as it synthesizes new information and meanings with previous interpretations of the legend. While Progressive period texts assert that Sacagawea understands the importance of helping Lewis and Clark in the conquest of the continent, Hebard additionally verifies that Sacagawea's attitudes and actions do not waiver in old age. Demonstrating her continued allegiance to the mission, she becomes an apologist of native assimilation. The elderly Sacagawea embodies principles of frontier traditions that apply to twentieth-century America.

Although other historians of the period criticized Hebard's scholarship and disputed her findings,[4] the work sold well throughout the United States. The Arthur H. Clark Company published and distributed approximately four thousand copies of the 1932, 1957, 1958, and 1967 editions of Hebard's text. Libraries and educational institutions purchased at least half of those volumes. Because this work was, for several decades, the definitive historical text of Sacagawea's life, writers and editors of grade school, high school, and college history books employed it as the primary resource for commentaries about Sacagawea.

Less than ten years after the first publication of Hebard's work, American writers and artists display a renewed interest in Sacagawea. Between 1940 and 1969, proponents write articles, paint scenes of the trip, erect monuments in her honor, and mark sights of the expedition trail. Historical novels are the most prominent and popular of these texts. Although not all novels of this period endorse the Hebard version of Sacagawea's life, each embraces frontier traditions. Sacagawea remains the essential helper in the wilderness, and in most cases, novelists declare that she is the key to the success of the expedition. Unlike the works of the Progressive Era, however, these works provide different reasons for the native woman's activities in the wilderness. In doing so, they offer variations and elaborations of the Sacagawea legend.

Rather than proposing that a nebulous commitment to manifest destiny is the sole reason for her actions, novelists of this period more often assert that a romantic attachment between Sacagawea and an expedition man is an impetus for her cooperation during the trip. Such works further argue that her affection develops because of Lewis's or Clark's considerate treatment of her. Although previous scripts scrupulously avoid references to Sacagawea's sexuality, writers in this period frame the story around the potential for interracial romance. The Indian princess of the trans-Mississippi West becomes a nearly perfect duplicate of her "sister," Pocahontas. Like Pocahontas, the legendary Sacagawea possesses a royal heritage and the physical characteristics of a princess. She helps white men in the wilderness, and beginning in the 1940s, Sacagawea also bears the burden of a hopeless love for a gallant and heroic captain.

To illustrate this addition to the plot, texts of this period feature different aspects of the trip than those emphasized in previous works. They highlight personal interactions between Sacagawea and her benefactor, whether it is Lewis or Clark. In an effort to present some descriptions of these interactions without too much dissonance, since Sacagawea is a married woman, most of the scripts adopt and embellish an interpretation first outlined by Coues. As the villain in these works, Charbonneau treats his woman with brutality. Lewis's and Clark's journals declare that Charbonneau beats Sacagawea on two different occasions during the trip. Reiterations of his behaviors not only legitimate Sacagawea's vulnerability to another man's attentions but also demonstrate the injustices of native existence and bolster arguments of civilization's rightful conquest of the wilderness.

Although Sacagawea texts of the 1940s through the 1960s share certain patterns of interpretations, they also record important differences that are especially evident in the ways men and women relate the narrative. As Tables 3 and 4 illustrate, men and women employ significantly different plot and character variations during this period.

While writers of both sexes praise Sacagawea for her helpfulness and cooperation, most male novelists also indicate that she acts from love alone. She possesses no real understanding of the mission or of manifest destiny. Neither the champion of a grand design nor an advocate of American destiny, this woman lives and thinks on a more basic level. She comprehends the world through the lens of her narrow life and limited emotions. The majority of male novelists furthermore frame Sacagawea's story around the tale of the expedition, implying that she is significant only in that context. Even within this framework, her most important legendary achievements, such as her guidance of Clark in the mountains, are not emphasized. Such actions are rarely, if ever, mentioned. More often acted upon than acting, Sacagawea depends on Lewis or Clark or another expedition man for direction and motivation. This woman is not in the least reminiscent of Dye's intrepid heroine.

Although female writers of the period concur with some interpretations advanced by their male contemporaries, these women attempt to avoid diminution of Sacagawea's accomplishments. Reiterating her heroic deeds, they highlight her guidance of the captains and her strength and intelligence. These texts agree that Sacagawea devoted herself to one of the men, but they offer additional motivations for her actions. As they argue, her esteem for a "civilized" man stimulates a real understanding of the superiority of Euro-American culture. Nearly all texts produced by women during this era also broaden the context of Sacagawea's story to include her

Table 3. Plot and Character in Sacagawea Texts Produced by Men,
1940–1969[1]

Date	Author	Guide	Evil Mate	Romance	Exped Only	Entire Life
1942	Peattie	x	x	Lewis		x
1944	Kingston				x	
1950	Adams	x			x	
1958	Fisher		x	Clark	x	
1959	Munves			Clark	x	
1963	Henry		x	Clark	x	
1965	Blassingame		x	Clark	x	

Table 4. Plot and Character in Sacagawea Texts Produced by Women,
1940–1969[1]

Date	Author	Guide	Evil Mate	Romance	Exped Only	Entire Life
1943	Emmons	x	x	Clark		x
1944	Ross	x				
1945	Seymour	x				x
1954	Farnsworth	x	x	Clark		x
1955	Pringle	x	x	Clark	x	
1964	Waltrip	x	x	Clark		x

[1] An x indicates that novelists emphasize Sacagawea's role as "guide," embrace her narrative as part of the "expedition only," and present events from Sacagawea's "entire life," and so forth. Texts portraying a love attachment are identified by the captain who purportedly receives her attentions.

lifetime before and after the expedition. These texts adopt the Hebard version of Sacagawea's later life and portray her early years by expounding on bits of information presented in original expedition scripts.

Not simply a character in the tale of America's epic journey, Sacagawea is the centerpiece of works written by women. Even before she meets Lewis or Clark or their men, the young princess possesses an indistinct sense that something is amiss in her savage world. Unlike male writers embracing the legend during this period, most women writers do not conclude that love alone inspires Sacagawea. Rather than being the sufficient cause for her actions, such emotions merely contribute to Sacagawea's intellectual grasp of more important cultural realities. After men of the Corps display the defects of native life, for example, Sacagawea champions native assimilation.

Of myriad texts offering variations and elaborations of the Sacagawea legend from the 1940s through the 1960s, I examine closely three historical novels. Typical of works written by men during this period, Donald Culross Peattie's *Forward the Nation* focuses on events of the expedition. He praises Sacagawea, but the import of her actions is reduced as a result of his disparaging comments about Sacagawea's sex and race. Although she remains the heroine of the tale, her accomplishments are overshadowed by the heroes, the civilized men of the Corps.

In *Sacajawea of the Shoshones*, Della Gould Emmons illustrates patterns embraced by other female writers during that time. Beginning her narrative with the young princess's capture and ending with the old woman's life among the Shoshones, Emmons presents an exceptional heroine whose awareness of civilization's virtues is awakened by Clark and the other men of the Corps.

While Will Henry's *The Gates of the Mountains* in some ways exemplifies male works of the period, it also departs from typical strategies. Henry, for example, omits large portions of the expedition story. Interested in questioning previous interpretations of Sacagawea's character, Henry also proposes that Sacagawea, Clark, and the narrator become involved in a romantic triangle. This situation offers Henry opportunities to examine mythic understandings of savagery and civilization.

Even as they forward variations of the Sacagawea legend, these representative works embrace and justify established frontier myths. Although the nation had completed its conquest of the continent and native groups had been placed on reservations long before this era, Emmons, Peattie, and Henry rehearse traditional interpretations of native savagery and mission. These texts also engage in the cultural discourse of native assimilation and acculturation.

To contextualize these works and to demonstrate that Sacagawea texts are not alone in embracing American mythic meanings, I additionally explore, in this chapter, how American film privileges similar representations during this period. As cultural conversations about savagery, intermarriage, and acculturation collide and coincide with actions and attitudes of this period, I subsequently describe how such concerns maintain prominence in American texts and policies from the close of the frontier to the end of the 1960s.

Although some critics have written that one phase of American history ended in the late 1800s, as Euro-American pioneers completed the settlement of the continent and as native groups from those territories were subdued and placed on reservations, not all writers and artists shifted their attentions to their own times or to the future. Many offered interpretations of the frontier past. Whether or not audiences accepted them as true portrayals of American origins (that is, whether or not rationalized frontier myths maintained a level of operational vitality during this period) is difficult to discern. Some people within America's complex and diverse populations probably viewed these texts as simple entertainments. Many undoubtedly believed that such narratives related absolute cultural realities. Still others might have consciously rejected frontier "truths" because many historical events conflicted with mythic conceptions. In spite of varied responses to frontier myths, creators offered tales of the wilderness, and large audiences enthusiastically embraced those stories. This association illustrated that frontier traditions sustained at least some level of emotional potency on the continent.

From the turn of the century to the end of the 1960s, American films have operated as one of the nation's most powerful purveyors of frontier mythic values and emotions. Reiterating notions previously illustrated and proliferated in captivity narratives, dime novels, Wild West shows, and other popular works, movies have reinforced common conceptions of the mission into the wilderness and of civilization and savagery. Films have not allowed notions of America's frontiers or their mythic meanings to fade from individual or collective memory.

Although Michael Hilger argues that silent movies of 1903 through 1929 are generally sympathetic to natives (6), other critics argue that Hollywood immediately adopted visual images that justified and rationalized the conquest of the continent. As Ralph and Natasha Friar assert, such works as Edison's "peep shows" and *The Great Train Robbery* feature ignoble savages (69–78). These characters show that civilization is obliged to eradicate paganism and barbarism in the wilderness.

In movies produced between 1930 and 1949, natives become vehicles to build the hero's stature. Raoul Walsh's film *They Died with Their Boots On*, for example, depicts the story of General Custer's heroic, albeit tragic, battle against unified Plains Indians. In this and many other films, savage hordes are almost exclusively male and have no tribal or individual distinctiveness (Bataille and Silet xxiii). Another famous work of the period, John Ford's *Stagecoach*, features Euro-Americans who bond together to fight off faceless, nameless savages who attack during their journey into the frontier. A few other westerns of this era are well known, but serials make up the bulk of films featuring natives during this period. Such works conflate all indigenous peoples into the definitive category of "savagery" and also relay the idea that they are incapable of communication, even with each other. Directors give them little, if any, dialogue other than "ugh" and "how" (Price 158). Images of savages thus become inseparable from portrayals of America's untamed landscape.

By the 1950s and 1960s, hostile natives become staples in American westerns. Jenni Calder contends, for instance, that familiar images of ignoble savages, female captives, and monstrous half-breeds preserve the glory days of the frontier (22). John Ford's *The Searchers* is a famous work capitalizing on all of these concepts. Not only is the protagonist, played by perennial western hero John Wayne, obsessed with rescuing his niece from captivity among natives, but when he does find her, he threatens to kill her because she will never overcome the taint of her contact with savagery.

Although such films display the power of frontier traditions, others appear to revise common portrayals of native peoples during this period. As Richard Brenzo and John Price argue, by the mid to late 1960s certain screenwriters and producers who conduct legitimate investigations of indigenous cultures provide glimpses of traditional native life on film (Brenzo 43; Price 160). Price also as-

serts, nonetheless, that even these few sketches reiterate that the
eradication of natives was unfortunate, but necessary, as civilization
was destined to progress across the continent (161).

The majority of these studies focus on images of male warriors,
captors, and torturers—the most common figures portrayed in
American films throughout the decades—but Indian princesses have
also played important roles in Hollywood productions. As Ralph
and Natasha Friar contend, Mona Darkfeather appears as the Indian
princess in twenty films produced in 1914 (109). Although the Friars
restrict their remarks about Indian princesses to Hollywood's early
years, data suggest that these images have also been important in
films produced in subsequent decades.

Tables 5 and 6 verify the Friars' assertions. As Table 6 illustrates,
between 1903 and 1929, 78 percent of films featuring a native woman
portray the young, beautiful, light-skinned maiden who helps to rescue one or more white men in the alien wilderness. Although the
proportion of works focused on any native woman drops during the
decade 1930–1940, the percentage of princess-oriented films remains stable. Such a statistic confirms the princess's persistent dominance of the screen. In the 1950s and 1960s, Hollywood focuses on
the princess in 65 percent of films about a native woman. Although
the number of movies that portray wives and/or mothers within
traditional native cultures rises over the decades, suggesting that
writers and producers incorporate historical research into their texts,
overall data illustrate that in all periods, Hollywood clings to Indian
princesses.

Besides restricting native images to a few common types, American films disseminate other pertinent information about indigenous
peoples. Because they focus almost exclusively on the nation's past,
such texts imply that natives were not really part of America after
they had been placed on reservations.[5] Although a few movies present historically accurate portrayals of indigenous peoples and their
cultures, even those films contribute to the cumulative effect of
Hollywood's obsession with the frontier period. According to such
works, whether natives are annihilated by the cavalry or are settled
peaceably on reservations, savages do not really matter as long as
they do not hinder civilization's progress.

Table 5. American Films Featuring a Native Woman[1]

Films	Period			
	1903–29	1930–49	1950–69	1970–84
Total	242	167	173	100
# about a native woman	60	29	40	28
% about a native woman	25	17	23	28

[1] Data derived from Michael Hilger's *The American Indian in Film.*

Table 6. Images of Native Women in American Films[1]

Film Images	Period							
	1903–29		1930–49		1950–69		1970–84	
	#	%	#	%	#	%	#	%
Indian Princess	47	(78)	23	(79)	26	(65)	15	(54)
Romantic Connection	22	(37)	8	(28)	14	(35)	8	(29)
Squaw/Fury	4	(6)	1	(3)	2	(.5)	4	(14)
Traditional Wife/Mother	0	(0)	2	(7)	9	(23)	11	(39)
Educated Woman	0	(0)	2	(7)	0	(0)	4	(14)

[1] Data derived from images presented in films featuring a native woman, as identified in Table 5.

Despite Hollywood's visual expurgation of native existence after the 1880s, many other texts produced after the turn of the century engage in a discourse about assimilation and acculturation. In "American Identity and Americanization," Philip Gleason claims that the idea of the "melting pot" dominated the cultural conversation about race and ethnicity for decades.[6] This vivid metaphor relays ideas of renewal and inclusiveness as it implies that the nation has been enriched by its diversity only as it forges a single "American" type.

Assuring that various peoples will become Americans in the New World, the melting pot proposes that the dominant culture dissolves differences, purges Old World imperfections, and melds and fuses everyone into a finer metal. Citing a newspaper clipping about the Ford Motor Company English School Melting Pot graduation of 1916, Werner Sollors emphasizes that these ideas were extremely popular and sustained great force during the period.

Initially dressed in foreign clothes and carrying signs that indicated their countries of origin, graduates walked across a stage decorated like an immigrant ship. They then descended into an immense caldron and emerged moments later in "American" clothes. Each carried a small American flag (*Beyond Ethnicity* 89–90). Ritually reborn through the melting pot, these students were Americans.

As some sources claim, discussions about cultural pluralism countered melting pot rhetoric beginning in the 1920s. Asserting that America has always been composed of culturally distinct racial and ethnic groups, proponents of pluralism further argue that diversity is a strength of the nation rather than a liability. In spite of these contentions, certain U.S. policies seem to have denied the inclusiveness of the melting pot. They also appear to discount America's acceptance of cultural pluralism. The 1924 Johnson-Reed Act, for example, restricted immigration based on nationality. With such quotas in place, America could not be construed as an asylum for the "other." Nor could it be seen as a place to melt all peoples into a finer metal. Instead, potent collective conceptions have designated that some groups were unqualified for melting. Their differences were unfusable.

Indigenous peoples, African Americans, and Orientals have been among the nation's "unmeltables." As Richard Polenberg writes, the melting pot has never reflected the reality of America. Also rejecting the reality of cultural pluralism in this period, he states that although diversity has always existed in the nation, various peoples have been excluded from participation in the dominant culture because of their race. In *Fire in the Streets: America in the 1960s,* Milton Viorst seems to oppose such conclusions as he describes the birth and growth of the civil rights movements of the 1950s and 1960s. Viorst nevertheless concurs that although civil rights legislation was one of the greatest achievements of the 1960s, such decrees did not eliminate racial exclusion in America. As Allen Matusow claims, the ideal of a multiethnic, multiracial democracy, a society that provides equal justice and equal opportunity, was imperfectly realized by the close of the 1960s (375).

Polenberg, Matusow, and Viorst, like most historians discussing race during this period, focus on issues and events concerning

African Americans. As other researchers point out, U.S. policies also contemplated concepts of indigenous peoples' assimilation and acculturation in this era. Francis Paul Prucha writes that policies have swung from encouraging native assimilation to embracing self-determination and then back to assimilation during the first six decades of the twentieth century. Although officials have seemingly reversed their objectives repeatedly, each policy has maintained a common thread. None understood, nor could they overcome, problems of racial exclusion.

Although previous programs like the Dawes Act of 1889 attempted to annihilate all forms of indigenous culture, the Indian Reorganization Act (IRA) of 1934 has been most often held up as the beacon of programs reflecting America's acceptance of native traditions. As Prucha writes, the IRA was a "watershed" policy that began with John Collier, America's most famous Commissioner of Indian Affairs (917). Encouraging indigenous forms to flourish and ordering the recovery of lands lost during allotment, the IRA, also known as the Wheeler-Howard Act, sought to protect traditional identities and native lands.

Graham Taylor nonetheless argues that differences between the Dawes Act and the Indian Reorganization Act were not absolute. According to Taylor, Collier appeared willing to recognize distinct native cultures, but he formulated monolithic theories of tribal organization based on conceptions derived from a visit among the Pueblos. Reflecting Collier's conflation, the IRA subsequently mandated that the tribe was the basic unit for the enactment of all federal economic and political programs. Because bureaucrats wrote native constitutions and because these officials also held a tight reign on most economic programs to assure tribal survival, they limited indigenous peoples' political and economic autonomy.

Even if the IRA did not espouse total native self-determination, these policies might be interpreted as being a pragmatic synthesis of pluralism and assimilation. In *The Roots of Dependency: Subsistence, Environment, and Social Change among the Choctaws, Pawnees, and Navajos,* Richard White contends that neither idea guided certain Collier programs. After Hoover Dam was built, for example, the Soil Conservation Service and the Army Corps of Engineers sought ways to protect the facility from silt accumulation. After determining that overgrazing on the Navajo reservation led to erosion and gullying, engineers suggested that herd reductions could eliminate the problem of silting. Collier and other officials accepted this solution despite the economic and cultural importance of such animals in Navajo society. According to White, this program devastated Navajo subsistence.

During the 1930s and early 1940s, although Collier sought to protect indigenous peoples and their traditional cultures, his support of native self-determination was limited and contingent. His championing of aboriginal rights and prerogatives also fell short if they clashed with Euro-American interests. While the IRA seemed different from Dawes, both embraced concepts of assimilation, at least to some extent, and both guarded the economic interests of the larger society. Other aspects of the IRA also coincided with those of allotment. Although Dawes implicitly assured that natives would be welcomed into American society if they adapted themselves to the dominant culture, that promise was not met in most cases. Proponents of allotment suggested that this failure arose from aboriginals' lack of acculturation. As Hoxie and others argue, however, even when natives accepted outward signs of "civilization" after their lands were divided, the melting pot could not eliminate the stigma of race. Most of the population had not accepted the idea that difference and diversity were the essence and strength of America.

The IRA of the 1930s and early 1940s did not eliminate, and perhaps exacerbated, the ambiguity of native positions and roles in American culture. Undoubtedly seeking to guard traditional cultures and the remnants of their homelands, the IRA also ironically reinforced the isolation of indigenous peoples. Collier might have envisioned a "harmonic orchestra"[7] or a stained-glass window or a quilt as the root metaphor for America, with diverse populations playing various "instruments" in unison or with groups of varying sizes, shapes, and colors adding depth and meaning to the culture. These visions nonetheless failed to reflect the national reality. Despite rhetoric extolling cultural pluralism, race continued to be a factor for exclusion in this era. The IRA made that exclusion easier. While Collier rejected the necessity of total assimilation, he could not guarantee that America would accept cultural pluralism.

After World War II, U.S. policy again promoted the physical and cultural integration of natives into the dominant culture. As Donald Fixico asserts, native involvement in the war, both in the military service and within industries at home, showed that indigenous peoples were ready to become full participants in a unified and homogenous society. Embracing such beliefs during Eisenhower's administration, government officials and legislators drafted and enacted a series of federal policies to terminate tribes and to "desegregate" reservations. Congress also funded relocation programs that encouraged natives to "melt" into the dominant culture by moving to urban areas.[8]

In spite of public controversy and protests by indigenous groups, the Eighty-third Congress passed a host of bills to terminate tribes. These acts cancelled any special tribal rights and privileges codified in treaties or other agreements with the federal government, including annuities and tax protection. Individual natives would simply join the general population after their tribes ceased to exist. While policy makers envisioned termination as a method for releasing the government from its obligations to tribes, they theorized that relocation would ease economic strain on reservation areas by integrating individual natives into American urban society. Former federal dependents would become productive members of an invigorated industrial city, to the benefit of the dominant culture and natives alike.

In "Private Property, The Indian's Door to Civilization," William Hagan asks Congress and other officials to reexamine their assumptions about native assimilation. As he foretells, persistent cultural differences would doom these programs. Despite the aspirations of their proponents, termination and relocation left thousands of natives more demoralized, more financially destitute, and more isolated than ever. Although only a few tribes were actually terminated, those groups relinquished their special status with the federal government, and they surrendered their homelands. Individual natives additionally lost their sense of self as their ethnic groups ceased to exist.

Relocation programs affected even more people. Convinced that aboriginals had finally assimilated, policy makers did not recognize that many had not adapted to the dominant culture, in spite of ex-

ternal appearances. Because relocation programs failed to prepare
natives to deal with the culture shock of living in big cities and because cultural biases flourished in cities like Minneapolis, Chicago,
and Los Angeles, most natives participating in relocation returned
to reservations after a short period.

Although William Brophy and Sophie Aberle agree that termination and relocation were ill considered and destructive, they propose
that assimilation could succeed if natives were given more responsibility in enacting such programs.[9] Brophy and Aberle do not realize, however, that many natives did not aspire to adopt Euro-American lifestyles. Although Hagan understands that reality, even he fails
to mention that American culture did not accept assimilated natives
as equal citizens.

From the 1930s through the 1960s, as U.S. policies appeared to
swing between mandating native self-determination and coercing
their assimilation, these strategies denied larger cultural realities.
Clinging to certain socially constructed meanings, the nation continued to separate savages from civilized peoples. In denial of cultural pluralism and in demonstration of its doubt about assimilation, "civilization" for the most part excluded native peoples from
full participation in American culture.

Dam projects undertaken from the late 1940s through the 1960s,
though not directly tied to U.S. native policies, also reflected such
ideologies. Interpreting this enterprise as progress on the continent,
the Army Corps of Engineers planned and executed the Missouri
River Basin Project, allowing Euro-Americans to use territories that
had previously been held hostage to the uncertainties of nature. As
the promotional brochure *Discover the Spirit!* reports, the Missouri
River was "too wild for the peace-loving farmers and ranchers working along its banks" (10). Not only containing unpredictable spring
floodwaters, the dams also yielded huge amounts of hydroelectric
energy, allowed for future irrigation, and provided new water recreation areas.

As Michael Lawson argues, such projects directly tied to native
concerns. Completed in 1966, the series of dams converted hundreds
of thousands of acres into reservoirs, flooding river-bottom lands
from twenty-three reservations. These reservoirs destroyed plants

and wildlife and displaced hundreds of aboriginal families (171–72). In spite of concerted efforts by natives to prevent the projects, engineers and legislators were unswayed. Because natives had not assimilated or because America denied the validity of cultural pluralism or from both causes, indigenous peoples had no political clout. Their protests had no effect even when the issue concerned their own territories.

When longtime U.S. senator from North Dakota Quentin Burdick introduced a measure in 1967 to name the reservoir formed by one of those dams for the state's heroine, the legislature approved. Lyndon Johnson immediately signed the bill. As the *Bismarck Tribune* reports, North Dakota residents endorsed the name that they considered to be "fitting" and "appropriate" ("Reservoir's 'Sakakawea' "). No one wrote of the irony that Lake Sakakawea, among the nation's largest and cleanest bodies of water with a "shoreline stretching 1,600 miles, a distance longer than the coasts of California" (*Discover the Spirit!* 10), flooded millions of acres that the historical woman had once walked. No one recorded that the flooded land had belonged to the Mandan, the Arikara, and the Hidatsa, tribes most closely associated with the historical Sacagawea. No one noted the irony that such groups again lost their homes in the name of progress that Sacagawea purportedly embodied.

From the 1940s to 1970, myriad texts embrace the story of the Lewis and Clark Expedition and include similar references to American progress. According to Cutright, although writers published fewer than eleven texts about the Lewis and Clark journals before 1905, over two hundred titles came to press between 1905 and 1976 (202). In addition, many histories, novels, and other American works present the narrative of America's "epic journey." Each of these works comments on Sacagawea and interprets her role in America's destiny.

Donald Culross Peattie combines all of these goals in *Forward the Nation,* a historical novel. Born in Chicago in 1898, a graduate of Harvard's history department, Peattie reflects frontier traditions and offers some new assertions about Sacagawea. Citing the original journals, the Biddle edition, and the Coues text, Peattie announces that no character is fictional. No incident is invented. Everything has been "provided by the unimpeachable reports of eye-witnesses," and whatever has not been stated in the records can be found between the lines (n.p.). American audiences accepted Peattie's "truths" with enthusiasm. Publishers attested to the novel's popular reception by printing several hardback editions and by offering a special "armed services" paperback for overseas consumption during World War II.

The "truths" that Peattie extends about the expedition are identical to those submitted in previous interpretations. The title *Forward the Nation,* for example, verbalizes and legitimates concepts of manifest destiny. Allowing for little ambiguity in the meaning of the expedition, the title testifies that the momentous journey has not constituted just a single event in American history. It also shows that the trip symbolizes the continuous, inexorable process of "civilizing" the continent. Such a designation reminds readers that America moved not only westward but also "forward" as western wildernesses became part of the nation.

Peattie reinforces these ideas in the narrative also. As he writes, "Lewis and Clark went forth, not to conquer, only to find the way in which a peaceful nation might march, by home and farm, by mill and mine, to the western sea that Nature set it for a boundary" (40). As Peattie's title and text report, the continent always belonged to the United States. In this passage, Peattie additionally describes the subsequent history of the region. Denying any negative intentionality by the captains, and thus by extension the "peaceful nation," he fails to mention who was vanquished.

Just as many other works do, Peattie ignores native existence prior to the expedition. Neither does he specify that settlers carry out the mandates of manifest destiny. Rather, the entire nation, through the personified "home and farm" and "mill and mine," marches toward the sea. Besides decontextualizing the actors in this vision, Peattie offers an illogical reversal of cause and effect. The products of "civilization" appear to drive the process and not to result from it. Assuring America that it has been justified in occupying the continent, Peattie engages in the cultural work Fisher describes. He rehearses the inevitability of the westward "march," and he encourages the culture to forget the realities of that conquest.

In addition to reflecting notions of manifest destiny, Peattie embraces the dichotomy of civilization and savagery throughout his work. Illustrating typical conflation of native peoples into a single ignoble savagery, Peattie claims that the "Indian" is an "alloy" of deceit, venality, and cowardice. Further defining all natives as male, the novelist claims that "he" is a creature whose loyalty runs no deeper than "mere advantage" (56). In stark contrast with this typical savage, Lewis and Clark and the other men of the Corps are above such petty considerations. Representatives of civilization, they aspire to complete America's destiny on the continent.

In a novel about America's glorious mission on the continent, immersed in common notions of savagery and civilization, Peattie relates the story of Sacagawea. Acknowledging his indebtedness to Grace Raymond Hebard, Peattie writes one of the few male-created texts that mentions Sacagawea's childhood and old age. Despite the potential for a broader narrative, he offers only cursory remarks about Sacagawea except within the context of the expedition. Similar to other facets of his novel, Peattie rehearses some typical conceptions about Sacagawea, but he also advances a new subplot of potential romance.

Like previous texts, Peattie establishes that Sacagawea is not a common savage. Physically distinct from other native women, the petite Sacagawea has a lovely face and obsidian, almond-shaped eyes. She is "beautiful," even by "white standards" (6, 72, 83). She is also bright and energetic, not a squaw who has been cowed by harsh treatment and the burdens of savage existence (70). Once the expedition members reach Fort Mandan, Lewis recognizes that this exceptional woman will help them in the wilderness. Fulfilling that function, Sacagawea "concerns herself thus earnestly over the men's comfort" (111). She also points out landmarks, saves essential instruments and medicines during the squall, and helps Clark to find a route through the mountains (108, 111, 122). As Peattie proclaims, Sacagawea "will be remembered as long as Americans love their country, for in its history no other woman ever served it better" (109). In these notations and others, Peattie reiterates the Sacagawea legend.

Interposed among these accolades, however, are commentaries

that diminish Sacagawea's heroic stature. Lewis, for example, reminds himself that Sacagawea is still "an alien, and a slave" (73). In
other passages, she is described as a "little savage" and a "Stone
Age woman" (11, 89). While Peattie employs many strategies of
Sacagawea's Progressive Era proponents, as he attempts to separate
Sacagawea from savage masses and as he vaunts her accomplishments, this text illustrates that Sacagawea is savage.

Peattie also expands the argument of her savagery. As he contends, Sacagawea is a savage and therefore part of nature. She is a
"small captive animal" and a "she-animal and her cub" when she
nurses her baby (70, 134). Extending his logic, Peattie reasons that
because Sacagawea is savage and part of nature, she is particularly
suited to serve the needs of the expedition. Because she was "born
a piece of aboriginal American Nature" (122), Sacagawea's heritage assures that "civilized" men of the Corps will survive in her
wilderness.

Commentary about the character of women affects Peattie's
estimates of Sacagawea's heroism as well. Although he asserts that
a man acts in his own interests or out of loyalty to a cause, he concludes that a woman "seldom has any genuine attachment to a cause.
It is a man she follows, and she espouses whatever cause he upholds.
. . . In serving, she serves him; this is her single purpose; this is her
strength. For him, she will walk barefoot on thorns, and carry great
weights upon her back" (56–57). Not limiting his remarks to savages,
Peattie suggests that no woman is capable of recognizing the importance of a meaningful crusade. Circumscribed by nature to simple understandings of a narrow sphere, a woman responds to the
world only through the filter of her man's dreams and loyalties.

Arguing that no female is competent to comprehend, much less
act upon, allegiance to a cause, Peattie rejects the explanation that
Sacagawea's devotion to manifest destiny spurs her to action during
the expedition. Incompetent to understand important cultural
meanings, Sacagawea becomes the "other." Peattie thus combines
comments about Sacagawea's sex with illustrations of her savagery
to portray a doubly removed "other." Not simply alien because she
is a native, Sacagawea is also isolated from "culture" and "civilization" because she is a woman.

Together with his pronouncements about savagery and woman-hood, Peattie specifically explores motivations for Sacagawea's co-operation during the expedition. As he asserts, Sacagawea is helpful because she finally discovers a man who is worth her love and devo-tion. Sacagawea's husband cannot exact her affection because of his savage brutality. Charbonneau kicks and hits Sacagawea numerous times during the trip (74, 125–26, 218–19). He additionally horrifies the entire Corps when he offers her sexual services to any man who wants her for the evening (144–45). In keeping with Coues's esti-mate of Charbonneau, Peattie writes that this squawman's immer-sion in savage life has brought him to the lowest levels of civiliza-tion. Although he quite literally possesses Sacagawea, such a product of cultural degradation cannot seize her heart.

Vulnerable because of her savage existence and her marriage to a brute, Sacagawea discovers a civilized man of noble spirit. Adding a subplot not hinted at by Progressive Era proponents, Henry pro-poses that Sacagawea falls in love with Lewis. This captain's virtues are so apparent, in spite of his stern, reserved manner, that he in-stantly commands all of Sacagawea's emotion. During their first meeting, "Sacajawea felt a strange new thing she had not felt for any man" (78). Although the exact nature of this "strange new thing" remains undefined in this passage, Peattie titillates the audience with a potential romance. Almost at the same moment, however, he attempts to quash those intimations by asserting that the sensa-tion that has overpowered Sacagawea is "loyalty" and "devotion" (78, 94).

Despite assurances of the platonic nature of Sacagawea's emo-tion, other references imply that she experiences a different kind of feeling. During that first meeting, for example, Peattie claims that her loyalty was "conceived as suddenly as life" and that it was "as vigorous in her" as her unborn baby (78). While a metaphoric "con-ception" need not point to a sexual response, the connection be-comes more perceptible and plausible when Peattie writes that Sacagawea "secreted" this "strange new passion" in her heart (94). She pledges her soul to Lewis. These excerpts combine to create a sense that the depth and intensity of her emotions are more than allegiance can contain. At the end of her life, when she recalls that she has acted from "love of a man—a white man" (233), Sacagawea substantiates that conclusion.

Despite allowing some ambiguities in the nature of Sacagawea's emotions, Peattie never veers from assertions of Lewis's feelings toward her. He mentions that Lewis becomes "more human" as he interacts with Sacagawea (134). In spite of this concession, Peattie summarizes Lewis's response as nothing more than "gratitude" for her singlemindedness during the entire mission (233). Not for one moment does he respond to Sacagawea in the same way she perceives him. He is superior, too removed from her savage world, to consider Sacagawea as a romantic partner. As far as Lewis is concerned, she is instead the key "of truest metal" that has been "shaped to fit an intricate lock" of the expedition (55). Through the passive voice, Peattie suggests that Sacagawea's objectification is nearly absolute. Despite his praise of the woman's "metal," Lewis sees her not as a person but simply as a tool. She becomes a device molded by external powers for his purposes. Not important as a person, much less a potential lover, Sacagawea is the means to accomplish the goals of the expedition and to serve the nation's best interests.

Donald Culross Peattie thus portrays a character who is far different from the heroic champion presented in Progressive Era texts. Not only confining her to the ambiguous position of the somewhat admirable, though obviously inferior, savage, this novelist also defines Sacagawea as an insipid, dependent woman. Even within the confines of those meanings, however, Sacagawea is further reduced because the man she adores does not return her love. Although Peattie celebrates the fact that "the continent, like a flag, was fully unfurled" (248) as a result of Sacagawea's efforts, he claims that she does not really understand the significance of that flag. No longer is she a heroine of inner strength and fortitude, the woman upon whom suffragettes focus for inspiration. Undercutting much of the praise he offers, Peattie defines Sacagawea as less a heroine than she has been depicted in any other narrative since writers initiated the legend in the Progressive period.

Accepting some "truths" Peattie relates about the expedition and about Sacagawea, Della Gould Emmons rejects others in her novel *Sacajawea of the Shoshones*. Born in Minnesota, Emmons became a music teacher and drama coach in a town adjacent to a Sioux reservation in South Dakota. She later moved to Washington state where she wrote and produced pageants, plays, and novels. In *Sacajawea of the Shoshones,* her most acclaimed work, Emmons centers the text around the story of the native woman. Citing Dye and Hebard as her sources, Emmons portrays Sacagawea from her childhood among the Shoshones to her old age at the Wind River Reservation. All passages embracing manifest destiny are inextricably tied to the narrative of this native woman in this novel, so Emmons perpetuates assertions about Sacagawea's American heroism. She also expands that tradition.

Like her predecessors, Emmons excludes Sacagawea from ignoble savagery by indicating her royal heritage (8) and by delineating her physical attributes. In accord with mythic precepts concerning Indian princesses, Sacagawea is vivacious and pretty with a luminous, sweet face (16, 183). Her skin is lighter than most natives, no darker than the hand of a tanned trader (57). Also possessing exceptional intelligence and energy (38, passim), this Sacagawea's superiority is so evident that Lewis and Clark immediately recognize her value. Like Peattie's subject, Emmons's heroine fulfills their expectations. Vowing that she will help in every way and pledging never to burden them, this woman digs artichokes, sews moccasins, and performs innumerable other tasks (156–57, passim).

She also saves the mission on several occasions, including the time she guides Clark through the mountains. In another incident, when Sacagawea sees items drifting in the river during the squall, she acts, "Those prized possessions! What matter if there was danger. She must save all that she could. Like lightning she worked. Quickly she grasped one here, two there . . . she tucked them into her lap and reached for more, oblivious to personal danger" (166). As Lewis proclaims, "we must not forget that our success was due largely to Sacajawea . . . I pray God that we will always remember it" (245). Acting rather than acted upon, Sacagawea is intrepid and capable.

Although these portions of Emmons's text do not depart significantly from Dye's account in *The Conquest,* other commentaries offer important changes to the narrative. Emmons, for instance, incorporates the subplot of a potential romance between Sacagawea and a truly civilized man. Employing strategies similar to Peattie's, Emmons justifies Sacagawea's feeling by enumerating Charbonneau's deficiencies. A much older man of forty-three, Charbonneau rapes Sacagawea when she is only fifteen (85). He displays his cowardice throughout the mission, and he also slaps and beats her (71, 148, 166, 203). Such actions differentiate Sacagawea's "master" from other men of the Corps.

Although Peattie contends that Sacagawea idolizes Lewis, Emmons and nearly every other writer embracing the romantic story submit that she adores Clark. This tall, square-shouldered, handsome man with red hair and blue eyes (79) is Sacagawea's chivalrous knight. Seeing that she is pregnant, he tries to help her with the heavy bison robes (100). He protects her during the journey (157) and chides Charbonneau for striking her (203). As Emmons contends, Clark's first "look of understanding and sympathy turned Little Bird Woman's starved heart over and over and upset her world then and there so completely that it changed the remainder of her long life" (100). From that moment on, Sacagawea's heart and soul belong to Clark. Constantly watching him "with a worshipping look" (132), Sacagawea sees him as "her God" (183). For hundreds of pages, Emmons illustrates Sacagawea's devotion to the captain.

While Peattie depicts a man who is unaffected by Sacagawea's presence and attentions, Emmons denies that interpretation. When Clark gives Sacagawea a beaded belt, for example, he is "stirred by the depth of her emotion; he felt as though he had touched a delicate instrument of infinite sweetness and a melody unforgettable and lonely vibrated within his innermost being" (124). At another point during the trip, a picturesque scene of the "young mother and her babe" (159) awes him. Employing similar language to Dye's, Emmons associates Sacagawea with the Madonna in this and other passages. She concurrently proves that Sacagawea's presence affects Clark. Unlike the remote Lewis, Clark does not see her as merely a means to an end or a tool to accomplish the mission. She is a person.

Despite her inclusion of the love story, Emmons does not allow Sacagawea's heroism to be diminished. Sacagawea adores Clark, but that emotion does not reduce her to an object. Nor do those feelings define the totality of her existence. Clark and the expedition serve as catalysts for a discovery of more comprehensive meanings about savagery and civilization. Sacagawea's affection is only a contributing factor to her heroic actions during the journey and for the remainder of her life. Clark, for instance, teaches her that women deserve better treatment than savagery allows (109, 159). Civilized men relieve women of their burdens and apportion them dignity. More important, Sacagawea learns that all native peoples will benefit from civilization's penetration of the continent. Just before her capture, the twelve-year-old Sacagawea perceives that her people are starving. Speaking with determination, she asserts that " 'A way *must be* found to free us from hunger and fear' " (original emphasis, 6). Although the young girl recognizes the problems of wilderness existence, only through her exposure to civilized people does she come to understand that savagery is inherently flawed.

As Sacagawea discovers, "civilization" will abrogate those faults. Extending her reverence beyond Clark, Sacagawea embraces the entire Corps and their mission into the wilderness. She embarks on the journey, not simply from love of a single man, but from her knowledge that he and his kind will change the continent. As Emmons writes, Sacagawea's "heart was singing, her face alight with worship for these white men going to her people, going to send traders to them, going to free them from hunger and fear" (106). Answering questions that Progressive Era proponents leave unasked, Emmons argues that Sacagawea learns about the justice of manifest destiny from the expedition men.

Emmons further illustrates that Sacagawea's allegiance persists and even grows. While holding a Jefferson medal after the Fort Mandan departure of the Corps, she prays to the "white man's God." As she pleads for guidance, "The Great White Father extended his hand and in warm friendship clasped hers and said, 'My daughter, you have served me well. Your people are now my children. Continue your work for them. I pledge you help and protection' " (264). Employing typical rhetoric of manifest destiny, Emmons adopts phrases like "Great White Father" and "my daughter" in reference to Jefferson and Sacagawea. This president, like others who preceded him, is the mythic paternal benefactor of all native peoples. They are his "children."

In this passage, Emmons emphasizes other concepts also. As Jefferson physically emerges from the medal to answer Sacagawea's prayers, Emmons overlaps religious and political imagery and fuses their meanings. Sacagawea registers no difficulty in accepting Jefferson as a God. Nor does she show dissonance in interpreting manifest destiny as a religion, or at least in welcoming its sacred purposes. Embracing these ideas for her lifetime, Sacagawea returns to the Shoshones in her old age to teach them to plant and to tell them about their "white friends" (304). As she exhorts, the Shoshone must now prove their sincerest gratitude for the "protection of the American flag." They must adapt to the white man's life (314). Sacagawea thus enters the cultural conversation that is most applicable to Emmons's own era. She argues for native assimilation.

Della Gould Emmons proliferates the notion that Sacagawea is an American heroine. She illustrates that this native woman cooperates during the mission, guides the men through the mountains, and later tries to bring civilization to the savages. Reaching an audience unlikely touched by Hebard's scholarly tome, Emmons's novel disseminates the story of Sacagawea's admirable and more comprehensive heroism to a broad readership. Emmons's text reached even more people than book sales document because her script was transformed into a screenplay for *The Far Horizon*, a major Hollywood film produced in 1955. The cast of major stars drew thousands of viewers. As Emmons enlarges the context of the Sacagawea narrative, in the book and the film, she extends its audience. So too does Emmons enlarge the legend.

Peattie and Emmons therefore present very different heroines. Despite certain dissimilarities, both novelists investigate an important aspect of frontier myths intersecting with the Sacagawea narrative. As Emmons and Peattie introduce a potential romance, they explore possible means of accomplishing native assimilation and acculturation, goals openly endorsed in American culture. Since intermarriage would appear to be a logical extension of assimilationist thinking, these writers test social restrictions against miscegenation.

The issue of interracial mixing has always been an integral aspect of American discourse on assimilation and acculturation. Focusing on Pocahontas myths, Werner Sollors argues that intermarriage was an important adjunct of early melting pot imagery. As he claims, Pocahontas has epitomized the abolition of "prejudices of descent," adding that through her, Americans established a legitimate connection with "noble Indian ancestry" (72, 79). Pocahontas's native blood purportedly ennobled rather than tainted her progeny and, through mythic extension, all Americans. Leslie Fiedler concurs with this interpretation, declaring that Pocahontas has served as a "symbol of White man's reconciliation with our land and its first inhabitants" (64). Including Sacagawea in his argument, Fiedler proclaims that both Indian princesses have supplied a "lovely American dream" that washes away fears of miscegenation in a single, cleansing metaphor (86).

Historical evidence and cultural texts, including those embracing the Sacagawea legend, counter such blithe claims. Although he illustrates the positive results of intermarriage between a Jew and a Christian in his play *The Melting Pot,* Israel Zangwill acknowledges that American culture has long forbidden interracial relationships (Sollors, *Beyond Ethnicity* 71). In the 1870s, for example, the U.S. Congress became disturbed by reports of miscegenation between army officers and native women, reports Sherry Smith in "Beyond Princess and Squaw: Army Officers' Perceptions of Indian Women." As Smith documents, Congress convened the Banning Committee in 1876 to investigate sexual immorality occurring at frontier army posts.

Despite congressional fears, however, frontier diaries point out that the officers were also immersed in frontier myths of savagery and civilization. Although the men might have had liaisons with native women, restrictions against miscegenation were so forceful that the officers' diaries and letters insisted whites would be degraded by sexual relations with native women. Post records also reveal that almost no officers married native women (69–72). As these and other data show, although adherence to social strictures has not always been upheld, taboos of miscegenation have functioned as a cultural "reality" in Euro-American society.[10]

Further illustrating the power of social taboos, many states have prohibited African American and/or indigenous peoples from marrying Euro-Americans, even into the twentieth century. According to a 1993 Associated Press news story, the number of interracial unions has doubled since the Supreme Court struck down state laws prohibiting them. In spite of the increasing reality of these relationships, "many Americans still seem fixated by interracial romance . . . and there is an occasional cross-burning or other acts of racial prejudice and hatred" aimed at couples who dare to challenge the taboo ("1 of every fifty marriages"). As this information would attest, the legacy of proscriptions against such relationships has not been entirely altered.

Describing literary portrayals of interracial relationships in "A Plea for Fictional Histories and Old-Time 'Jewesses,' " Alide Cagidemetrio asserts that Sir Walter Scott and James Fenimore Cooper also embrace, reiterate, and justify taboos of miscegenation. Several of Scott's English heroes, for instance, marry Scottish women, and those unions result in a strengthening of disparate traditions. In one narrative, however, that beneficial match is possible only after the hero casts aside the beautiful, alluring, but dark "Jewess." Although some forms of mixing might be beneficial, each society defines its own acceptable limits.

Cagidemetrio further claims that several of Cooper's plots, including *The Last of the Mohicans,* also hinge upon an obsession with racial purity. Black or native "blood," according to Cooper, is neither noble nor redeemable. Too much the "other," the alien Indian princess does not illustrate the coalescence of different races. She instead verifies restrictions against such mixing. As Clark Wissler writes, although Pocahontas and Smith are paired romantically in a profusion of American texts, John Rolfe, not the gallant captain, becomes her husband. Wissler further asserts that works depicting Smith's heroism denigrate Rolfe because the latter succumbs to the seductive temptations of the wilderness (183). In these literary works and others, writers point out the limits of acculturation for anyone deemed the "other."

The idea of miscegenation has pervaded American films as well. As Table 6 illustrates, a high percentage of American films featuring a native woman have portrayed a romantic connection between the Indian princess and the "civilized" hero. Silent movies, for instance, pair 37 percent of Indian princesses with Euro-American men. These figures remain relatively stable in the 1930s and 1940s, and in the 1950s and 1960s,[11] as 28 percent and 35 percent of later princesses, respectively, are involved with "civilized" males. Although many films have illustrated the prospect of such relationships, interracial romance ends tragically in all of these stories. Film princesses have a special ability to recognize the superiority of the Euro-American men and their culture, but their love cannot come to fruition because of taboos against miscegenation.

Peattie and Emmons also uphold such cultural proscriptions as they depict Sacagawea's relationship with either Lewis or Clark. Because he clearly traces Sacagawea's savagery and Lewis's emotional indifference to her, Peattie does not appear to suggest that such a romance is even remotely possible. Other commentaries, interjected throughout *Forward the Nation,* nevertheless point out the potent sexuality of this young, native woman. Her body and, in particular, her breasts become the focus in several scenes. Aware of her physical presence, Lewis notices that she reveals the "round bronze apple of her breast" when she feeds the baby (121). In another scene, the captain observes that Sacagawea's breasts possess "a brave young lift to them" (148). She is not simply the mother nurturer but also a sexual being, and the novelist does not eliminate the possibility of Lewis's involvement with Sacagawea.

Although Peattie hints at a potential romance, he ultimately declares that interracial relationships are unacceptable. Writing of Sacagawea, he declares, "In her own blood ran an unalterable devotion to them . . . the marriage of the American soul with the soul of aboriginal America" (236). Offering the only acceptable alternative to the obscenity of interracial mixing, Peattie condones a "marriage" of disparate souls, but not of bodies.

Emmons also examines the concept of miscegenation in *Sacajawea of the Shoshones.* Less circumspect than Peattie, Emmons admits that Sacagawea affects Clark. As Clark has contact with this marvelous woman, he becomes emotionally involved, and in several scenes he seems prepared to put aside disparities of heritage. Disconcerted by his feelings for Sacagawea, Clark wonders if race is really so important, asking, "was she so different temperamentally from a white girl?" (135). Continuing this examination in a dream, he visualizes "a bewitching composite" of a civilized woman and the "savage Sacajawea" (137). Despite his musing, Clark answers his own question. The difference not only exists; it is too important to challenge. Engaging in the discussion that has absorbed American culture, Clark arrives at the commonly held conclusion. Because savagery demarcates Sacagawea from himself and civilization, Clark cannot cross the barriers of race. Emmons consequently assures her audience that Sacagawea arouses "chivalry" in Clark (136). Other emotions are unacceptable.

As previously described, the heroine of Emmons's tale embraces manifest destiny and accepts the superiority of "civilization." Her most disturbing, if not most important, discovery is acknowledging the evil of miscegenation. From the time the Corps arrives, she possesses a vague awareness of cultural contrasts, and she "sighed at the impassable canyon that yawned between" herself and Clark (157). Until she learns that the "canyon" is legitimately "impassable," however, Sacagawea hopes to win him. Thrilled by Clark's protective embrace after the flash flood, she asks him why he has rescued her. When he states that any "self-respecting civilized man" would have done the same thing, her "glow died slowly out and left her cold and weary. Gently, but firmly, she drew away from him" (189). Despite her pain, Sacagawea accepts that the chasm between savagery and civilization must never be breached.

Emmons thus tests the concept of interracial mixing. Because Clark is civilized and Sacagawea is not, Emmons concludes that such a relationship must not be consummated despite the native woman's heroism. The noble captain is acutely aware of the tenets. Although she cannot cross or erase racial lines, Sacagawea's innate wisdom and superiority ironically assure that she can learn that restrictions against miscegenation are just. Arriving at the same conclusion that Peattie and so many others have before her, Emmons illustrates that interracial relationships are unconscionable.

Twenty years after Emmons and Peattie produce their texts, Will Henry publishes *The Gates of the Mountains,* his version of the Lewis and Clark Expedition. Henry Wilson Allen grew up in Missouri and eventually moved to California where he has written many novels illustrating events from the nation's history. Writing under the pen name Will Henry, he is the winner of the Spur Award of the Western Writers of America, Wrangler Award of the National Cowboy Hall of Fame, and the Levi Straus Golden Saddleman Award. Henry has focused on the "great westward expansion" (*Gates* n.p.). His title garnered from Dye's *The Conquest,* Henry's *The Gates of the Mountains* exemplifies his interest in western history and his fascination with America's cultural heroine, Sacagawea.

Seemingly unconcerned about advancing intricate details of the trip or restricting himself to "truths" proposed in previous scripts, Henry presents his novel from the viewpoint of a "half-breed" narrator, Frank Rivet. Though no one by that name or description accompanied the Corps of Discovery, this character allows Henry to explore cultural meanings of the expedition. Frank, for example, highlights questions about the nature of savagery and civilization because he is half-Pawnee and half-French. Like other writers, Henry illustrates that most, if not all, squawmen on the continent were French. Unlike American heroes, these men capitulate to savagery and produce monstrous progeny. In addition, the narrator becomes one part of a romantic triangle. Frank loves Sacagawea, but she adores Clark. Through this love story, Henry not only illustrates and examines previous assertions concerning Sacagawea's royalty and her savagery but also explores miscegenation.

Henry defines distinct cultural levels throughout *The Gates of the Mountains.* Assessing various peoples' positions based on their purported level of "civilization," Henry provides an image of a cultural "ladder." Although this metaphoric vision generally implies movement, no group or individual climbs or descends Henry's ladder, because status is established by birthright. Lewis and Clark and other "civilized" men of the expedition are fixed at the top. At the opposite extreme are aboriginals that the Corps meets during the journey. Although natives are all savages, Henry asserts that even that classification has gradations. The Sioux, for example, are the most savage (71) while the Mandans are nearly civilized (113).

Through the character Frank, Henry illustrates that a "half-breed" is neither savage nor civilized. Struggling to find his appropriate "rung" throughout the novel, Frank suffers from rootlessness and isolation. As Lewis and Clark discuss the prospects of hiring

Frank for the expedition, they illustrate American feelings about the products of interracial relationships. Lewis claims that "heathen impurities" (11) taint Frank. Although Clark attempts to counter Lewis's comments by asserting that the young man is also half Rivet, with "good, strong and steady" blood, Lewis argues that nothing can redeem the menace of mixed heritage (12). Dismissed from civilization because of his birth, Frank is nonetheless higher on the cultural "ladder" than any native. While this might appear favorable, Frank has no identity, no people of his own.

The only other character who shares Frank's predicament is Sacagawea. Examining the ambiguities of her position, Henry questions whether she is a savage or a princess or if she can be classified at all. As the narrator interacts with Sacagawea, he observes her associations with others, and he always interprets her and her actions. According to Frank, this native woman is the prototypical Indian princess in every way. Unlike the "lean and hungry-looking she-weasel" Otter Woman, Sacagawea is beautiful and compelling (120). Providing extensive physical details, Frank describes her as slender with a small, round "Caucasian-shaped head" and "Caucasian features." The short, straight nose and soft, well-shaped mouth deny Sacagawea's native heritage. Her hair is a "rare dark auburn," and her skin is so light that "each blush was to be seen . . . as vividly as in the face of the fairest French or American girl." As the narrator testifies, Sacagawea's eyes are neither black nor brown, but gray with a "certain hint of green-blue seen in deep clear water" (126). Just as every other writer has done since the turn of the century, Henry describes a woman who looks Euro-American.

Frank declares repeatedly that Sacagawea is "not at all like an Indian" (126, passim). Peerless among savages, possessing qualities "no Indian maiden ever knew," Sacagawea is "a regal woman by any standard" (126). She also has "no crown but her auburn hair, no gemmed circlet save the brightness of her smile, no scepter but the crude stone" (127). Such descriptions have undoubtedly prompted Raymond Stedman's remarks that Henry's novel serves as one of the best examples of "sheer adoration" of Indian princesses in American literature (30). According to Frank, Sacagawea is an incomparable Indian princess.

Henry does not permit Frank's assessment of Sacagawea to stand unchallenged, however. Questioning previous assertions of Sacagawea's royalty and superiority, Henry emphasizes what other Sacagawea texts have not, the idea that perception precedes interpretation. Frank's descriptions of the princess and his understandings of her actions are not automatically valid because he knows her and has interacted with her. Instead his meanings become suspect because he is obviously in awe of her.

As Frank later discovers, not all the men of the Corps see Sacagawea as he does. Lewis states, for instance, that she is "a simple savage employed at government expense to gain us an audience with the Shoshone Indians" (217). In keeping with other texts that attempt to decipher Lewis's responses to Sacagawea, Henry illustrates that the captain objectifies her. Clark also apparently shares some of Lewis's perceptions. As he tells Frank, she is a "squaw, a Shoshone slave, serving an aged French white who bought her and worked her" (286). These "civilized" men observe a woman whose position on the cultural "ladder" is far below their own.

Neither Lewis nor Clark supplies the most vivid portrait of Sacagawea's savagery, however. Instructed by Clark to look at her carefully, to see the realities of her life, Frank eventually realizes that she is a woman "in full Shoshone pigments" (286). She no longer appears to be the same person he thought he has beheld previously. Her face is elongated, her nose is bridged higher, and her cheekbones are more pronounced. Neither does Sacagawea act like a princess. Chewing burley tobacco "as contently as any buffalo cow," she spits into the fire and dribbles brown juice down her chin. Moments after she plays with a puppy, Sacagawea "knocked out its brains on the nearest cottonwood and dropped it still jerking—ungutted, unskinned" into the stew pot (286–87). When he sees the "real" Sacagawea and the gulf between her existence and civilized life, Frank is disgusted by the scene. He realizes that she is savage.

Presenting extreme portrayals of Sacagawea, Henry questions previous interpretations of this American heroine. Is she the extraordinary princess or the repulsive squaw? As he stresses, both definitions are imperfect, incomplete, inherently flawed. Although Frank eventually realizes that the perfect, royal woman never existed, except in his own imagination, he at first believes that his comprehension of her savagery is accurate. He later discovers that Sacagawea "was never the dream of beauty which I had seen. . . . No more was she in actuality the brute female shown by the campfire" (301). Providing his protagonist with insight, Henry accentuates the concept of perception. Because observations are filtered through individual "realities," perceptions are conditional. All comprehension, as well as all interpretation, is contingent. As Henry insists, Sacagawea is neither squaw nor princess. She is whatever her beholder believes her to be.

Will Henry, therefore, approaches the character of Sacagawea, in addition to her legendary status as an American heroine, in a way that no other text has done. By demonstrating that context affects text and by questioning whether anyone can really know and understand another human being because of the importance of perception, Henry casts doubts on previous understandings of this native woman. Henry's conclusions about Sacagawea fall short of an absolute denial of meaning, however, for depictions of her intersect with another concern. Although he stresses that Sacagawea is neither ideal princess nor brute squaw, Henry does not extend his theories about perception into the realm of socially constructed understandings of savagery and civilization.

These classifications, unlike Sacagawea's character, are not contingent. As he illustrates throughout his work, each group occupies a fixed position on the cultural ladder, and each individual knows his/her place through group identity. Clark has his position, and natives occupy their respective rungs, depending upon fixed factors that show their level of savagery. As Henry maintains unequivocal categories and as he furthermore highlights the love triangle of Frank, Sacagawea, and Clark, he also explores implications of interracial relationships.

Like Emmons's heroine, Henry's Sacagawea adores Clark. When she "gazes" at the captain's handsome face for the first time, Sacagawea claims that "fire leaped" in her heart (128). That love grows as Clark saves her life and her baby's, during the breech delivery (145–46). Employing a novelist's prerogative in this scene and others to emphasize Clark's contact with Sacagawea, Henry contradicts the original expedition journals. In this novel, Clark, and not Lewis, ministers to Sacagawea during the difficult delivery. Although Henry provides a great deal of evidence illustrating Sacagawea's attachment to Clark, her desires are not as important as the effect she has on both Clark and the narrator. Their responses provide the framework for an analysis of miscegenation.

Despite his perception of Sacagawea's savagery, Clark is not impervious to her presence. According to Frank, when Clark first meets Sacagawea, "that granite carving of a man" felt her power and "trembled" to it (118). Later Clark admits that she was "enough to uncenter any man alive" (133). Although he is aware of her allure, Clark is also acutely conscious of the reality of his situation. He is a civilized man and the nation's ambassador, and she is a savage woman. Any entanglements with her would be indecent. Reflecting on a conversation he has had with Clark, Frank asserts that Sacagawea's feelings for the captain are unimportant because Clark thinks first of his men and the mission, and "no Indian girl would change that" (133). As he refers to Sacagawea's "Indianness," Henry emphasizes that if Clark succumbs to the lure of savagery, he can never fulfill his duties to the mission. The gallant captain gently tells Sacagawea that he could never love her in "an untrue way," the way a man loves a woman (210). Although Clark never explains why their love would be "untrue," the reason is clear. It is not because of Charbonneau, a virtually nonexistent husband in this text, but because of cultural prohibitions.

The story of the narrator's adoration for Sacagawea is quite different from the tale of her passion for Clark. When Frank meets the "tawny" princess, he is instantly smitten. As he proclaims, "I loved her . . . my heart stopped beating. For other women, from that moment, it never beat again" (118). Although Sacagawea confesses that she adores Clark and in spite of Frank's vow to forget her, the half-breed narrator loves Sacagawea throughout the novel. At the end of the novel, they are united in an idyllic scene. While some might view this subplot as nothing more than an attempt to satisfy the reader's desire for a happy ending, Henry registers other significant meanings. Contrasting impossible love with one that is possible, the novelist proposes and justifies strictures against interracial relationships.

Like Clark, Frank is aware of and responsive to the dichotomy of savagery and civilization and to taboos against miscegenation. Because Frank is a half-breed and because Sacagawea is neither savage nor civilized, his feelings are not truncated by cultural prohibitions. Facing two "truths," Frank realizes that "Sacajawea could no more be his [Clark's] mate in reality than I could be his [Clark's] son" (129). In this sentence, Frank summarizes the ambiguity of his own position on the cultural "ladder" and reiterates his acceptance of the proscriptions against interracial relationships. He can love Sacagawea because he too is not civilized.

Other passages in the novel reverberate with messages about the differences between savagery and civilization. Prior to his participation in the expedition, for example, the narrator realizes that, as a half-breed in a civilized world, he has no people. He witnesses a contrasting vision in the midst of their travels, however. As he asserts, no one is classified; no one is an "Indian" or a "half-breed." Rather, they are all "Americans together" (304). Projecting the promise of cultural pluralism, Frank declares that each person is distinct, and he affirms that those differences do not repudiate the shared identity of being Americans.

Frank's emotions arise from ritual experience. As ritual participants detach from fixed social structures, they enter a "liminal" phase, which creates a state of "communitas," according to Victor Turner. During liminality, previously fixed classifications no longer adhere and "equality and comradeship" become the norm (232). Although Frank wishes that the journey can last forever, he knows that such "equality and comradeship" will end with the mission. As Turner explains, rituals are temporary, and social positions are reestablished after the liminal period ceases. Although many ritual participants welcome the reconfirmation of previous statuses, Frank does not. Explaining that reluctance, Turner claims that "marginals," including people of mixed heritage, "have no cultural assurance of a final stable resolution of their ambiguity" (233). Frank summarizes his own dilemma. He knows that when the ritual ends, he will again be the "half-breed," not a member of the Corps, not an American.

Considering these conditions, Frank's choice to live with Sacagawea at the end of the journey illustrates and reinforces collective notions about savagery and civilization and interracial mixing. Prior to his decision, he asks himself a series of questions. Should he live in the "white man's" world, destined to be as miserable as he has been because, as an emblem of the monstrous results of miscegenation, he can never belong? Should he stay among the natives, adopting a people he has never viewed as his own? Arriving at the only logical conclusion in a world that ranks people on a cultural "ladder" and affixes them to a particular position according to their racial heritage, Frank affirms that natives are "his people" (303). He leaps from the expedition boat into Sacagawea's arms not simply from love but from a desperate need to belong.

Henry thus emphasizes how intensely people within a culture, and even those considered outside it, cling to "realities" that the dominant culture constructs. Such traditions not only indicate significant differences among social systems and classify them according to certain criteria but also promote codes of behaviors based on those categories. Shared understandings of the dichotomy of savagery and civilization prevail in this novel. Even from his marginalized position, Frank knows that Clark must not consider Sacagawea as a potential lover because both men have internalized social classifications and their meanings. For the same reasons, the narrator realizes he may consummate his passion. Henry depicts the marginality of both Sacagawea and Frank, and because civilization cannot absorb or accept that marginality, their position on the cultural continuum is within savagery. Endorsing the "one drop" theory of racial identity, Henry verifies that American "civilization" denies miscegenation as a legitimate means of creating a "melting pot" nation.

Within this novel, Henry concurrently explores the possibilities of cultural pluralism. As he describes Frank's vision of complete and perfect equality during the expedition, with diverse participants sharing hardships and offering unique knowledge and skills, Henry appears to endorse pluralism. Despite what seems to be a promise for America's future, lapses in the text disprove the validity of that potential. If the communitas of the mission were so powerful and so pervasive, if the breakdown of social institutions were complete,

distinctions between savagery and civilization would never have applied during the journey. Culturally constructed restrictions against
miscegenation would not have directed Clark's and other members'
attitudes and behaviors. Though Frank admits that this state of
shared "Americanness" is temporary, that ephemeral moment of
bliss never really occurs. Frank's vision is flawed by his own desire
to belong, and Henry documents that cultural pluralism is perhaps
nothing more than wish-fulfillment.

Paralleling his denials of the efficacy of the melting pot and skepticism of cultural pluralism, Henry highlights Sacagawea. While he
provides little commentary about her specific activities and accomplishments during the mission, he nonetheless defines her as an
American heroine. As Frank summarizes, "We were the strangers in
her land. Unto us she was bidden by her inner light to show the way,
to lead us through the wilderness, to guide us and go with us" (301).
Advancing her legendary attributes of helpfulness and guidance,
Henry implies that some innate "inner light" causes her to act.
Sacagawea is "beyond the imaginations of either captain to ensnare,
or any of us to describe" (302). As Henry suggests, this American
heroine belongs to legend.

He also extends the meanings of Sacagawea's presence. Informed
by that inner light, this native woman never struggles against her
heritage. She accepts her position on the cultural "ladder" with
grace and calm. Not simply the guide to the Corps during their
physical travels, she is an additional guide, the spiritual mentor to
the young half-breed. She helps Frank to understand and embrace
his own situation as well. Upholding the dichotomy of savagery and
civilization, she realizes that pluralism is impossible, and she per-
suades others to accept their destinies.

Although every text from the 1940s through the 1960s proclaims
that Sacagawea is an American heroine, proponents offer variations
to and elaboration of the legend. As DeVoto writes in *The Course
of Empire,* no evidence verifies that Sacagawea had a love affair with
any member of the Corps of Discovery. Neither has anyone discovered materials suggesting that she wished for a relationship. From
the time Peattie first intimates the connection, however, the love
story has assumed the air of "truth" in novels, histories, and articles.

While some critics may argue that such information provides one more scrap of the "realities" of the native woman's life and of her motivations during the mission, that plot has also influenced the Sacagawea legend.

Each text presenting the love story defines the nature of Sacagawea's heroism. Works claiming that her emotional attachment inspires her activities during the expedition reduce the significance of Sacagawea's accomplishments. Others embrace the romance but connect that sentiment to Sacagawea's discovery of the rectitude of manifest destiny. Asserting her devotion to the sacred mission and portraying her later advocacy of native assimilation, these texts extend Sacagawea's heroic stature. Whether devaluing or augmenting her contributions, such works do not overcome ambiguities about savagery and civilization that have been observed in previous works.

In connection with such predicaments, each text additionally explores an issue not addressed in the Progressive Era. Investigating the idea of a potential romance while maintaining the strict dichotomy between savagery and civilization during this period, Sacagawea works examine taboos of miscegenation and uphold those proscriptions. Although American culture struggled with ideas of the melting pot and cultural pluralism in the 1940s, 1950s, and 1960s, Sacagawea remains an American heroine, the useful emblem of manifest destiny. Still the essential helper in the wilderness during this period, she also becomes the superior native who recognizes her place and accedes to cultural constraints against interracial mixing.

5

THE SACAGAWEA LEGEND SINCE 1970

Proliferation of Popular Traditions
and Dissenting Portrayals

PROPONENTS OF THE Sacagawea legend offer variations of the narrative from the 1940s through the 1960s. While some writers extend the plot to incorporate the native woman's entire life, nearly every novelist proposes a love story. Critics might argue that such portrayals present a more accessible and understandable Sacagawea, a woman who implicitly denies objectification or characterization as a lesser being. Certain texts of the era accomplish that goal, but others, especially those suggesting that Sacagawea acts solely from a hopeless love for a civilized man, achieve the opposite effect. Such works instead diminish Sacagawea's stature and minimize the importance of her actions. In spite of particular narrative differences, nearly every text of the period grants that Sacagawea led the Corps of Discovery into unknown western wildernesses. They all proclaim her "American" heroism.

As evidence confirms, the popularity of the Sacagawea legend does not abate from the 1940s through the 1960s. Histories, novels, monuments, a major motion picture, and other works reinforce common assumptions held by people who are already aware of Sacagawea's story. These works also introduce and disseminate the tale to populations that have not previously honored her.

Exemplifying this phenomenon in the mid-1940s, a group of Sacagawea's champions embarked on a publicity campaign. According to the news story, "Statue of Sakakawea May Be Put in Hall of Fame," proponents of her legend sought to erect a Sacagawea statue to stand among likenesses of George Washington, Abraham Lincoln, and Daniel Webster on the New York University campus. Although the effort did not come to fruition, this crusade reinforced certain people's perceptions of the native woman and spread her renown to others.

Since 1970, writers, sculptors, and artists have offered a wealth of texts about Sacagawea. As in the previous era, scholars and creators advance diverse interpretations of the native woman and her actions. Historians, for example, have written scores of articles and books investigating Sacagawea's existence, including the date and place of her death and the spelling, pronunciation, and meaning of her name. These researchers additionally interpret and reinterpret evidence of Sacagawea's purported "guidance" of Clark during the mission.[1]

Two historical texts of the era, Harold Howard's *Sacajawea* and Ella Clark and Margot Edmonds's *Sacagawea of the Lewis and Clark Expedition,* devote many pages to analyses of this question. As they ask, does Clark not already know the route since the Corps passed through the gap the previous year? Is he simply embroidering her importance when he writes that she is his "pilot"? Does the captain not give her more credit than is her due? Arriving at different answers, Clark and Edmonds deny that Sacagawea was a guide while Howard asserts that although she did not constitute "the" guide of the expedition, she lead the party at certain critical moments.

Despite controversies surrounding the details of Sacagawea's life and specific "truths" of her activities during the expedition, recent histories agree on one point. They unanimously praise Sacagawea's courage and heroism. Not only perpetuating cultural discussions about this native woman, such works also proliferate the Sacagawea legend. *Lewis and Clark at the Great Divide,* a film produced by CBS as part of the "You Are There" series for young people, illustrates this dissemination. During the twenty-one-minute program, Walter Cronkite pops in and out of several vignettes, describing events and interviewing members of the Corps. Featured in the climactic moments of the film, Sacagawea arrives at the Shoshone camp, and expedition members discover that she is a princess. As Cronkite declares at the conclusion of the film, Sacagawea was the guide to

America's most important continental exploration, a true American heroine.

Justifying western conquests and outlining the bifurcation between savagery and civilization, most Sacagawea texts produced within the last two decades maintain the connection between Sacagawea's story and sacred traditions of manifest destiny. Not only do many refer to her as an Indian princess, but they also portray her physical, intellectual, and emotional preeminence, qualities associated with that "royal" image. Because of these offerings, works embracing Sacagawea during the period primarily tender traditional narratives of an Indian princess, a character who earns her title as an American heroine by helping civilized men in the savage wilderness.

Certain indications, on the other hand, seem to suggest that frontier myths have not preserved their previous potency during this period. As events on the continent and around the world have generated questions about race and conquest, as visionaries have confronted such traditions more often and more vigorously, the nation has engaged in a debate about frontier "realities." Countering secondary legitimations attempting to sustain commonly held assumptions, several works have offered other interpretations of the national mission and of native savagery. At least one script adopts the Sacagawea story to interrogate such "truths."

Because American populations have embraced competing realities during this period, I first review events and cultural texts intersecting with and commenting on frontier traditions. I then examine three Sacagawea works produced within the last two decades. Anna Lee Waldo's *Sacajawea* is a historical romance that articulates typical notions about the legendary heroine. In addition to reiterating manifest destiny, Waldo explores concepts arising from the rebirth of the American feminist movement in the late 1960s and 1970s. Also featuring Sacagawea in this period, an advertisement for a plate from The Hamilton Collection reflects the most common version of the Sacagawea narrative. She is a beautiful, gentle, helpful, and cooperative Indian princess, an American heroine because of her actions in the wilderness. In *Sakakawea: The Woman with Many Names*, librettist William Borden and composer Thomas Peterson produce a musical drama that draws upon the story of a heroic woman. Unlike many proponents, they question assumptions of frontier traditions. In this iteration of the Sacagawea narrative, Borden and Peterson ponder the rectitude of America's conquest and challenge the inherent differences between peoples who encountered one another during the frontier period.

Like all cosmogonic myths, frontier traditions have been part of a complex, interactive, cultural process. Such narratives have created and reflected, as well as illustrated and reiterated, social knowledge. Although primary and implicit frontier myths sustained power to determine cultural meanings and to define models of behavior for nearly two centuries, these stories could no longer wield totalizing potency as the nation underwent significant changes in the mid-nineteenth century. Illustrating that the vitality of traditional narratives varies over time and demonstrating the compulsion to maintain mythic potency, secondary legitimations sought to contain new conditions within old systems of comprehension.

While rationalized myths accommodated large segments of the American population for decades, stories justifying the sacred mission and upholding the dichotomy of savagery and civilization eventually lost their cultural consensus. No longer able to suppress discontinuities highlighted by historical events and illustrated in cultural texts, myths of manifest destiny have competed with other narratives of America's past. While this struggle undoubtedly began after World War II, frontier conceptions sustained at least some level of force for certain audiences, as evidenced by the popular reception of works submitting those "truths." Within the last two decades, nonetheless, contrary realities have gained vitality. Large segments of the populace have questioned, if not rejected, traditional frontier beliefs and behaviors.

Domestic and international events have facilitated these discussions and dissension since 1970. Although some people might not see the connection between frontier traditions and the Vietnam War, this profound national experience accentuated issues of conquest and race. Anti-war activists, for example, revolted against American interference in the internal problems of another country. Challenging previous assumptions about the national mission, protesters proclaimed that the war signified cultural imperialism. As they argued, the United States was culpable in its attempt to impose its own idea of "civilization" on other peoples.

While some historians might argue that manifest destiny never held sway outside the continent, they have noted that the Vietnam War fostered widespread discussions about race. In seeming response to demonstrations against the war, President Richard Nixon announced a policy of "Vietnamization." This program mandated the replacement of American troops with forces from South Vietnam. Although many citizens applauded plans to bring American soldiers home, certain critics pointed out that these policies simply made the war more palatable as "expendable" peoples fought and died.

Several specific incidents of the war also encouraged the examination of racial questions, but none so strongly as My Lai. The wanton slaughter of Vietnamese civilians from the small village shocked the nation, and a military court initially sentenced William Calley to life imprisonment for ordering the deaths. In spite of that decision, shortly after the conviction, Calley's sentence was reduced, and he was free in less than a year. Some Americans commended his release, explaining that peculiarities of the war had mitigated Calley's guilt. Others claimed that this incident simply illustrated that America still considered some lives to be more precious than others.

In response to these and other events in Vietnam, multitudes of Americans protested against the war. Not simply consisting of members of radical counter cultures, activists represented all ages, races, classes, and both sexes. Two prominent incidents in 1970 precipitated widespread confrontations with common assumptions about race. In April of that year, when National Guardsmen shot at student protestors at Kent State University, they killed four people and wounded nine. Also in 1970, policemen and highway patrolmen killed two and wounded many more as they "poured automatic weapon fire" into a women's dormitory at Jackson State University (Nash et al., 950). Across the nation, people denounced the violence, and many became involved in a reexamination of the premises of the war. Addressing another aspect of these incidents, a few commentators noted that the attack at Jackson State, committed against African Americans, drew far less media attention and public outrage than was expressed after the Euro-American student deaths. As reporters and other writers pointed out, racism probably motivated such disparate responses.

Connected to national discussions concerning race, a variety of studies and news stories, as well as popular songs, have focused on the racial and age composition of America's fighting forces in Vietnam. The Selective Service Act of 1940 mandated the first peacetime draft, an action that purportedly universalized military service of all able-bodied males in the nation. Although the intent of the act seemed clear, most college students received deferments during the Vietnam War. Moreover, when the lottery system was implemented, students with low lottery numbers secured most of the available National Guard slots. Because the largest percentage of college students were Euro-Americans from the middle and upper classes, the war had a disproportional impact on very young men from minority groups and/or lower classes.

As retired Admiral W. Norman Johnson submitted in a speech at Embry-Riddle Aeronautical University, Vietnam era draft boards, composed 95 percent of white males, conscripted thousands of Hispanic and African American inner-city youths during the war. Other data demonstrate that minorities served and died in large numbers in past wars, but the issue of systemic racism through selective service was not an important part of the national discussion until the Vietnam era. While America may not have rejected assumptions of conquest and commonly held ideas about race in the 1970s, the Vietnam War helped to bring the debate of those issues to the nation's attention.

Events on the continent generated similar dialogues about race and ethnicity during this same period. As Richard Polenberg argues, ghetto riots and rhetoric articulated by radical groups such as the Black Panthers led to a backlash in large segments of "mainstream" America. Partly because of those heightened emotions, subsequent school desegregations and busing engendered volatile verbal discussions and physical confrontations. Also tied to issues of race, affirmative action programs drew many protests from Euro-Americans.

In addition, racially motivated incidents have swept across American campuses since the late 1980s. Analyzing such hate crimes in "Bigots in the Ivory Tower," Naushad Mehta, Susan Tift, and Richard Woodbury write that many students have responded negatively to affirmative admissions policies, tuition waivers for minority students, and other school programs addressing issues of race and ethnicity. According to William Henry in "Beyond the Melting Pot," recent racial conflicts, on and off the nation's campuses, have arisen because of changing demographics in the United States. Anger over affirmative action and power-sharing has accompanied realizations that Euro-Americans will very soon make up a minority among diverse populations of American peoples (30).

These responses invoke frontier conceptions, verifying that the potency of such traditions has not entirely dissipated on the continent. Some cultural commentators have also relied on common understandings of manifest destiny during these decades of the "browning of America." As demographer Ben Wattenberg states, "We're a people with a mission and a sense of purpose, and we believe we have something to offer the world" (qtd. in Mehta, Monroe, Winbush). Although he does not specify the nature of that "mission" or provide a definition of the national "purpose," Wattenberg taps into emotions that have guided Euro-American populations for centuries.

Despite Wattenberg's rhetoric, frontier traditions have not maintained absolute potency on the continent in the past two decades. But neither has a new consensus overtaken those "truths." Through the push and pull of cultural discussion and change, the nation has engaged in a volatile polemic. Testing one version of the nation's beginnings against another, weighing their meanings in light of other interpretations, citizens have scrutinized America's story.

As U.S. populations became introspective over the national involvement in the Vietnam War and as they confronted notions of race at home and abroad, America's indigenous peoples became one focal point of the cultural discussion. Engendering the "Red Power" movement in the 1970s, natives contradicted the "reality" that aboriginals disappeared after the close of the frontier. Some tribes sought justice in federal courts. During this period, for example, the Three Affiliated Tribes of the Fort Berhold Reservation protested the Corps of Engineers' control of hunting and fishing

on and around Lake Sakakawea. Citing the losses that natives suffered because of the dam project, tribal leaders claimed that their
rightful jurisdiction over the area had been ignored (Johnson,
"Indians Seek Control").[2]

Other natives adopted different means of verifying their existence as they demonstrated against federal control and for self-determination in this era. Individuals and tribal groups launched a series of protests, including "fish-ins" in the upper Northwest, a
takeover of Alcatraz Island, the march of the Trail of Broken Treaties in Washington, D.C., and the 1973 occupation of Wounded
Knee. The last incident resulted in deaths on both sides of barri-
caded streets in the small reservation town in South Dakota. The
seventy-one-day armed confrontation at Wounded Knee intensified
discussions about the conquest of the continent and racism toward
indigenous populations.

Media were instrumental in connecting Wounded Knee to this
national polemic. As journalism professor Sharon Murphy contends,
newspapers before the twentieth century contributed to native
stereotyping by projecting common images of savagery. From the
turn of the century until the late 1960s, news media provided little
coverage of indigenous affairs. As "Red Power" flourished, however,
television, radio, and newspapers across the country focused on
native protests. Because the 1973 Wounded Knee occupation was the
most violent and one of the most protracted of these episodes, local
and national correspondents covered the story, bringing the news
to millions of Americans.

Then a resident of Bismarck, North Dakota, and wife of a newspaper reporter, I observed the controversy from close range. Media
commentators swarmed through the capitol, for its airport was relatively close to the besieged town, and many returned to Bismarck
to discuss the events, to decide their story "angles," and to wire
their interpretations of the occupation to their services. Through
the lens of Wounded Knee, such men and women framed the
national debate about native peoples.

Although most reporters registered shock at the violence at
Wounded Knee, they also recorded that the occupation was on the
exact site of the 1890 massacre of hundreds of innocent natives.

Most stories additionally highlighted contemporary injustices cited by the American Indian Movement (AIM). Manifold people across America, including members of other native groups, embraced this narrative. Not long after the end of the siege, an editorial group from the Mohawk nation published *Voices From Wounded Knee, 1973*. According to this text, Wounded Knee symbolized "a suppressed and oppressed people getting themselves together to restore some dignity to their lives" (1). Endorsing a story that countered common frontier traditions, the editors quoted Ellen Moves Camp, a native woman who had joined in the occupation. As she states, "They [the Oglalas] don't have no income—what little income they do have, maybe it's $19 a month . . . they're still living on rice and beans . . . our Indian people—are not going to be left out any more" (251). By the 1970s, as media and cultural texts presented images of native oppression and resistance, many Americans learned that myths of manifest destiny obscured or eliminated conflicting stories of the nation's past.

Other versions of the incident nonetheless reiterated and vindicated frontier conceptions. After holding eleven hostages, after negotiating with federal officials for more than two months, after declaring themselves a sovereign nation, the occupiers of Wounded Knee surrendered their weapons to federal troops. Many people publicly and privately commended federal agents and prosecutors for arresting and charging nearly three hundred people, including AIM leaders Russell Means and Dennis Banks, with a variety of crimes. Although many charges were dismissed, 185 native defendants were indicted. Only fifteen were convicted.

According to the editors of *Voices from Wounded Knee, 1973,* these trials, especially the proceedings against Means and Banks, served as a forum on issues of false arrest, illegal wiretaps, and perjury by federal agents. As the Wounded Knee trials dragged on, debates about racism and oppression continued in peoples' homes, in local newspapers, and on regional television stations, but national media paid far less attention to these proceedings than the incident begetting it. Wounded Knee, an episode that embodied local and national discussion concerning frontier myths, established that neither version of America's past held a cultural consensus.

Providing further evidence of the debate about native people's savagery, Ronald Trosper conducted a study of ranching efficiency in an area of Montana in 1978. As Trosper concludes, data showed that native and Euro-American ranchers had equal managerial knowledge and efficiency. He also admits, nevertheless, that neither ranching successes nor statistical proofs superseded problems stemming from assumptions about aboriginal laziness and ignorance. Such attitudes, for instance, continued to determine loan and land rental policies in the region. Although Trosper's conclusions point to a persistence of frontier mythic traditions, the existence of his study proves that not all Americans are immersed in these implicit "truths." As Trosper and many others have documented, America has been engaged in questioning frontier traditions.

Creators of historical fiction, television programs, and Hollywood films have also joined in such inquiries in the past two decades. Many popular texts have embraced myths of manifest destiny, and just as in the past, these stories have attracted large audiences. Gretchen Bataille and Charles Silet contend that American films of the 1970s and 1980s provide "a fascinating study of white America . . . trying to come to grips with itself and, in some measure, with its past" (xxv). As these comments imply, popular works have begun to debate frontier traditions.

Certain movies, produced in the last two decades, imbue native peoples with humor and dignity. According to Michael Hilger, screenwriters and directors present characters who possess a "significance in and of themselves" (140). Critics nearly unanimously cite *Little Big Man* as one such movie. According to film critic Louis Giannetti, the protagonist's native grandfather, played by Chief Dan George, embodies qualities of intelligence, morality, and humor, characteristics that contradict frontier assumptions (294). Commenting on the film in *Flashback: A Brief History of Film*, Giannetti and Scott Eyman write that producer Arthur Penn's sequences of the Battle of the Little Big Horn rebuke previous conceptions of General George Armstrong Custer and his actions. The critics also contend that Penn "rejected the heroic dimensions of these traditional American materials, converting the myth into a tragic parable of American racism and genocide" (478). When films like *Little Big Man* capture scenes of frontier warfare and provide images of the slaughter of innocent native women and children, they offer revisionist views of national beginnings.

Native women also receive different characterizations in recent films. As illustrated in Tables 5 and 6, presented in the previous chapter, of one hundred films depicting natives between 1970 and 1984, 28 percent feature a native woman. Although there has been no significant rise in this percentage over the decades, many of these works display a different type of woman. Portrayals of a traditional aboriginal wife or mother, depicted within the context of her own culture, have risen from 0 percent in silent films to 39 percent in movies produced in the 1970s and 1980s. Although such a woman might not appear heroic on a large scale, these representations contradict assumptions of native savagery as defined by frontier narratives. In *Dances with Wolves,* for example, the wife of the protagonist's native friend possesses subtle powers. Her presence and actions suggest that traditional native women were not totally subordinated to men.

Despite an increase in portraits of traditional native women's lives, American film makers have nonetheless delivered many stories about Indian princesses as well. Of works featuring a native woman in the 1970s and 1980s, 54 percent depict the young and beautiful Indian maiden who ventures into the wilderness to save the civilized man or men. Evidence would suggest that some recent American films reflect a new openness to native cultures, advancing legitimate questions about western conquests and savagery, but others cling to those very ideas.

Conducting a study of Utah college students' perceptions of indigenous peoples, Tim Shaughnessy verifies that the transformation of Euro-American responses to natives is not complete. As Shaughnessy learns, Euro-American youth consistently stereotype natives as inarticulate and inferior. He also concludes that media images of native savagery have contributed to that phenomenon. This study and others stress that although conquest and savagery have been subjects of debate in recent years, frontier myths continue to influence belief among significant numbers of Americans.

Within the last two decades, various artists advance Sacagawea's story to the American public, even amid contentious discussions about the national mission and about native savagery. Most of these narratives embrace Sacagawea, not because she provides an opportunity to counter traditional meanings, but because she reiterates frontier mythic conceptions. Most of Sacagawea's latest advocates present Sacagawea's story in the most typical way. She remains the Indian princess, vital proof that manifest destiny has been just.

Submitting a narrative that reflects the traditional legend, Anna Lee Waldo pens a 1,407-page romance novel, *Sacajawea,* the saga of an American heroine's lifetime. Although the book received unanimously negative reviews from historians and literary critics, it was extremely popular with American audiences. Commenting on this tome, Raymond Stedman claims that it provides evidence that this heroic figure from western history continues to appeal to America. As he asserts, Sacagawea's story sounds "inviting echoes of the ancient forest maiden" throughout the land (31). Verifying the attraction, Waldo's text was on the *New York Times* bestseller list for more than eight months in 1979 and 1980 and sold over one million copies in less than four years. Even as late as ten years after its initial publication, people who sold historical materials and memorabilia on the capitol grounds during North Dakota's state centennial celebration in 1989 testified that *Sacajawea* was one of their fastest-moving commodities.

The success of Waldo's novel is linked, in part, to a recent phenomenon of American popular culture, the explosion in production and consumption of romance novels. In *Reading the Romance: Women, Patriarchy, and Popular Literature,* Janice Radway investigates marketing strategies of romance fiction and interviews individuals from a "community" of romance readers. A professor of American civilization, Radway enumerates the most important qualities of romance fiction. One factor in the popularity of such narratives is marketing. Women, primarily from working-class families, make up nearly 100 percent of romance readers. Targeting this audience in various ways, publishers print novels in paperback, to produce and sell them at reasonable prices. In addition, the books are marketed in drugstores, supermarkets, and mall bookstores where millions of women shop every day (32–38). *Sacajawea* illustrates the efficacy of such marketing strategies. Waldo's publishing company, Avon, printed *Sacajawea* in paperback only and sold it in assorted "women's" shopping locations.

Undoubtedly as important as marketing techniques, the plots of romance novels must adhere to specific criteria for popular acceptance. As Radway contends, romance readers want "chronicles of female triumph." Searching for assurances about their lives as females and their roles as wives and mothers, consumers embrace a "utopian vision in which female individuality and a sense of self are shown to be compatible with nurturance and care by another" (55). According to Radway's research, this community of readers demands historical narratives of an independent and defiant woman (56). The tale must also illustrate the heroine's connection to a handsome man, and she must be successful in attaining his attention and in "establishing herself as the object of his concern and the recipient of his care" (84). Waldo's novel incorporates these demands.

Combining marketing strategies and the promise of an acceptable plot to draw readers' attention and to inspire spontaneous purchases, the cover art of the 1984 edition of *Sacajawea* relates the subject's strength and independence. It also alludes to the historical context of her story. As the picture relates, several frontiersmen are resting in the background, cradling their guns across their arms. In the foreground, a beautiful woman strides ahead, confidently leading the weary men. As her fringed buckskin dress and her dark, flowing hair exemplify, Sacagawea is moving forward, with purpose. Even before readers encounter the Sacagawea story, the book cover declares that a strong and determined woman is the subject of this novel, not the men.

The plot of *Sacajawea* fulfills romance readers' requirements for an incomparable heroine as it simultaneously presents a traditional tale of the legendary Indian princess. Clever and curious as a child (8), Sacagawea vows to conduct herself as the daughter of a great chief even in the face of terrible treatment by her captors (66–67). As a young woman, she is alert and intelligent (273). She has shiny black hair, full lips, widely spaced dark eyes, high cheekbones, and "creamy-brown," silky skin (146, 499). Graceful and slim (146), Sacagawea is beautiful, even by "white standards" (154). Although Waldo does not describe a woman that is as Euro-Americanized as Henry's heroine, this Sacagawea possesses all the physical and intellectual attributes of a true Indian princess. Consistent with all other interpretations of Sacagawea's efforts during the mission, Waldo's tale emphasizes that the heroine provides food, mends clothes, and cares for the men and her baby (313–14, passim). In one scene, this wise native woman teaches the men to protect themselves against mosquitoes with buffalo grease (329). Leading them forward into the wilderness, saving their lives, Sacagawea is an American heroine.

Continuing a tradition begun in texts of the 1940s, Waldo highlights a love story. She also adopts her predecessors' strategies in portraying an evil Charbonneau. A half-breed abomination in this novel (218), Charbonneau is a lascivious old squawman who wins Sacagawea in a game of chance, hits her, and tries to sell her "favors" (154, 231, 296, 318). Yearning for real fulfillment, Sacagawea finds Clark, and he wants her also. Despite their passion, which is illustrated in hundreds of pages of heart-throbbing, impetuous embraces, this heroine and hero do not consummate their love.

Demonstrating how easily Sacagawea's story, as well as social proscriptions against miscegenation, can be molded to nearly every requirement of the romance novel, Waldo portrays the traditional tale of the Indian princess who loves a civilized man and saves the mission but who can never participate in civilization because of her native heritage. As Waldo asserts, "this feeling had roots between them, but the roots could never be nourished and kept alive" (664). The impediment to their relationship is not Charbonneau, nor is it the baby. Taboos against interracial mixing prevent Sacagawea and Clark from fulfilling their desires. Even as late as the 1970s, despite debates about frontier traditions, Waldo confirms that the intrepid heroine cannot win Clark, even temporarily, because of racial differences.

Not only does *Sacajawea* reinforce American frontier myths; the novel also attempts cultural work for the nation's future. Just as Dye has done in the Progressive Era and as Emmons undoubtedly does in the 1940s, Waldo participates in the protracted conversation about women's roles and positions in American society. Employing Sacagawea as a model for American women of their own times, each of these female writers exemplifies a heroine who rises above the constraints of her day and takes control of her life. As they submit, other women can do the same.

For more than two centuries, myriad texts have engaged in the cultural discourse about women's positions and roles in American society. Even before the rise of the feminist movement during the Progressive Era, certain writers have questioned the idea of women's circumscription within the home. In *Woman in the Nineteenth Century,* for instance, Margaret Fuller focuses on commonly cited "women's differences," their bodies, emotions, and roles as wives and mothers. Although many texts of Fuller's era declare that such distinctions certify women's weakness and inferiority, Fuller stresses that feminine characteristics prove women's superior intuition, a quality that counterbalances men's brute sensuality. Employing traditional arguments to sustain her viewpoint, Fuller contends that women deserve equality because they are in some ways better than men. Although she does not avoid the trap of relationality (that is by defining women primarily through their association with their fathers, husbands, and sons), Fuller is one of the first American writers to interrogate concepts of a "woman's place" and to encourage ideological revolution.

By the turn of the twentieth century, some of Fuller's ideas served as foundation arguments for woman suffrage. As the movement expanded from a few women on the fringes of American society to incorporate moderate reformers during the Progressive Era, proponents employed Sacagawea as a standard bearer of suffrage, as has been previously discussed. After suffragists achieved their objective, American feminism declined, according to William Henry Chafe. As he argues, activists for women's rights gained the vote but lost their impetus to act in unison.

The debate about women's roles did not die after the 1920s, however, since the ballot did little to eliminate women's economic or social inequality. Another critical moment in the feminist movement occurred during and after World War II as American women supported the war effort. They embraced sundry occupations, including employment in heavy industry. In *Out to Work: A History of Wage-Earning Women in the United States,* Alice Kessler-Harris documents that Euro-American women earned wages since their arrival in the New World, but she also asserts that World War II offered unprecedented opportunities for women. Necessity mitigated traditional attitudes about female circumscription. Such transformations could not have occurred, asserts Chafe, without the approval and encouragement of the government and the "principal instruments of public opinion," newspapers, radio, magazines (146, 148). Through every possible avenue, American culture promoted women's entry into the war effort and legitimized female employment.

Despite certain inroads for women in the work force during the war, traditional attitudes did not change unconditionally. As Chafe writes, "most citizens preferred to retain traditional definitions of masculine and feminine spheres," even as they allowed modifications of the "content of those spheres in practice" (194). Chafe's comments coincide with Ruth Milkman's conclusions. As Milkman contends, women invaded the work force at the culture's encouragement, but women's pay, the type of labor they were allowed to do, and prohibitions against their enrollment in unions pointed to ideological separation and hegemony. Other evidence of the persistence of this orthodoxy occurred after the war. When soldiers returned home, many women workers lost their jobs and were told to return to their homes.

Although the women's movement may have appeared to be dormant in the 1950s as American culture disseminated idyllic images of the homemaker, family, and the stay-at-home mother, these were not the only realities on the continent. Kessler-Harris argues that during this decade more women became part of the work force than at any previous time in the nation's history. By the 1960s, women were among America's most important wage workers, especially in clerical and service sectors. During this decade, many women became inspired by the rhetoric and action of the civil rights movement, student revolts, and Vietnam protests. Whether they were employed or not, such women demanded a reexamination of traditions that restricted female roles in American society.

Chafe, Kessler-Harris, and others agree that Betty Friedan's 1963 *The Feminine Mystique* helped to focus the nation's attention on cultural assumptions about women's biology and psyche, as well as their social and economic statuses in America. Striking a responsive chord in multitudes of women and men across America as it highlighted the destructive effects of women's circumscription, this work and others helped to spark a resurgence of the women's movement in the 1970s. Kessler-Harris argues that feminists "pushed the ideology of the home from the center of consciousness. In its place women at the edge of change began to search for new perceptions of self and new relationships to power and authority" (319). Fighting against deeply rooted traditions, activists in the women's movement focussed on several issues, including sexual freedom, the ability to control reproduction through access to birth control and abortion, and the Equal Rights Amendment (ERA). As feminists achieved some of their goals and as ERA activities escalated, other men and women adhered to established ideologies and fought against reform. The women's movement was privately and publicly debated across America during the 1970s.

According to Janice Radway, romance readers have participated in this contentious conversation. Disputing other interpretations of romance fictions, Radway contends that reading romances does not enforce female dependence, nor does it rationalize women's repression. She argues that these ritual readings instead express participants' remonstration of the very institutions that have attempted to limit their roles in a patriarchal culture.

Embracing such ideas in a novel about one of America's most renowned Indian princesses, Anna Lee Waldo employs Sacagawea as a model of and argument for modern feminism. Unlike Peattie's heroine, Waldo's Sacagawea is not a weak, little object to be manipulated by men. Pointedly connected to the cultural conversation about women's place, she serves as an ideal figure to investigate issues of repression and circumscription, in addition to female control of sexuality and reproduction. Despite various men's attempts to subjugate this remarkable heroine, Sacagawea becomes an independent woman.

Early in the novel, Waldo emphasizes the evils of male domination as she presents scenes of rape, an act of violence marking the victim's impotence and the perpetrator's control. Treated as a sex object by the age of ten or eleven, Sacagawea is repeatedly raped by her Minnetaree "grandfather" and "father" and nearly every other man around her (88, passim). Although she protects herself from Charbonneau when she first meets him (156), he forces himself on her after he wins her in a game of chance (235). With no means of resisting or escaping her "master's" will, Sacagawea is pregnant by the time she is twelve or thirteen.

Waldo accentuates the portrait of female vulnerability in many ways. Pointing to an analogy between Sacagawea's life and those of contemporary American wives, Waldo emphasizes that Charbonneau is a "master" who owns and controls a slave. Young and small, Sacagawea is physically unable to overcome her slavery, but perhaps more important, she is also defenseless because of her economic dependence. She has no alternative other than compliance. In addition, among the portrayals of rape, Waldo submits that Sacagawea's master/husband committed many of them. As the novel demonstrates, sexual assaults are no less loathsome even if they are perpetrated within legitimate social institutions.

Sexual control is not the only indication of female repression in this text. Nearly every man in Sacagawea's life attempts to circumscribe her existence and to discount her importance. Captain Meriwether Lewis is among Sacagawea's worst detractors. When Clark argues that they should take her along on the mission, Lewis is horrified. Although he admits that she would be an invaluable asset, Lewis notes that they would never be able to hold up their heads if Washington ever found out that a woman took part in this military mission (277). In another incident, he refuses to follow Sacagawea's advice at Three Forks and wastes several days on the wrong tributary because he "could not trust a woman" (336). Finally, when the Corps leaves the Mandans, Lewis does not pay her. As he states, " 'we can't list a woman on our Army payroll—no way!' " (682). Discounting her knowledge, scoffing at her contribution, Lewis is not significantly different from the men who rape Sacagawea. In each case, these attitudes and actions suggest an underlying fear of Sacagawea's strength. All men seek to control her.

Despite male attempts at domination, Waldo's heroine prevails. Employing scenes from the original journals, Waldo reveals that Sacagawea is a woman of remarkable power and intelligence. She knows, for example, that there is no waterway across the continent and laughs at the men who are naive enough to hope that it exists (258). During the squall, she does not simply sit in the boat rescuing valuable articles that float alongside her. This Sacagawea plunges into the river, baby on her back, to save the irreplaceable stores (318). Attesting to Sacagawea's courage and potency, Waldo capitalized on an ambiguity in the original scripts. Because Lewis proclaims that Charbonneau and two other men would perish if the boat overturned, the novelist interprets the captain's failure to comment on Sacagawea's presence as evidence that she can swim. Her purported ability is even more impressive when Lewis concedes that he would drown in the powerful current.

The squall marks only the first of a series of incidents in which Sacagawea displays her power. Reversing most scripts' interpretations, Waldo claims that she saves Clark from certain death during the flash flood (358). Not limiting Sacagawea's potency to such grand events, Waldo depicts a woman who defies male authority throughout the mission. When she demands the right to see the whale, Clark acknowledges that nothing will stop her (569). In other scenes, she does not allow her husband to punish her child (580), and she tries to convince other native women that they should form their own social organizations, for such institutions should not exist just for men (602).

Articulating Sacagawea's feelings about Charbonneau and extrapolating those ideas to all men, Waldo argues that "she wanted to be as free of him as possible so that he could not cast a net over her made of the strings of his dependence on her" (557). As Sacagawea reasons, women become circumscribed because of men's dependence upon them. Not allowing herself to be subordinated by any male, Sacagawea recognizes that "she would not be content to stay in this place [Fort Mandan] long. She had goals and a horizon to follow. She had hope" (689). This unfettered heroine leaves Charbonneau and leads a long and fulfilling life. Although she marries again, she does not allow herself to be repressed, and when she returns to the Shoshones in old age, she bears the name Porvino, which means "chief." She is the only woman who speaks with authority among males. In innumerable scenes, Anna Lee Waldo presents a woman of bravery and courage, a heroine able to fight against male domination. A model for modern feminists, Sacagawea seems to promise that strong women can triumph.

Waldo tries to universalize the potential of such feminism by showing that Sacagawea is "everywoman." To establish the identity between Sacagawea and Euro-American women, the novelist attempts to collapse differences between savagery and civilization. Representative of all womankind as she endures the pains of labor, Sacagawea experiences emotions that were "as primitive and as civilized as any woman's. There was no distinction between primitive and civilized in the event of birth" (284). Denying the notion that savage women "enjoy" easy labors, Waldo claims that all women share equally in the life-giving experience.

This effort to ignore or discount Sacagawea's native heritage ultimately fails, however, because Waldo emphasizes her heroine's racial identity so often throughout the text. Racial differences doom Sacagawea's and Clark's love. More significantly, Waldo consistently depicts native culture as primitive and savage, and she suggests that savagery is the root of Sacagawea's subordination. When Sacagawea is a child among the Shoshones, her brother says that she asks too many questions, "more than a girl-child should" (5). She is not allowed to paint on stone, for that activity is reserved for men (6). Illustrating the ways in which female repression is passed from one generation to the next, Sacagawea's mother chastises her curiosity (11).

Women's worst subordination, so vividly depicted in the series of rapes, is inherently connected to native culture. Because she is a slave among savages and because savages do not differentiate between little girls and women, Sacagawea is subject to male sexual domination by the age of ten. None of the men of the Corps commits such acts. Acknowledging the correlation between female repression and savagery, Sacagawea proclaims, " 'I do not want to be a slave squaw forever. . . . I cannot live like a caged bird always' " (113). As this statement implies, Sacagawea is not so immersed within savagery, even before her contact with civilized men, that she cannot recognize the truth about native existence. She simply must learn how to escape her savage subordination.

Similar to Emmons's subject, Waldo's Sacagawea discovers that civilization offers female independence. As she states during the journey, "There is pleasure for me being here with you white men" (480). Although she does not specify, at this point, the exact nature of her satisfaction nor its cause, Sacagawea defines her feelings more thoroughly in a subsequent scene. As she reflects, "she was feeling more and more as though she belonged with these white men. They accepted her as one of them. . . . She had acted as an interpreter and was treated more like one of the men than like a squaw. . . . These were things done only by men [playing the fiddle, firing a rifle, singing in public]. But here, with these people, it made no difference. Life was good here" (526). Articulating her contentment with the companionship and equality that civilized men offer, Sacagawea envisions the journey and its achievement of communitas in much the same way Frank Rivet does in *The Gates of the Mountains*. In Waldo's text, however, that dissolution is grounded in gender-based statuses rather than racial differences. In spite of such positive images, certain questions remain. Can Waldo filter out race as she presents the story of an Indian princess? If she cannot, how does that affect her portrayal of feminism and/or her characterization of a heroine?

Adopting common assumptions concerning women's roles and positions within traditional tribal cultures, Waldo is unable to separate the issues of race and gender. As she claims, savagery institutionalizes the subordination of women. Implicit in this reasoning is the notion that civilized society is, and was, open to women of power and intelligence. While Waldo might concede that Euro-American women are confronted by some measure of male domination or diminution, as evidenced by Lewis, she confirms that many "civilized" men can accept female autonomy.

Instead, Waldo highlights the repression of native women, arguing that Sacagawea escapes the strictures of savagery, not that of universal male domination. As the plot reveals, Sacagawea learns to resist the confines of primitive societies. Through her contact with the men of the Corps, she evolves into something greater than she has been. When she translates for the captains, for instance, Sacagawea feels that she has "reached a height of esteem never before dreamed of by women" as the "great medicine of white men" transforms her (618). Clark, a man who is not afraid of female power, muses over her metamorphosis and realizes that she is "no longer cowed by the shackles of Shoshoni or any other native tradition or behavior" (664). Through such an educational process, Sacagawea discovers that savagery must change so that native women's talents and ideas can be accepted, just as they are in Euro-American culture.

As these notations suggest, Waldo attempts to collapse racial categories to define the universality of Sacagawea's heroism, but she concurrently emphasizes disparities between savagery and civilization in an effort to prove Sacagawea's development as a woman. In effect, this novelist presents irreconcilable images. Is Sacagawea "everywoman," a person whose race is unimportant to her identity as a powerful female? Or is she a native woman who must escape the limitations of her primitive culture and embrace the freedoms that civilization bestows on all its citizens? While Waldo obviously wishes to blend these questions, she cannot.

Stressing Sacagawea's transformation at the same moment that she denies her heroine's real acceptance by civilization, Waldo does not transcend savagism/civilization dichotomies. Accepting and reiterating proscriptions against miscegenation, illustrating the savagery of native life, especially as it affects women, and contrasting that existence with civilization, Waldo upholds and justifies frontier myths. As the back cover of the novel proclaims, Sacagawea "stood straight and proud before the onrushing forces of America's destiny." Through this "great woman," Waldo tells the story of this "great nation." In various ways, *Sacajawea* disseminates many traditional meanings of manifest destiny and illustrates ambiguities of the Indian princess.

Waldo's approach to Sacagawea and her activities is not an aberration even in an era that has witnessed strident dissension over issues of conquest, race, and gender. A 1989 advertisement for a commemorative plate, offered for sale by The Hamilton Collection, also testifies to the force and attraction of traditional representations. Although Olivia Sayer, a product specialist for The Hamilton Collection, provides no specific data about the number of "Sacajawea" plates that have been fired or sold, she asserts that "American Indian subjects" are the company's most popular products. This information would appear to coincide with the manifold Indian images that The Hamilton Collection markets in almost every Sunday's *Parade* magazine. Among those offerings, "Sacajawea" is a commodity that combines nostalgia for "Indian" objects with positive messages about America's past.

Attempting to appeal to broad audiences, the advertisement for the "Sacajawea" plate establishes the connection between the native woman and her "American" heroism. The advertising copy presents the tale of a traditional Indian princess. As the script reads, "Gentle, serene and knowledgeable, Sacajawea helped lead her party over plains and rivers and through Montana mountain passes." Familiar with America's uncharted wilderness, she guides civilized men through the perils of the frontier. Although none of the western states existed at that time, copy writers record no apparent dissonance in naming the territory "Montana." The text additionally explains that the plate is a "tribute to this American heroine" of the Lewis and Clark Expedition. Reinforcing that message, the advertising banner reads, "Sacajawea: A Brave and Noble American Heroine." Just as in other works produced during the Progressive and subsequent eras, this advertisement declares that Sacagawea was and is an American heroine because of services she performed during the expedition.

The advertisement also provides a color photograph of the collector plate. A representation of a graphic print designed and executed by David Wright, the plate displays a woman possessing all the physical attributes of the Indian princess. She is young and beautiful, and her skin is lightly tanned. Her clothing of fringed buckskin may not indicate a "royal" station, but the accoutrements adorning her dress, such as fur trim, extensive beading and quill work, jewelry, and other ornaments, verify Sacagawea's sovereignty.

The plate additionally illustrates the context of Sacagawea's "American" heroism. Directly associating this Indian princess with the frontier West, Wright places her in the wilderness, with snow-peaked mountains in the distance, a river somewhat closer, and a primitive campsite just behind. This portrait also denotes Sacagawea's connection to the men of the Corps. Two frontiersmen, no doubt Lewis and Clark, look at a map or chart in the background, and a few other men talk by the boat. There is no doubt, however, that Sacagawea is the subject of this vignette. Sitting gracefully and serenely in the foreground, the beautiful Indian princess dominates the print.

No dissonance interrupts the visual harmony of the scene or Sacagawea's association with the American mission on the continent. Nowhere does the ad register conflict between Sacagawea's nobility as an "American Indian Woman" and her role as an "American Heroine." Colors of red, white, and blue are prevalent. The baby's cradleboard is decorated with red beads or quills, the design appearing remarkably similar to stripes of an American flag. Sacagawea, a picturesque heroine, holds her baby's cradleboard in her lap, her arms surrounding him protectively. As the portrait confirms and the advertisement copy echoes, she simultaneously fulfills her obligations as a protective mother and as an American heroine of the Lewis and Clark Expedition. A "bold and brave Indian woman," this Indian princess assures the nation of the rectitude of manifest destiny.

In the same year that The Hamilton Collection first advertises the "Sacajawea" plate, two Euro-American men produce another iteration of the Sacagawea narrative, the musical drama *Sakakawea: The Woman with Many Names*. Unlike other proponents of the Sacagawea legend, librettist William Borden and composer Thomas Peterson use the story of the expedition and Sacagawea's role in that mission as a means of interrogating narrative traditions of America's western conquests and the dichotomy of savagery and civilization. As this play demonstrates, frontier myths no longer maintain compelling power among certain, possibly widespread, American populations. Instead, contrary narratives compete for "reality" status on the continent.

According to William Borden, the inspiration for the musical drama was Thomas Peterson's. As Borden writes, the composer/conductor wanted to create an opera that related something of North Dakota's history (1 Oct. 1991). Peterson, who grew up in Grand Forks and attended the University of North Dakota, reported in a telephone interview that the 1989 state centennial celebration offered funding for a dramatic production. Declaring that he hoped to write "larger-than-life music" to fit a "larger-than-life narrative," Peterson said that he was not interested in Teddy Roosevelt or other "modern" state personalities because a vision inspired his choice of a subject.

He saw a picture "of a young native woman, standing alone, looking off, feeling the burden of great responsibility." Acting on that vision, Peterson selected Sacagawea as the subject of his drama. As he asserts, "she is already a myth—one of the true great myths of our country." Elaborating on his choice, Peterson stated that Sacagawea was a "powerful character," one who has elicited "intense universal emotions" in many audiences. Playwright and English professor at the University of North Dakota, William Borden collaborated with Peterson. Borden writes that although Peterson initially suggested Sacagawea as the subject of the drama, he too became intrigued by the story of this "mythic and universal figure" (1 Oct. 1991). Like other creators of the past century, Thomas Peterson and William Borden embraced the Sacagawea legend.

Despite possibly typical reasons for Peterson's choice of subject matter, *Sakakawea* was affected by America's dialogue about race. As Borden asserts, he prepared to write the libretto by reading the expedition journals, a few biographies, and historical articles debating Sacagawea's name. He also claims that he did not read any of the historical novels, because "I didn't want other fictions in my head. I especially didn't read that huge novel that was so popular"

(1 Oct. 1991).[3] Blending information gathered from these sources with the need to cast two former North Dakota women who have received national recognition as professional singers, Borden wrote a tale of a native woman who lived to old age.

That decision roused controversy. As Borden notes, "The Lewis & Clark Assoc. were very upset that we even considered that she might have lived to 89; the party line is that she dies much earlier" (1 Oct. 1991). The association's response should not be surprising, for Hebard's version of Sacagawea's life has inevitably directed attention away from the expedition and toward the native heroine. Adding another reason for their preference, Borden writes, "I regard the party line as a white bias that privileges written records over oral testimony" (1 Oct. 1991). As these comments suggest, historical debates about Sacagawea's death have not abated. More important, Borden points out that Euro-American conceptions of "evidence" no longer persuade all populations.

Another conflict surrounded the production of *Sakakawea,* one directly tied to the national debate concerning western conquests and interpretations of native cultures. Once Peterson and Borden selected Sacagawea as the subject for the drama and outlined the narrative, they sought funding from the North Dakota Council on the Arts. The council refused their request, though an earlier version of Borden's script was the 1987 winner of the "Opera Now!" libretto competition in Minneapolis, Minnesota (*Sakakawea* Playnotes 10). As the council explained, the world had "enough white versions of Indian stories" (Gail S. Hand). Decades prior to this production of the Sacagawea story, such comments would probably have never taken place.

Despite these controversies, Borden and Peterson persuaded the council and others that *Sakakawea: The Woman with Many Names* was not just another "white version" of an "Indian" story, and many state and national associations provided grants for the production. They included the University of North Dakota, the North Dakota Council on the Arts, the National Endowment for the Arts, the North Dakota Humanities Council (*Sakakawea* Playnotes 1). The reversal in agency support partially hinged on Borden's and Peterson's concession to the North Dakota Humanities Council's demands. As they insisted, the playnotes would include two scholarly commentaries on the Sacagawea story, one provided by a person schooled in Euro-American history and the other knowledgeable in native traditions. More significantly, council directors undoubtedly came to understand that *Sakakawea* interrogates frontier myths.

Produced in celebration of North Dakota's centennial year, *Sakakawea: The Woman with Many Names* played before sellout crowds at the Chester Fritz Auditorium in Grand Forks, North Dakota, in September 1989. As reviewer Gail Stewart Hand writes, the drama was "clever, moving, riveting," a "striking and brilliant" musical celebrating the legend of Sacagawea. Three years in production, enveloped in a cultural debate, *Sakakawea: The Woman with Many Names* employs flashbacks and two Sacagaweas, one old and one young, to move back and forth from the Wind River Reservation in Wyoming in 1884 to scenes of the Lewis and Clark Expedition in 1805 and 1806.

In some ways, Peterson and Borden do not depart from previous versions of the legend, as they incorporate activities inscribed in the original journals and other texts. The heroic Sacagawea is a cooperative helper in the wilderness. She translates for the captains (I-3) and signifies the expedition's peaceful intentions (I-9–12).[4] When the men are starving because they cannot find meat, she arrives with vegetables and roots that she has dug, and the entire chorus sings, "What would we do without you?" (I-19). Peterson and Borden also illustrate Sacagawea's bravery. As she sings, "If I can be someone, if I can do something, if I can wander beyond mountains to the farthest sea—I will be remembered, I will be remembered by someone. . . . I can grab chances like berries, like limbs on a tree I can climb. Every chance is a path somewhere, every gamble a mountain to climb to see what lies beyond. The unexpected the juiciest berry to bite" (I-21). This woman is nothing like the person Lewis describes on several occasions. She is a courageous heroine, one who possesses aspirations beyond her immediate surroundings.

Again, in keeping with other Sacagawea texts of the past five decades, *Sakakawea* reflects a love story between the heroine and Clark. Charbonneau is more an object of pity than of scorn in this production, as he is a coward and weak in comparison to any other member of the Corps. He offers Sacagawea no consideration or tenderness, and she yearns for "a little love" and finds it in Clark (I-18). Clark returns that emotion. As he sings when she is ill, "I don't need you to buy horses. I don't need you to find food. I need your bright laugh, I need your warm hand in mine. I need you close to me" (I-25). Just as other works previously contend, this drama of the Sacagawea legend also asserts that their love is doomed.

Arguing with Sacagawea over the hopelessness of their situation, Clark explains that he has plans when he returns to civilization. As he states, "It's different in the city. It's different in the white man's world. I love you, Janey, but it's not a city love. A General can't have a People wife" (II-17). While he might not agree with cultural taboos of miscegenation, Clark acknowledges that being married to a native woman would destroy his political ambitions. Outlining the character and actions of a heroic woman, illustrating her husband's faults, citing her doomed love for Clark, Borden and Peterson appear to submit another example of the traditional legend.

Despite certain typical approaches to the narrative, *Sakakawea* inscribes other concepts that question Euro-American assumptions about native peoples. The play also interrogates the nature and results of the nation's sacred mission on the continent. Such commentaries mark significant departures from previous interpretations of the legend. Borden and Peterson, for example, confront a passage in Lewis's journal that implies Sacagawea's savage impassivity. Overlapping each other's disparate conversations, Sacagawea and Lewis sing,

Lewis: Here she was captured by enemies only a few years ago . . . [5]
Young Sakakawea: Only a few years ago, horses thundered over that hill. An arm scooped me up . . .
Lewis: I cannot discover . . .
Young Sakakawea: I rode behind him . . .
Lewis: . . . that she shows any emotion . . .
Young Sakakawea: . . . all day, the horse's spine . . .
Lewis: . . . of sorrow in recollecting this event . . .

Young Sakakawea: . . . hard against my buttocks . . .
Lewis: . . . or of joy in being restored . . .
Young Sakakawea: . . . the man's back sweating, his smell heavy in my nostrils.
Lewis: . . . to her native country.
Young Sakakawea: It was like dying— (II-1–2).

By juxtaposing these "stories," Borden shows that perception presupposes interpretation.

As Sacagawea relates, she not only registers the peril and anguish of her past capture but also recollects the pain and horror of that experience years later. Lewis, nonetheless, is a man whose realities have been informed by frontier myths, and he implicitly knows that savage women are unemotional creatures. Although he sees Sacagawea and hears her tale, he also understands that she is unquestionably savage. Nothing, not even her own testimony, sways his opinion that she is impassive. He perceives what he must. Because the audience witnesses two intersecting, yet conflicting narratives, Lewis's judgments become pointedly ironic. Sacagawea's remain heroic.

Although other writers have also cast doubts on Lewis's interpretations of Sacagawea's impassivity, most have not countered broader notions of native savagism. In this drama, Borden and Peterson question that assumption. When Clark first meets Sacagawea, they talk about the mission. As she asks, "You'll see many Peoples? We call ourselves People. You call us Indians" (I-8). Not simply rejecting the Euro-American designation for natives, Sacagawea also points out that aboriginals' conceptions of themselves differ sharply from those submitted from outside. First, she establishes the error of conflation, as conceived and proliferated through frontier myths. As Sacagawea states, natives are "peoples," many groups that embrace different traditions and different customs. She further emphasizes that native people are not less than human.

Borden and Peterson explore the concept of America's peoples and human dignity in another scene as well. While every text embracing the Lewis and Clark Expedition at least mentions York,

Clark's slave, his presence becomes an integral part of *Sakakawea: The Woman with Many Names.* When Sacagawea meets York, she wants to know his relation to Clark, asking if he is a friend or a brother. Clark says he owns York, but she cannot comprehend what that means (I-12). When she persists in her attempt to understand the nature of one human being's ownership of another, York at first proclaims, "Oh, it's an easy life. No responsibilities. I'm happy when I work. I sing, I dance" (I-13). However, the moment Clark moves away, York asserts, "A man takes away your freedom, he takes away your heart. You got to make your own heart, You got to keep it beating, and every beat cries 'Freedom! Freedom! Freedom!' " (I-13). This short scene is a pivotal moment in the play for a variety of reasons.

Sacagawea's inability to comprehend the word or meaning of institutionalized slavery would seem to deny that she was a slave or that she had been treated as a slave. Although Borden accedes to Sacagawea's captivity, he suggests that this tradition must not have implied a captive's total subordination. Secondly, York's changing testimony about slavery, attesting to the joy or pain that accompanies it, certifies the power of socially constructed realities. Because he is a slave and thus totally dependent on the will and whim of his master, York is forced to reiterate culturally accepted meanings of that condition in his master's presence. The irony that the victim must propagate those ideas becomes manifest when York feels safe enough to tell Sacagawea his true feelings. This short exchange about slavery also intersects with commentaries about the purpose of the expedition. By designating what the Euro-American institution of slavery has afforded African peoples, York foreshadows what will happen to native populations that occupy lands in the West.

As the play embraces the cultural debate about America's conquest and Euro-American visions of race, *Sakakawea: The Woman with Many Names* questions the intent of the journey and documents the destruction of native cultures in other scenes as well. A moment after the young Sacagawea pleads with her brother to provide horses for the Corps, the setting switches to the old Sacagawea. As the elderly woman recollects, "They were very strange, and they meant well. But they did not understand the consequence of their journey. None of us understood. We did not know that traders would follow. We did not know that railroads would follow. We did not know that treaties would follow, that reservations would follow, that Wounded Knee, boarding school, BIA would follow" (II-7). Although Sacagawea claims that neither she nor anyone else of the Corps planned or could have foreseen the results of the expedition, she addresses issues that other Sacagawea texts do not raise. Unconcerned with Euro-American settlement or progress accomplished by "civilization," unpersuaded by arguments about the need for native assimilation, her account highlights the effects that the mission has inevitably wrought on America's indigenous peoples. As she lists outcomes suggesting confinement and paternalistic authority, Sacagawea echoes York's declarations about slavery.

Not simply delivering a message about the horrors of conquest, *Sakakawea* also relates a tale of what might have been in the West. If America had been different, for example, Sacagawea's and Clark's love could have flourished. Never accepting the validity of Clark's reasoning, Sacagawea sings, "The way to my heart is straight as an arrow. Why do you walk 'round and 'round as if you're following a river in and out? Can't you walk straight into my heart? I walked straight into yours" (II-15–16). As far as Sacagawea is concerned, Clark's people might be different from hers, but their love is simple and pure. Despite Sacagawea's efforts, Clark is unable to set aside his ambitions. He cannot shed the meanings and proscriptions of his own culture.

Sacagawea's and Clark's love affair is a small, yet vivid example of unnecessary loss. As the play illustrates, there are more significant failures than this doomed love. Also lost are opportunities for various peoples to come together to learn about one another and to understand each other's points of view. Cognizant of the explosive potential of any meeting of "others," Borden and Peterson relate that prospect through dance. Early in the trip, the Corps encounters a group of native men. As the entire troupe dance around the campfire, they are "full of wariness and fear . . . the dance represents not fighting but the fear and ignorance that can lead to battle" (I-20). The dance never develops into violence, but the potential is evident.

In another scene, Borden and Peterson display what might happen when people rid themselves of fear and suspicion. After the Corps' arrival at the Shoshone camp, native men and women perform a dance of welcome. Eventually, all the members of the expedition join the festivity. As Borden writes, "There is a spirit of communality and celebration, a recognition of differences and a transcending of differences, a glimpse of what was, for a brief moment, and what might have been, had history played itself out differently than it did" (II-9). Not simply recreating the liminality that Frank Rivet envisions in Henry's *The Gates of the Mountains* and that Sacagawea feels in Waldo's *Sacajawea,* this production proclaims that communitas can be real. Borden and Peterson also suggest that the ritual might include more participants than other texts consider. This dance does not engage members of the Corps only; it involves all peoples in the wilderness. As the ritual conveys, everyone might exist without barriers that preclude human communion.

Although the communitas of this scene is ephemeral, it occurs in the center of the play. The promise of that experience underscores the poignancy of subsequent loss, an ill-fated love and implications of many lost lives and cultures. As history professor Gordon L. Iseminger writes of the production, "Borden suggests that the differences between Clark and Sakakawea—that differences between the white man and the Indian—could have been bridged had people listened to their hearts. Lamentably they did not" (*Sakakawea* Playnotes 14). Because of the emphasis on a lost love and missed opportunities, *Sakakawea* might seem a gloomy production, but in important ways it is not.

Borden and Peterson write, instead, that the convergence of music, script, actors, and audiences "reflects something essentially American . . . the spirit of exploration and the meeting of diverse cultures that characterized the Lewis and Clark Expedition and, indeed, characterizes America today and gives America—and North Dakota—extraordinary potential" (*Sakakawea* Playnotes 6). The brief experience of communion at the Shoshone camp expires, but the play itself is a ritual, one recreating that liminal moment of America's past. Although Borden and Peterson propose that the repetition of lost communitas results in repeated regret, the ritual itself might serve another purpose. Addressing that possibility, the playwright and composer assert that "perhaps Sakakawea's journey of friendship can guide us unto our future" (*Sakakawea* Playnotes 6). As Borden and Peterson propose, America is constantly changing, perpetually remaking itself. *Sakakawea: The Woman with Many Names* reminds ritual participants—actors, producers, musicians, and audiences—that diversity could have been, and still can be, America's strength. The nation continues to meet "others," because it is made up of different peoples, so America can someday assure that the promise of diversity transcends the evanescence of ritual. Cultural pluralism can become a reality.

Borden and Peterson retell the legend of one of the nation's most celebrated women. Inspired by the story of her heroic actions, as many other Americans have been in the past century, these men nevertheless interrogate common understandings of that historic moment. As they connect their text with America's cultural debate about conquest and race, Borden and Peterson ask questions that most Sacagawea works have not posed. In doing so, they illustrate the ambiguous results of western conquests and racial interactions on the continent. They do not place particular blame for that past, but instead suggest possibilities for America's future.

Encountering contentious national dialogues about manifest destiny and race relations in the last two decades, each Sacagawea text written within the past two decades establishes that this historical native woman has remained an important figure of the American West. As Waldo's *Sacajawea,* The Hamilton Collection plate "Sacajawea," and Borden and Peterson's *Sakakawea: The Woman with Many Names* also illustrate, contemporary writers and artists have adopted her story for disparate purposes. Although historians have debated specific "truths" of her life and actions, most Sacagawea texts created for popular consumption continue to vaunt her as the Indian princess. The collector's plate advertisement certifies that she is the heroic native who helped in the great civilizing project of the nation's untamed wildernesses. The bestselling romance novel *Sacajawea* combines such rhetoric with confirmations of the power and strength of American women. Although many Sacagawea proponents have continued to reiterate rationalized frontier myths in this period, at least one text attempts a different kind of cultural work. In *Sakakawea: The Woman with Many Names,* disparate images and meanings emerge from the story of America's epic journey. Despite narrative variations and diverse purposes, these works testify that Sacagawea remains an inviting subject for American scholars, painters, novelists, and sculptors.

6

THE SACAGAWEA LEGEND
Past Images and Future Prospects

THE JOURNALS OF the Lewis and Clark Expedition originally capture Sacagawea's story, and her legend arises from texts produced during the Progressive Era. Offering variations and elaborations of the tale since that time, many Euro-American works subsequently reproduce the narrative of the heroic Indian princess. As Bernard DeVoto writes in *The Course of Empire,* Sacagawea "has received what in the United States counts as canonization if not deification" (618). Many scholars continue to puzzle over her enduring popularity. But as this study illustrates, Sacagawea's initial renown and legendary importance emerge from the seemingly inextricable link between her story and Euro-American myths.

The Sacagawea narrative, in addition, has proved useful in addressing significant timely concerns on the continent. As an example, many proponents of the legend, especially female writers and speakers, have employed Sacagawea's story to examine women's positions and roles in American society. Some of these same texts and others embracing the narrative have explored concepts of native assimilation and miscegenation. Each Sacagawea work demonstrates that textual production has constituted both timely and timeless responses to and assessments of situations, people, and ideas on the continent. The Sacagawea legend, born of an intersection of the nation's history, ideologies, myths, and individual textual production, provides extensive information about Euro-American culture since the early 1800s.

Guiding the project, as William Doty exhorts in his work *Mythography: The Study of Myths and Rituals,* is the principle that a multilayered, multifunctional approach to interpretation results in far richer knowledge and understanding than any single tool of analysis could ever produce. I have employed three intersecting methodologies to engage and comprehend Sacagawea texts: New Historicism and sociocultural and psychological myth criticisms.

All cultural productions are caught within a context of historical conditions, relationships, and influences. As New Historicists contend, an analysis of such ideological meanings furnishes understandings of the works themselves and knowledge about the cultures from which they have been produced. Individual creators do not simply adopt a coherent body of ideas, beliefs, and attitudes imposed on them by society, writes Catherine Bell. Artists constantly and actively, through struggle, negotiation, qualification, and accommodation, engage in constructing and reconstructing cultural realities. The critic's job is to uncover these influences, to make sociohistorical issues and significances central to the understanding of all texts.

Because of its ideological emphasis and its acknowledgment that popular works aid in discovering cultural meanings, New Historicism has served as one methodological prong in this study. Such ideas are essential in the interpretation of scripts that establish and disseminate the Sacagawea legend. When examined through New Historical questioning, for example, comments like G. S. Snyder's become suspect. Snyder argues that scholars can discover "truths" about the historical Sacagawea by reading original expedition journals. Everything is made clear in these diaries, he claims. By accepting their authorship as nonideological, Snyder depicts Meriwether Lewis and William Clark as disinterested recorders of facts. Purportedly unswayed by personal beliefs or emotion, they supposedly present the entire story without lapses, omissions, or breaks. New Historicism rejects such notions.

If all works are historical artifacts born of an individual's necessary relation to cultural ideologies, then recorders reveal information and ideas they may have never contemplated. The Lewis and Clark Expedition journals, for example, are fruitful sources for the discovery of many meanings. These texts expose comprehensions of the producers and their own cultures more so than intended subjects. Like the expedition scripts, each work that has engaged the Sacagawea story points to significant ideological underpinnings in Euro-American society. Nearly all confirm the ease with which Sacagawea's story has been woven into the nation's orthodox narrative.

Despite insights that New Historicism has offered this project, ideological inquiry does not serve as the sole means of investigating Sacagawea texts. Because her story has been enmeshed in, and intermingled with, one of the most important stories of America's sacred beginnings, I have also employed myth criticisms to interrogate the Sacagawea legend. Myth and ideology are inherently interconnected, according to Peter Berger and Thomas Luckmann's pioneering work *The Social Construction of Reality*. As they argue, everyday knowledge or cultural "realities" are ideological meanings—illustrated, explained, and justified through a variety of social institutions, including myths. The most comprehensive bodies of social tradition, myths integrate meaning and institution into symbolic totality, supplying a cohesive and meaningful world to its citizens.

To produce a more comprehensive study, since the Sacagawea legend has been inextricably tied to mythic meanings, I have examined Sacagawea texts through lenses of psychological and sociofunctional myth criticisms. Focusing on a sanctified story's point of origin as it emanates from individuals who are motivated by various fears, needs, and desires, psychological myth critics trace the outward radiation of a culture's sacred narratives. Such scholars argue that only when a myth has psychological significance for the individual can it develop a shared relevance for a general population. According to critics employing this methodology, myths burgeon as individual experience is codified into meaningful patterns of cultural understanding.

Attending to the collective aspects of sacred narratives, sociofunctional myth critics explore the cultural "work" accomplished by mythic texts. As they contend, traditional narratives serve as "cement" or "charters" to solidify common understandings of particular social "realities." Although incongruities emerge in any cultural system and threaten the "truth" status of constructed knowledge, myths may overcome potential social chaos by explaining away discrepancies and justifying traditional meanings. Because myths function to maintain cultural equilibrium, sociofunctionalists contend that myth studies can reveal significant information about dynamic social systems and changing cultural "realities."

Because of vital interrelationships between myths and ideologies, as seen in sacred narratives of the American frontier, myth criticisms and New Historicism have proved to be particularly worthwhile methodological partners in the analysis of Sacagawea texts. Reverberating profoundly within Euro-American society because of the nature of their formation and function, ideological/mythic works such as Eva Emery Dye's *The Conquest* and Della Gould Emmons's *Sacajawea of the Shoshones* and others have disclosed their convergence with and commentary on frontier traditions. In addition, because they have sustained an examination of the consequences of their production, each text relating the Sacagawea narrative also points to the effects of that immersion and its causes.

Psychological and sociofunctional myth criticisms emphasize meanings associated with sacred narratives. New Historicism focuses on ideological investigation. These methodologies have provided the means to evaluate individual production, to explore personal and cultural factors helping to spawn such responses, and without privileging one area over the other, to negotiate the space between the two. As this study establishes, Sacagawea's story has not functioned to illustrate native peoples' existence on the American continent. Nor has her legend pointed to indigenous interpretations of the mission of manifest destiny. Neither does it impart understandings about the historical woman who accompanied the Corps of Discovery. Sacagawea's persistent animation instead has addressed timely and seemingly timeless needs and aspirations of Euro-American culture, an association that has endured for nearly two hundred years.

After summarizing the history of the Sacagawea narrative in this chapter, I present further evidence that her legend continues to attract creators and audiences. I then examine the ramifications of such narrative endurance and flexibility, especially as it points to the lasting acceptance of frontier traditions. To conclude this study, I begin to explore ways in which America might come to remythologize Western myths and native women.

Just after the turn of the nineteenth century, Lewis and Clark

Expedition diaries and the earliest editorial compilations of those
journals reflect and reinforce implicit frontier traditions. The scripts
substantiate that America was embarking on a sacred mission to civi-
lize the continent. All indigenous peoples, alike in their ignoble savagery, were excluded from that process. In nearly constant contact
with Sacagawea for two years, the diarists of the Corps also confirm
that they generally perceive her to be part of that savagery. She is a
squaw, virtually indistinguishable from innumerable other native
women. Although the expedition narratives particularize Sacagawea's activities to a certain extent, diarists and editors do not
define her as a heroic woman. Nor do they declare her an "American" heroine.

American novelists, researchers, sculptors, and other creators of
the Progressive period transform this woman from a savage squaw
into an Indian princess. They initiate and proliferate the Sacagawea
legend. Many texts combine declarations of Sacagawea's royalty
with evidence of her noble character and heroic actions to document
female power and to justify suffrage for women. Not simply a vehicle
for suffragists, however, Sacagawea also becomes an emblem of
manifest destiny. As Progressive Era texts continue to reflect conceptions evinced in rationalized frontier myths, they proclaim that
Sacagawea was an "American" heroine based on evidence of her cooperation and helpfulness during the wilderness mission. They validate Sacagawea's cultural usefulness to explain and justify sacred
frontier traditions.

Although rationalized frontier myths lost much of their compelling potency by the middle of the twentieth century, many popular
texts, including works reflecting the Sacagawea legend, illustrate
that those traditions continued to inform at least certain populations on the continent. Rehearsing assumptions about civilization's
progress on the continent and indigenous peoples' savagery, proponents of the Sacagawea narrative offer variations and elaborations
of the legend from the 1940s through the 1960s. Most male novelists
depict a Sacagawea significantly different from the heroic woman
that female writers portray. As the narratives exemplify, all concepts
of savagery may not have applied directly to concerns of their own

period, but some ideas associated with native peoples were pertinent to cultural conversations of the times. As they examine ideas of native assimilation and taboos of miscegenation, nearly every script incorporates the plot of a romantic entanglement between Sacagawea and one of the captains. All defend social restrictions against interracial relationships. The Indian princess of the trans-Mississippi West reiterates tenets of frontier myths that relate to this period.

Since 1970, as events on the continent and abroad have encouraged cultural dialogues about the nation's frontier conquests and the "other" cultures and peoples, proponents of the Sacagawea legend advance her narrative for various purposes. One text features Sacagawea as a proto-feminist, a model for the modern, emancipated woman. This work and many others uphold frontier mythic traditions. Another text proves, nonetheless, that Sacagawea's story can be used to question social "truths" that her name and image have previously sustained. Even as the popular legend has encountered narrative dissension in this period, Sacagawea has endured as an important cultural figure in America.

An example of representative works embracing and disseminating the Sacagawea legend, the 1974 "Young People's Special" television production *Sacajawea* testifies to the story's intersection with American frontier myths. Sacagawea was one of America's preeminent heroines, according to the script and photography. Highlighting Sacagawea's devotion to the nation, the production presents the most wonderful moment of the expedition, 4 July 1805. In a break from the arduous trek, all members of the Corps dance and laugh together, celebrating the independence of the United States. Their joy is an expression of "American" communitas.

Conceivably without conscious intent, the "Young People's Special" also points to other "truths" of the legend. This piece hints that the jubilation of Independence Day and other common understandings of Sacagawea's existence are perspectival. As the film begins, snapshots of Sacagawea's intrepid actions flash across the screen. The camera zooms in on a woman dressed in buckskin. She is laboriously paddling a boat, and a woman's voice begins to tell the story in a native language. Her narrative lasts for only a moment, however, as a man's voice-over translates her words into English. In the next instant, the man speaks alone. He recounts the rest of the tale.

Although producers commonly employ this kind of sequence to suggest a continued translation, the scene also signifies the root metaphor of the film and the entire Sacagawea legend. Euro-American culture, the audience long maintaining a fascination with this native woman's story, initially relied upon white, male translations and appraisals of everything surrounding the expedition—the people, the events, and Sacagawea herself. As this text intimates, Sacagawea's legend is, and has been, based upon a proliferation of Euro-American observations and interpretations, fulfilling the needs, dreams, and desires of the dominant culture.

Scholars from several academic disciplines have called for a suspension in America's naive acceptance of such interpretations. Among those advocates, Sharon Murphy asserts: "The story of America's birth and coming to nationhood is laced with accounts of how white men tamed the wild land . . . and gradually assumed benign dictatorship over nomadic people unable to control their own destiny" (43). Robert Berkhofer claims that it should not be surprising that Euro-Americans formed these ideas and images. The remarkable feat is that frontier traditions have been so capable of adapting the idea of "Indian." For more than two centuries, that image has been repeatedly adjusted to fit the nation's political, economic, and social needs and circumstances (31). Commenting on conquest and native savagery, tales of Indian princesses have constituted an important facet of America's sacred narratives. These stories have also contributed to the persistence of frontier traditions.

In "The Pocahontas Perplex: The Image of Indian Women in American Culture," Rayna Green cites the damage that these narratives have wrought upon native peoples. According to Green, stories of princesses not only stereotype native women but also provide people with a warped understanding of native women's compliance, even complicity, with Euro-American agendas on the continent. As Green exhorts, "It is time that the Princess is rescued . . . [from] her obligatory service" to the dominant culture (714). Since so many Americans have embraced the Sacagawea narrative for so long and for so many varied purposes, Green's admonitions might appear to be futile.

Signaling that reality, many people persist in circulating the Sacagawea story. Harry Jackson, a celebrated artist who produces sculptural images of America's western frontier, has successfully marketed works featuring Sacagawea for more than a decade. Commissioned by the Buffalo Bill Historical Center of Cody, Wyoming, Jackson completed *Sacagawea* in 1980. The ten-foot, polychromed bronze monument, donated by Mr. and Mrs. Richard Cashman, stands in the courtyard of the Center.[1] As Donald Goddard asserts, "the monument places Sacagawea firmly at the 'crossroads of the American frontier' " (14).

Reflecting that critical placement, the statue is surrounded by four museums: the Whitney Gallery of Western Art, the Buffalo Bill Museum, the Plains Indian Museum, and the Winchester Arms Museum. Although she does not mention *Sacagawea*, Jane Tompkins reports her reactions to the museums. She acknowledges that, at the entrance to the Center, visitors are told that perceptions of the West are perspectival, that the West has been a mythic place, steeped in and vivified by stereotypes. Despite this acknowledgment of sacred narratives, Tompkins writes: "The Buffalo Bill Historical Center did not repudiate the carnage that had taken place in the nineteenth century. It celebrated it . . . it helped us all reenact the dream of excitement, adventure, and conquest that was what the Wild West meant to most people in this country" (*West* 192). Jackson's *Sacagawea* is integral to that celebration.

Although the statue carries no inscription, *Sacagawea* circulates common understandings of the native woman who guided Lewis and Clark into unknown wildernesses. Not simply identified with the frontier period, the subject of Jackson's work becomes part of that landscape. As Goddard writes, *Sacagawea* was "created by the wind, which sweeps her hair and the enshrouding blanket into diagonal ridges and contours that suggest geological formation. . . . [She is] herself a landscape, a promontory of primordial human consciousness shaped by the elements" (15). Just as many other texts retelling the Sacagawea narrative, Jackson's sculpture depicts a native woman who is connected to the earth. She is essentially an aspect of the frontier. Such portrayals illustrate Annette Kolodny's assertions in *The Lay of the Land*. As Kolodny contends, Euro-American males envisioned the West in terms of female compliance, a feminine territory awaiting and anticipating male exploration. Employing similar terms, Stan Steiner argues that the Euro-American male romance with the land has been a "frontier fantasy." Although Steiner adds that perceptions of a "compliant and passive" earth were inaccurate (205), texts reiterating the idea of the female land and its eager submission to that conquest perpetuate the "fantasy." Jackson's monument relays those very ideas. Sacagawea becomes an emblem of that magnificent volition, not simply her own, but the territory's willingness for conquest.

News articles and other promotional materials about the statue illustrate the same ideas. In *A Monument in Bronze:* Sacagawea *by Harry Jackson,* historian Larry Pointer cites Sacagawea's contributions to the success of the expedition and writes that "Wyoming is justifiably proud of her progressive native Americans and of Sacagawea, the Shoshone woman who typifies the sterling qualities of her people" (original capitalization, 19). Echoing arguments of the Dawes era, Pointer insists that Sacagawea's people were "progressive" because they were friendly with Euro-Americans throughout the frontier period. Not simply "leaders in diplomacy," the Shoshones also displayed great abilities to adapt to "new challenges" on the Wind River Reservation by becoming farmers and "productive" citizens.

In the same bulletin, Marjorie Spitz writes that the monument is dedicated to "a woman of great patience and indomitable spirit. She is the artist's gift to untold future generations" (20). Perhaps not surprisingly, the monument was presented to those future generations on July 4, 1980. As *Sacagawea* was unveiled, no one recorded any dissonance that the statue of a Shoshone woman was dedicated on the anniversary of America's independence. No one noted she was not a citizen of that country; nor did anyone hint that the mission of "discovery" might not have been her own. No one wrote of the irony that Euro-Americans, not natives, crowded the courtyard to see the dedication.

Perhaps unconscious of that incongruity as he writes about the unveiling, Carl Bechtold suggests another motivation for Jackson's desire to embrace Sacagawea, one that other proponents of the legend have shared. Texts conveying images of and information about Sacagawea reap large profits. To be more precise, works that reflect and proliferate *traditional* images of Sacagawea have proved extremely lucrative. As Bechtold reports, Jackson sold twelve bronze castings of the two-foot studio model in less than thirty minutes after the unveiling. Within twenty-four hours, Jackson had taken orders for more than double that number. At $15,000 apiece, this limited-edition work recorded sales of just under $500,000 in less than a day. By early 1993, according to the Harry Jackson Original Sculpture price list, these forty bronze pieces realized an estimated market value of $60,000 each. Twenty other small versions of the monument, painted like the larger work, also sold out rapidly. They are now purportedly worth $55,000 apiece.

Since the unveiling of the original statue, Jackson has produced more than eight hundred limited-edition sculptures depicting images of Sacagawea. Although many of these works are sold-out and are now reportedly worth between $53,000 and $60,000 each, some are still available. The eighteen-inch bronze *Sacagawea II,* pictured in Figure 3, retails at $4,900, the lower price undoubtedly reflecting the fact that Jackson produced 350 castings. Completed in 1992, Jackson's latest Sacagawea work, the twenty-seven-inch polychrome, *Sacagawea with Packhorse,* sells for $25,000.

Because Jackson's limited edition sculptures are costly, his pieces are unquestionably outside the reach of many potential Sacagawea enthusiasts. Several other enterprises have addressed that problem, however. As The Hamilton Collection announces in an advertisement in *Parade* magazine, anyone can own a "meticulously crafted and skillfully hand-painted" sculpture of Sacagawea and her infant son. A three-dimensional interpretation of the David Wright Sacagawea plate, this five-inch work is available for three installments of $18.33, plus handling and shipping. Also targeting audiences of modest means, Books on Tape recently mailed out a brochure of new releases, among them an unabridged "Exclusive!" of Anna Lee Waldo's *Sacajawea.* Offering the exhaustive portrait of the remarkable Indian princess, this tape provides renters fifty-four hours of mythic

Figure 3. *Sacagawea II,* patinaed bronze, by Harry Jackson, 1980
Photo courtesy of Harry Jackson Studios

listening for only $38.00. Whether created by Harry Jackson or marketed by The Hamilton Collection or Books on Tape, these texts testify that American producers and consumers are not ready to give up images and narratives of Sacagawea.

Although the legend is flourishing, common meanings of that story have been subjected to interrogations about conquest and the savagery of native peoples, as *Sakakawea: The Woman with Many Names* exemplifies. In addition, I have witnessed other evidence of this dialectic. In 1989, when I examined a copy of the 1906 *Sakakawea (Bird Woman) Statue Notes* in the North Dakota State Historical Society archives, I discovered that the booklet had been interlined. Someone had crossed out each reference to "squaw" and "papoose" and substituted the words "woman" and "baby." As these changes reveal, images and commentaries that have attested to native peoples' savagery no longer convince everyone on the continent.

The May 1993 edition of *Country Living* offers further evidence that America is continuing its dialogue about native peoples. Two advertisements, ironically placed on facing pages, yield disparate, perhaps mutually exclusive, understandings of tribal women. One advertisement solicits contributions for the American Indian College Fund while the other pitches yet another "Princess of the Plains" limited edition collector's plate. The all-too-familiar plate, offered by The Hamilton Collection, features an exotically beautiful, buxom Indian maiden decked out in buckskin and fringes. As is typical of Indian princesses, "Prairie Flower" is an aspect of nature. Flowing grasses, delicate flowers, and a gentle stream surround her; her horse, also adorned for the princess's upcoming wedding, bows its head in apparent awe of her charm and "regal" bearing.

On the opposite page, the American Indian College Fund presents a photograph and script that conflict with such mythic images. The half-page photograph of Tina Begay, a "Tribal College Student," displays a young woman attired in dark slacks, a plain shirt, and cowboy hat. She seems to be wearing no make-up, and her long, dark hair is braided. Smiling broadly, she leans slightly forward, a posture that deemphasizes her breasts. Although Tina's typical Western clothing does not certify a particular ethnicity, her silver belt and silver and turquoise ring and bracelet hint at her Navajo heritage. The text of the advertisement solidifies that connection, and it also declares the power and authority that Navajo women have held within their own culture. Nothing in the advertisement, neither photograph nor script, harkens back to images or ideas associated with Indian princesses or squaws. Tina Begay is a Navajo, a modern woman who knows and treasures her heritage; she is also a college student. Such identities commingle comfortably and convincingly in this text.

These examples illustrate that the cultural debate about native peoples often provides a conglomeration of disparate concepts. Stereotypical images exist alongside significantly different meanings. Portrayals of opposing "realities" confront each other. Although the College Fund advertisement bears signs of authority and legitimacy, Americans who have been immersed in Indian princess myths still might not reject traditional meanings. As the discussion broadens and intensifies, however, "readers" attending to the discontinuities of those messages might begin to renounce particular "realities" in favor of others that make more sense. If the emotional power of mythic traditions can be countered, the Sacagawea legend and narratives of all Indian princesses might someday be superseded. But, as this study demonstrates and as Bataille and Sands assert, "The old stereotypes still thrive in the American imagination, still do harm to Indian women" (xvi). New understandings have not overtaken sacred narratives of America's frontier conquest.

Emphasizing the potency of narratives that rationalize manifest destiny and the difficulty of superimposing new understandings upon them, many scholars contend that other meanings have only started to gain a voice or an identity within the dominant culture. What then may come of Rayna Green's exhortations to desert Indian princesses? What can be done to ameliorate the reality that few dissenting portrayals of native women have ever been produced because Americans seem unwilling to abandon emotionally satisfying and/or economically rewarding traditions?[2] How can Green's belief that native women deserve better definition come to fruition? Can the nation remythologize not only Sacagawea, but all Indian princesses and indigenous women and men? If so, how can those portrayals and interpretations be legitimated and proliferated? Furnishing definitive answers to such confounding questions may be beyond my, or possibly anyone's, capability. A comprehensive inquiry into these issues is outside the scope of this text. Nevertheless, a study of the Sacagawea legend would be incomplete without considering, even briefly, the potential for, and possible means of achieving, significant cultural change in American understandings of its past and present.

For the transformation to occur, discussions must not center on Sacagawea alone because she is not the only Indian princess. Nor has she been the sole native who has been captured in the web of myths. Different understandings of native women and men will be embraced only as they coincide with new, widespread comprehensions of frontier narratives and the ideologies that have helped to engender them. As cultural historian Michael Kammen writes, Euro-America must somehow come to terms with "the sheer force" of myths relating the colonists' covenant to convert wildernesses into sacred spaces (28). To do so, Americans must stop digesting mythic texts uncritically. According to Robert Scholes, people can learn that interpretative meanings are codes. Readers can defend themselves "against the manipulative exploitation of received opinion" (*Semiotics* 14). He also insists that cultural interpreters must relinquish the pleasures of absorption in and by mythic texts. They must situate themselves outside those traditions to perceive alternate meanings (*Protocols* 131).

One possible means of realizing critical detachment is through exposure to works that question traditional assumptions and recast accepted ideas. While folklorists and myth specialists have long written about the importance and power of American sacred traditions, only recently have literary and historical researchers pursued this kind of ideological inquiry. Arnold Krupat writes in the foreword to the latest reissue of Roy Harvey Pearce's *Savagism and Civilization* that this extraordinary text was not afforded the attention it deserved when it was first published in the 1950s. As he asserts, the critical community of that era was not particularly interested in ideological analysis. Within the last two decades, a number of historical and literary scholars have indeed entered that conversation. They have begun questioning the "received" meanings of the nation's westward movement, the tradition that Friedman terms "the most potent, pervasive, and ramified American myth—*the* American myth" (original emphasis, 41). These studies have highlighted the constructed nature of frontier myths and their connections to cultural production.

Annette Kolodny's *The Land Before Her*, for example, explains that culturally condoned images of violent penetration and conquest have never been the sole Euro-American response to the continent. If the nation can accept the fact that pioneer women envisioned different ideas of the frontier, that they interpreted their actions through metaphors of community and home, Kolodny argues that America may someday remythologize the West and rethink the nation's relation to the land. Also focused on female experience, Susan Armitage and Elizabeth Jameson present *The Women's West*, an anthology of essays that scrutinize stereotypes of Western women. These works aim to identify and correct omissions in historical understanding of female roles in the American frontier experience.

Presenting another critical analysis of frontier myths, Jane Tompkins deconstructs the Western. She contends that popular films and novels of the American West have articulated questionable values as they have condoned violence and conquest. Westerns have advanced an obsession with pain, a celebration of the suppression of feeling, and a need to dominate the land. Culturally pervasive and overpowering, Westerns are "compacted worlds of meaning and value," transmitting "codes of conduct, standards of judgment, and habits of perception that shape our sense of the world and govern our behavior without our having the slightest awareness of it" (*West of Everything* 6).

These critical works and others examine the existence and consequences of frontier myths, very often in conjunction with inspections of images imposed on the native "other." As they shed light on the power of America's sacred narratives, they have also encouraged a reexamination and rethinking of mythic realities. In spite of a marked increase in these investigations, their power to achieve widespread revisioning of conquest "realities" would appear to be limited.

The insufficiency of scholarly texts to recast frontier myths occurs, at least in part, because these works reach limited audiences. Testifying to his ignorance of cogent reexaminations of traditional frontier messages, *Voice Literary Supplement* reviewer Stuart Klawans admits that his connection with, and knowledge of, native cultures had been limited to novels by James Fenimore Cooper and films produced by John Ford, with small modifications after seeing such popular productions as *Little Big Man.* He became aware of his limited and mostly erroneous understandings only after reading Jack Weatherford's *Native Roots: How the Indians Enriched America.* As Klawans writes, his previous "crudities" were possible only because of the power of American frontier traditions (11). Despite his confirmation of the potency of myths, Klawans's experience might imply that if the word were spread far enough, if messages were repeated often enough and with sufficient authority, alternate realities might someday preempt sacred narratives.

History professor Nancy Shoemaker argues that superimposing new understandings cannot be accomplished without great difficulty. When she offered university students an opportunity to reexamine and rethink traditional meanings in a course entitled "The American West: Myth vs. Reality," Shoemaker discovered the "mythological baggage" that her students carried to class. Although they read historical and literary works that tendered irreconcilable evidence and disparate viewpoints about Euro-American conquest of the wilderness, her students remained devoted to myths of the West. As Shoemaker advances, "My students *knew* the frontier was a place of raw opportunity, where individuals flourished and men could prove they were men" (original emphasis). Convinced of the essential masculinity of the Euro-American wilderness experience, Shoemaker's students additionally confirmed their attachment to culturally condoned images of native peoples, notions that have invariably accompanied the Western narrative tradition. "They take the course because they want their stereotypes about Indians confirmed, not torn away," she writes.

As Shoemaker's experience implies, offering contradictory inter-pretations of people, actions, and ideas about America's frontier ex-perience does not necessarily block the absorption of and devotion to sacred stories. Because these narratives continue to captivate cer-tain segments of the American population, alternate viewpoints might never effect significant enough cultural change to override mythic power. Michael Kammen points to one reason for this power in "The Problem of American Exceptionalism: A Reconsideration." As he contends, the idea of America's sacred mission into the wil-derness has been one of the most important ways of proving the nation's exceptionalism. Anyone who grapples with meanings and realities of frontier traditions also engages in a wider struggle. Per-haps Shoemaker's students and many others have been unable to adjust their understandings of Euro-American western experiences and their conceptions of Indian savagery because they cannot ac-knowledge the possibility that American superiority has also been socially constructed.

If frontier myths are inextricably linked to "realities" of national preeminence, can America ever reenvision the mission on the con-tinent and reassess native peoples? If the psychological force of tra-ditional stories is so significant, can America ever countenance al-ternate viewpoints of the conquest of the West? Are there other useful avenues to increase awareness of, and critical thinking about, mythic traditions?

Devoted to rereading texts and their underlying assumptions, Jane Tompkins affirms the difficulty of achieving epistemological certainty. After encountering widely differing historical accounts of native and Euro-American interactions, Tompkins writes of her di-lemma in " 'Indians': Textuality, Morality, and the Problem of His-tory." As she asks, if all renderings emerge from a particular per-spective, conferring different accounts of human motivations, actions, and responses, how is the reader to know which version(s) to believe? Tompkins argues that readers can "know" only that which can be pieced together "according to what seems reasonable and plausible," based on evidence available (118).

While Tompkins does not propose a practical method for arriving at what seems "plausible" and "reasonable," various researchers argue that multicultural education can help Americans to avoid emotional allures of mythic meanings.[3] As James Banks insists, American schools have functioned to force acculturation to and acceptance of a supposedly monocultural nation. A school board in Florida recently proved that such an orthodoxy thrives in at least some pockets on the continent. In May 1994, school board members proclaimed their distaste for multiculturalism and passed a decree that teachers must instruct their students that *the* American way is superior to all others.

Gerald Pine and Asa Hilliard claim that most educational institutions have never acknowledged the multicultural realities of American society. They further assert that schools have instead served as "sites for producing and making acceptable myths and ideologies that systematically disorganize and neutralize the cultural identities of minorities" (197). Because schools have played such an important role in proliferating and reinforcing traditional narratives, institutional acknowledgment of alternate meanings could facilitate their acceptance and dissemination through America.

Such arguments, and hopes, are not new. Scholars interested in native cultures have long advocated the introduction of native cultures into school curricula.[4] Anna Lee Stensland, for example, asserts that materials by and about native peoples deserve a place in all American classrooms, as they are essential to understanding the history and heritage of the continent (8). Shoemaker adds that the best means that educators have of demythologizing native peoples is to "insure an Indian presence in the classroom, as teachers, students, and guest speakers." Although some schools have instituted innovative multicultural programs, more have not. Illustrating the effects of such deficiencies, several Chippewa teenagers describe their marginalization and their frustrations with prejudices that arise from ignorance. As Angela Charwood comments, "It's like American history is only about white people, like we weren't even there, you know?" Elizabeth Day relates that she has never felt that she has been part of America, and Brenda Lang adds that all Americans should "try to appreciate the people we honor and respect, to appreciate us" (Minton).

If school programs and curricula were to present indigenous peoples' past and present literatures, histories, geographies, languages, and rituals, Americans of all ages might begin to appreciate the tribal "other." They might see through "received" meanings of manifest destiny. If students were to discover the diversity of native cultures, they might no longer accept concepts of undifferentiated savagery. If children and adults were to realize that frontier "realities" are perspectival, they could begin to reject culturally mandated visions that people were and are good only if they or their ancestors aided the national mission into the wilderness.

Although I do not outline a comprehensive plan for the integration of native materials into school curricula, I highlight one important means of achieving that difficult goal. Students of all ages, races, and ethnicities must be encouraged to interpret diverse, multicultural American texts, to ask difficult questions, to ponder cultural assumptions. All populations on the continent would benefit from this kind of learning and thinking. Not only would children and adolescents of every race and ethnicity discover the existence of "others," but they would be more likely to continue critical explorations long after their formal education ends.

Like Tompkins, interpreters will encounter different versions of American reality as they engross themselves in paintings, sculptures, ethnologies, histories, and literary texts depicting native life and Euro-American and indigenous interactions. The exploration will produce confusion as neophyte "decoders" discover the lack of simple, straightforward information. But the process of discovery can be worthwhile. Ambiguity and uncertainty can help to prove that relentlessly consistent traditional meanings of manifest destiny—understandings that Euro-American culture has attempted to make obvious and irrefutable—have encouraged reductive thinking. Cultural interpreters can also realize that frontier myths have distorted and misrepresented the "other" on the continent.

As part of this process, students must encounter portrayals that contest traditional understandings of tribal cultures and the frontier "conquest." Ethnographies and ethnohistories are one source for this kind of revisitation. Although many anthropological studies conducted by non-natives are grounded in Euro-American cultural assumptions, the best ethnographies and ethnohistories seek meanings that are significant to the cultures being observed. Some excellent works have focused on native women. Jane Kelley's *Yaqui Women: Contemporary Life Histories,* for instance, is framed around questions of her female informants' roles and statuses within contemporary Yaqui society.[5]

In addition to anthropological texts, various novels based on solid ethnographic research have provided integrated portraits of complex, indigenous cultures and have described native peoples as individuals. According to Leo Olivia, such portrayals have been offered in Adolf Bandelier's *Delight Makers,* a story of Pueblo life; Elliott Arnold's *Blood Brother,* a novel describing Apache culture; Hal Borland's *When the Legends Die,* a narrative depicting Ute social customs (98–106).

Some artists have produced sensitive portrayals of native life although they have not shared the same ethnicity or race as their subjects. Philip Butcher nonetheless argues that "for the fullest expression of the minority presence in America" there must be texts produced by peoples "who are part of the culture they depict and products of the tradition they describe" (23). As Mary Dearborn asserts in *Pocahontas's Daughters: Race and Ethnicity in American Culture,* literature by people who are "on the edges of American culture can perhaps best represent what happens within that culture" (4).

Within the last two decades, ethnographic and ethnohistoric studies conducted by native men and women have added significantly to understanding tribal life. Escaping the potentially distorting double bias of Euro-American male observers whose investigations cross barriers of race and gender, female anthropologists and ethnohistorians of various native heritages offer studies focusing on indigenous women. Lakota scholar Beatrice Medicine, for instance, probes neglected subjects in "Indian Women and the Renaissance of Traditional Religion" and "Indian Women: Tribal Identity as Status Quo." Attempting to amend cultural distortions, Priscilla Buffalohead claims that females were prominent in traditional Ojibway political, economic, and social life. Buffalohead describes Ojibway women's labor, their property, and their social rights and obligations. As she asserts, this egalitarian society was based on sexual complementarity and mutual respect between men and women.

Like anthropological texts produced by non-natives, many ethnographies and ethnohistories by native men and women reach select audiences. Rayna Green's *Women in American Indian Society,* however, targets general populations. Written in nonspecialized vocabulary and displaying an array of photographs, this text orients readers to essential issues that have surrounded native women. In an early chapter, Green highlights mythic images that have traditionally defined native women. She also recontextualizes the legend of Pocahontas. As Green declares, the Euro-American story of the first Indian princess is "far from the truth." Native accounts assert that John Smith was "chosen by Powhatan to be adopted into the chief's family. As the daughter of the tribe's leader and a woman of considerable status, Pocahontas served as Smith's 'mother,' for he had to be reborn, after a symbolic death, as one of the tribe. Thus, Pocahontas was not delaying Smith's execution and thwarting her own people when she threw her body over his. She was in fact acting on behalf of her people" (35). By reframing the familiar story in terms of Pocahontas's own culture, Green shows that other interpretations are possible. Different meanings do exist. As native perspective purports, Pocahontas did not concede Euro-American superiority nor colonists' rights to the land. She instead acted from tribal world views and value systems. Not simply denying its usefulness as an adjunct to frontier mythologies, this version of the Pocahontas narrative also provides a glimpse of a traditional native culture.

Green repudiates the conflation of tribal cultures throughout *Women in American Indian Society.* As she submits, women held diverse statuses and possessed different kinds of power and authority within precontact native societies. In another chapter, Green features histories of several native women who resisted national policies during the late nineteenth century. They included Sarah Winnemucca, a Paiute who donned a fanciful "princess" outfit during her lectures to Euro-American populations; Susan LaFlesche, the first female physician of native heritage; and Susan's sister Suzette, who dressed in Omaha ceremonial clothing as she lectured in America and Europe.

Green also presents information about contemporary native women and their cultures, extending specific commentary about such tribal leaders as Wilma Mankiller. As she insists, "Indian women have in large part been responsible for their people having something to celebrate in the modern era. They have taken on the work of reviving traditional languages and ceremonies, hoping to preserve and distinguish their heritage. They have fought for their people's rights in and out of court. They have returned to their traditional native environments to lead their people through renewal" (99). By stressing twentieth-century tribal life, Green avoids the implication that native peoples only existed in the past. She additionally underscores crucial roles that tribal women have played in the recent history of indigenous cultures and of America. Clearly expressing her belief that the continent must embrace new understandings, Green writes that non-native peoples can "recognize that the vision and strength of Indian women [are] essential to the American identity" (101). Green's ethnohistory and other anthropological studies by native authors can facilitate that discovery.

Suggesting another avenue for investigating tribal cultures, Robert Scholes insists that the best opportunity to learn about any society is through examining its literary works. As he claims, important cultural knowledge emanates from its grammatical, semantic, and syntactic codes (*Semiotics*). Gerald Haslam adds that literature is "an integral part of all human cultures, reflecting through the special use of language subtle values unique to each. In many ways literature offers the sharpest available view of a given culture's soul" (1). A. LaVonne Ruoff, a critic who has published numerous articles and two book-length analyses of native literatures, argues that indigenous rituals and songs, oratory and autobiography, poetry and fiction convey meanings that other genres cannot replicate.

Within the past few decades, creative works produced by native artists have begun to receive critical attention in America and around the world. A few of these texts directly oppose traditional understandings associated with Pocahontas and Sacagawea.

Paula Gunn Allen, a poet, novelist, and scholar of Laguna/Lakota heritage, rethinks one of the nation's most significant legends in "Pocahontas To Her English Husband, John Rolfe." Unlike Green's ethnohistory, Allen's poem does not assume a scholarly tone, nor does it maintain academic distance. The work instead offers a first-person account of Pocahontas's own story. Only after death is she allowed to speak for herself, to verbalize her experiences in her own way. When she states, "I spoke little," but "you listened less" (31–32), Pocahontas addresses her husband and all America. Others, primarily white males, have spoken for her and translated her actions to each other. Now she can finally reveal herself.

Pocahontas's long-delayed account denies mythic interpretations that have accompanied her name. Not the noble princess of Euro-American mythology, not the genteel woman who supposedly captured the hearts of British royalty, this narrator is filled with accusation, brimming with vituperation. She enumerates the times she saved her husband from "certain death" (5) and elaborates on the wrongs that he reaped upon her. Relishing a splendid revenge, Pocahontas reports that Rolfe's "descendants" (18) are dying as they indulge in tobacco, the "golden" crop that natives taught them to harvest.

Allen attempts several purposes in this work. She redefines a famous native woman's life. In addition, because Pocahontas's narrative has never really been about familial transgressions or local concerns and because her story has instead constituted an allegory of native and colonial interactions on the continent, Allen also reassesses that allegory. She displays the inadequacies and inaccuracies of the Pocahontas legend. As this poem declares, generosity was repaid with treachery, and trust was answered by betrayal. Allen submits that Pocahontas's story can be useful to invalidate American claims of the glorious frontier "conquest."

Pocahontas is not the only Indian princess to receive attention from Paula Gunn Allen. In the lengthy poem "The One Who Skins Cats," Allen employs Shoshone oral tradition, the Lewis and Clark Expedition journals, and other historical and literary sources to interrogate meanings associated with the Sacagawea legend. Again adopting the first-person point of view, Allen allows the native woman to tell about her many names and the many things she did in her lifetime. She participated in the Lewis and Clark Expedition, saw a whale, left her treacherous husband, found another among the Comanches, eventually returned to the Shoshones, and became Porivo, Chief Woman.

Although these incidents are presented in any number of Sacagawea texts, Allen's poem does more than reiterate the story. She introduces a woman who openly acknowledges the import of the legend that arose after her death. This narrator, with frank nonchalance, recounts her life, recites the history of the legend, and reflects on meanings of that narrative tradition. Without projecting any sense of pride, Sacagawea describes how and why suffragists embraced her as their heroine, how "white women" first claimed that she led the expedition. She also reports dispassionately that she has subsequently become a "mountain pass" and a "river woman" (37–38), results of the spread of that story.

Although Sacagawea intermingles the tellings of her life and legend, she never allows reality and invention to blur. In the first stanza, Sacagawea clearly states that "they" call her Bird Woman, a seeming deference to external definition. But then she repeats the phrases "I am" and "I am the one who" throughout the stanza. These mantra-like utterances serve as declarations of identity. She is a wanderer, a speaker, a watcher, a teacher, a mother, a wife, a slave; one who weeps, and meets, and runs away. Because she completes these phrases in so many ways, Sacagawea explores the multiple facets of her life. She expresses the complexity of self-definition. But never does she obscure the difference between ascribed meanings and her own.

As she does in "Pocahontas To Her English Husband, John Rolfe," Allen undertakes cultural reclamation in "The One Who Skins Cats." She empowers Sacagawea to reveal truths about herself, a right that has often been denied native women. Allen also privileges native testimony. Like Hebard, Waldo, Borden, and others, the poet presents a woman who lived to be nearly one hundred years old. Unlike most works embracing that account, Allen's poem is a conversation about competing meanings. Echoing the title of the poem, Sacagawea points out that there are many ways to "skin a cat." Her story can be told in many different ways (168); she can be seen as the guide, a patriot, a chief, a traitor.

Despite the narrator's apparent detachment in enumerating these identities, Allen denies that all characterizations of Sacagawea are equally true. She instead draws attention to the clash of disparate meanings and interpretations. Because Allen labels specific elements of the story as legend, clearly differentiating fact and purposeful fabrication, she questions why Euro-American culture has had such difficulty separating the two. She underscores the perversity of the narrative tradition that has defined Sacagawea and interrogates ideological assumptions that have inspired that legend.

"The One Who Skins Cats" obviously comments on issues examined in this study, and the poem certainly contributes to the reconsideration of the Sacagawea legend. Allen verifies that the narrative tradition has a history. The legend has had a life of its own. As she insists, that existence must not be confused with the life of the native woman who resided for a time among the Mandans and accompanied Lewis and Clark to the Pacific Ocean. Despite such worthwhile commentaries, other questions radiate from Allen's poems. Do "The One Who Skins Cats" and "Pocahontas To Her English Husband, John Rolfe" serve to remythologize native women? Because these works aim to recast the stories of America's most important Indian princesses, are they not trapped by that objective? Essentially reactive, the poems still converse about the two women who have captivated Euro-American audiences for centuries. The works become entangled in a dialogue driven by interests and desires that are far removed from most native concerns. Although redressing specific distortions about these women is no doubt cathartic and probably beneficial to some extent, such efforts, by themselves, cannot achieve widespread reassessments of tribal women.

A number of native artists help to achieve that objective as they present texts arising from their own cultural dialogues. These works ask questions and advance meanings garnered from native contexts. Produced within the last three decades, several novels written by tribal people have won a variety of national awards, among them N. Scott Momaday's *House Made of Dawn*, Leslie Silko's *Ceremony*, and Louise Erdrich's *Love Medicine*. Although the protagonists in

House Made of Dawn and *Ceremony* are males, these and other texts written by native peoples have featured tribal women's lives.

Acclaimed writer James Welch describes eighteenth-century Blackfeet existence in *Fools Crow*. He focuses on the Lone Eaters, a subgroup of the larger nation, at a time when greater numbers of Euro-Americans begin to arrive on the high plains. While Welch's novel features a heroic male, the story also highlights the lives of Blackfeet females: his birth mother and his father's two younger wives, his own spouse, and other women of his camp. Offering a contextual presentation of the Lone Eaters' existence, Welch describes the importance of female chastity and virtue. He also relates images of polygamy and sexual complementarity and how those practices correlated with traditional native society.

Other works written by natives have addressed indigenous women's existences also. Ruoff, for instance, cites Ella Deloria's *Waterlily* as an "invaluable portrayal of nineteenth-century Sioux life—told from a woman's perspective" (71). Raised as a traditional Dakota, Deloria eventually worked with Franz Boas in conducting ethnographic studies of native cultures. She penned *Waterlily* in the 1940s. Although the script received positive reviews at that time, publishers declined to print the novel because they felt that it could not attract significant readership. Finally published in 1988, *Waterlily* relates a tale of three native women: Blue Bird, her mother, and her daughter Waterlily. Men enter into the narrative, but the text features the separateness of male and female spheres, emphasizing the complementarity of gender relations within traditional Dakota culture. More significantly, Deloria highlights women's rituals, such as the hunka and buffalo ceremonies, female kinship obligations, and other realities of plains existence before the arrival of Euro-Americans. Expressing admiration for the novel in his introduction to the work, Raymond DeMallie insists that *Waterlily* contributes greatly to comprehensions of Dakota women's traditional lives.

While portrayals like *Fools Crow*, *Waterlily*, and others undoubtedly contribute to reforming Euro-American conceptions of native peoples, especially those of tribal women, exclusive reliance upon historical revisioning could perpetuate another element of frontier traditions, the notion that indigenous peoples and their societies existed only in the past. Concerned with that possibility, Rayna Green writes that Euro-Americans need to learn about contemporary native women, such as the "tribal chairwoman in blue jeans" ("Review Essay" 265).

Writers of native heritage have produced accessible texts characterizing contemporary tribal cultures. Providing American populations with opportunities to consider current native realities, these works testify that America's indigenous peoples have not vanished, even if the dominant culture would seem to verify that notion. Several recently published anthologies confirm native existence. They include Paula Gunn Allen's *Spider Woman's Granddaughters: Traditional Tales and Contemporary Writing by Native American Women*, Geary Hobson's *The Remembered Earth: An Anthology of Contemporary Native American Literature*, and Rayna Green's *That's What She Said: Contemporary Poetry and Fiction by Native American Women*.[6] Some texts within these collections present accounts of indigenous existence prior to the arrival of colonists or depictions of early interactions between natives and Euro-Americans. Many characterize twentieth-century native life.

One successful anthology, *A Gathering of Spirit: Writing and Art by North American Indian Women*, presents poetry, songs, drawings, photographs, short stories, essays, and other works produced by native women. Beth Brant declares in the introduction that she was at first reluctant to edit the collection. Despite that initial uncertainty, which arose from her belief that she lacked enough formal education and practical experience to edit other writers' work, Brant assumed the task. As she asserts, "I wanted to hear from the women yet unheard. I wanted the voices traditionally silenced to be a part of this collection" (10). She wanted native women's stories from reservations, from rural areas, from cities, and from prison to be told and heard.

Brant sought and received contributions from such well-known writers as Paula Gunn Allen, Beatrice Medicine, and Wendy Rose, and from lesser-known creators as well. All relate vivid portrayals of tribal women's lives. One text depicts a mother's internal struggles with her daughter's desire to fit into Euro-American culture, to conform to that society's idea of beauty. Also detailing the unique challenges of being a native woman, a short story relates a family's removal from their home and land as the U.S. government prepares to test nuclear bombs in the area. Another work describes a little boy's pain at being labelled a half-breed. His anguish brings back his mother's memories of taunts she received when she was a child. One of the most powerful texts in the collection is a series of letters between Brant and Raven. An inmate on death row in Maryland, Raven has been convicted of a murder that she claims she did not commit.

Contributors to this anthology are individuals with unique experiences, but Brant asserts that they also share a "continuity of spirit" and a belief in community (12). As Brant writes in the introduction to the text, "We are not 'stoic' and 'noble,' we are strong-willed and resisting. . . . **We are not victims.** We are organizers, we are freedom fighters, we are feminists, we are healers. . . . For centuries it has been so" (original emphasis, 12). Although such realities are not new, the collection documents a recent change. Brant proclaims that we "are the ones who do not allow anyone to speak for us **but us**," using "our pens, our paints, our cameras" to keep "**us** a culture" (original emphasis, 13–14). Through their creative efforts, these native women reveal themselves to each other. They simultaneously disclose their fears, dreams, frustrations, and successes—their lives and meanings—to others.

Evidence suggests that many people have welcomed their messages. Adopted as a required text in native studies and women's studies programs on the continent, the anthology has also been translated into several languages other than English and is available in braille and on tape. The first edition sold more than 5,000 copies in less than a year. As Brant's collection verifies, native women's "testament is out there now, part of the wind, part of people's minds and hearts" (15).

Tribal writers also reach substantial audiences as they compose novels of contemporary native existence. Many of these works highlight female characters and their lives. Michael Dorris's *A Yellow Raft in Blue Water*, for instance, introduces three related women, each narrating truths about contemporary tribal life on and off a Montana reservation. An adolescent of African American and native heritage, Rayona Taylor must come to terms with her mother's life and identity. She and her mother must additionally discover their connection to Rayona's great-aunt.

Also concerned with contemporary reservation life, James Welch relates a tale of a young Blackfeet man's separation from traditional tribal meanings in *Winter in the Blood*. As Ruoff writes in "Alienation and the Female Principle in *Winter in the Blood*," the work hinges on the man's relationships with native women, especially his grandmother. Weaving into the account of the protagonist's life the story of the devastating 1862 Blackfeet migration, Welch indicates that the man's alienation may be healed only as he acknowledges his grandmother's past.

Winner of the National Book Critics Circle Award for Fiction, Louise Erdrich's *Love Medicine* relates the complexity of modern tribal life. The best-selling novel features two Chippewa clans of the Turtle Mountain Reservation in North Dakota. The opening episodes of a native woman's unsuccessful return to the reservation serves as a unifying concern in *Love Medicine*. According to Robert Silberman, June Kashpaw's death affords other characters important opportunities to explore the meanings of her life and their own. June's previous lover, her unacknowledged son, her adoptive father and mother, her sisters, her niece, her former neighbors—these are some of the tribal people inhabiting the novel.

Although a few reviewers have criticized the novel for its multiple narrators, who relate seemingly isolated vignettes spanning three generations, others have applauded that variety of articulations. Karl Kroeber writes that *Love Medicine* extends "the speech-systems of different age groups, genders, occupations, modes of acculturation, political attitudes, religious commitments colliding, overlapping, intersecting, contradicting, fusing" (2). Polyphony is achieved as characters engage in community gossip. According to Kathleen M. Sands, this kind of storytelling identifies group membership, differentiates appropriate and inappropriate behaviors, and reinforces cultural values (14). As Sands argues, gossip is "the very method of the novel, individuals telling individual stories" (19).

Although Erdrich presents many interesting characters in *Love Medicine*, the women are particularly intriguing. Marie Kashpaw and Aurilia are among the tribal women who live and flourish on the Turtle Mountain Reservation. One of Erdrich's most compelling and vivid characters, Lulu Lamartine is a mother, a lover, a rival, and a friend. She projects none of the "savage" qualities long associated with "squaws." Lulu is not a drudge; nor is she vicious. She is certainly not an Indian princess. Emanating a sense of wildness, Lulu has intense appetites and experiences. She is a vibrant, life-affirming woman. Through Lulu and other characters, Erdrich's *Love Medicine* documents and celebrates the survival of native peoples and their cultures.

Biographies and autobiographies are also exceptionally useful in disseminating meanings about indigenous cultures and tribal people. Many eighteenth- and nineteenth-century native "autobiographies" are as-told-to narratives, and too often, Euro-Americans who wrote and edited the scripts filtered textual meanings through external value systems and assumptions. Some native men and women nonetheless composed stories of their own lives. At the turn of the twentieth century, for example, Zitkala-Sa wrote a series of articles for the *Atlantic Monthly.* Within the last three decades, a considerable number of tribal women have published autobiographies, communicating their lives to each other and to the world. As Green writes, they "tell their stories as they wish, drawing upon the multiple perspectives—both traditional and non-Indian—that have shaped their life" (*Women* 29).

Two autobiographies by contemporary native women relate twentieth-century tribal experiences. Although Mary Crow Dog and Wilma Mankiller present very different histories and employ distinct narrative styles, these works also share some remarkable similarities. Both women have lived as the "other" in America, and they have survived personal crises that have arisen, at least in part, from the intersection of race and gender. Both women have witnessed, and at times participated in, local and national politics that have concerned native peoples. These tribal women tell about their public and private selves.

Mankiller: A Chief and Her People is an autobiography and an ethnohistory written by Wilma Mankiller and collaborator Michael Wallis. Juxtaposing public and private contexts, this work recounts significant portions of Cherokee history as it intersects with Mankiller's family and personal narratives. Mankiller, the principal chief of the Cherokee nation, details major U.S. "Indian" policies from the 1840s to the present, including the Indian Removals, the Dawes Act, Indian Reorganization, and Termination and Relocation. Unlike many other works that characterize the nexus of Cherokee and American histories, this text illustrates how national policies have affected particular tribal families and individuals.

Mankiller describes her early life in the 1940s on an Oklahoma allotment that her family obtained during the Dawes Era. As the chief writes, she and her eleven brothers and sisters attended school dressed in clothing made of flour sacks. Mankiller claims that she did not realize the poverty that marked her childhood. As she asserts, her youth was filled with the richness and wonder of ceremonial dances and secret Cherokee rites and rituals. That connection was disrupted, however, when Mankiller's family moved to California in the 1950s.

Their relocation experience, she asserts, was not significantly different from the difficulties that her forebears endured during the Trail of Tears. Besides suffering from culture shock, she and other family members immediately encountered ethnic intolerance. Mankiller hated the area and ran away to her grandmother's home repeatedly. Despite the many problems associated with urban life, she also notes that the Indian Center ameliorated the alienation that many natives felt during relocation. Mankiller nonetheless insists that relocation was a disaster for most tribal peoples because the program robbed them of cultural cohesiveness and their sense of place (112).

Because of her interest in politics, particularly in native empowerment, Mankiller inevitably returned to Oklahoma. Her family's allotment provided that sense of place and served as a base for her involvement in community activities. In 1981, for example, Mankiller supported and directed a program to rebuild homes, lay pipelines, and conduct renovations. Writing of the Bell Community Revitalization Project, the chief asserts that this venture and others illustrate tribal peoples' desire for, and movement toward, self-sufficiency. Since her return to Oklahoma, Mankiller has suffered personal setbacks, but she has also realized significant victories, including election and reelection as the principal chief of the Cherokees.

As it documents the endurance and florescence of an individual and the continuity of the Cherokee nation, *Mankiller* also focuses on native women. Wallis writes that Mankiller "proudly describes herself as a feminist, a leader who is concerned with women's issues worldwide" (xxiv). She displays that concern in her autobiography. Like Rayna Green, Paula Gunn Allen, and others, Mankiller refutes squaw/drudge and Indian princess imagery. She describes traditional tribal women's powers and discusses the importance of women's councils. As Mankiller argues, Cherokee women have always maintained prominent positions within the nation. The chief also discusses the many challenges facing contemporary native women. She writes:

> Each day, they face daunting problems as they struggle just to survive. They are mothers not only of their own children but of the entire community. Poverty is not just a word to describe a social condition, it is the hard reality of everyday life. It takes a certain tenacity, a toughness, to continue on when there is an ever-present worry about whether the old car will work, and if it is does, whether there will be gas money; digging through piles of old clothes at St. Vincent de Paul's to find clothing for the children to wear to school without being ridiculed; wondering if there will be enough to eat. But always, there is hope that the children will receive a good education and have a better life. (110)

If, as Mankiller asserts, native women are especially strong, then she is an exemplar of that strength.

In many ways strikingly different from *Mankiller, Lakota Woman,* written by Mary Crow Dog and Richard Erdoes, is an explicit and oftentimes disturbing narrative of contemporary native existence. Although the text does not always maintain a straightforward chronology, major experiences of Crow Dog's life emerge sharply. She describes a childhood marked by family disruptions, poverty, and long periods spent with her grandmother. As was typical of many native adolescents of that period, Crow Dog attended a Roman

Catholic boarding school. Providing vivid details of mental and physical cruelty, she reports the sisters' renunciation of everything "Indian" and the physical punishments meted out for such sins as holding a boy's hand. Because she was unwilling to capitulate to external expectations, Crow Dog eventually dropped out.[7] Astonishingly frank about her experiences with alcohol and drugs after she quit school, she also reports that she shoplifted and spent some time in jail. Crow Dog insists that her attitudes and problems emanated from the cultural impoverishment of her life. That deficiency, she claims, resulted from her status as "other" and her alienation from traditional Lakota values.

Crow Dog's outlook and life changed when she became part of the American Indian Movement in the 1960s. Telling the rest of her history through the context of significant national events, she asserts that AIM leaders, Dennis Banks and Russell Means, and her future husband, Lakota holy man Leonard Crow Dog, helped her to forge a connection with tribal meanings and hopes. She participated in the march on Washington and the takeover of the Bureau of Indian Affairs building. She gave birth to her first child during the occupation of Wounded Knee and later fought for her husband's release from jail. *Lakota Woman* intertwines reports about such highly publicized episodes with narratives of more personal occurrences. These revelations, of horrific episodes of prejudice and racial confrontation, express the power of the narrative. Hatred revealing itself in raw language and accusation, Crow Dog's story seethes with anger. She tells about an armed stand off at a South Dakota motel, and she exposes proprietors who refuse service to natives.

At several points in *Lakota Woman*, Crow Dog describes her friend Anna Mae Aquash with great warmth. Fury and anguish always accompany her reflections as she divulges the details of Aquash's death. Rejecting the official report that her friend died of exposure, Crow Dog writes that Aquash was raped and murdered after the occupation of Wounded Knee. Her murderer(s) left her body on the South Dakota plains.[8] The pain that Crow Dog and Aquash's family felt at her death was compounded by the irreverent treatment her body received from government officials. They cut off her hands and sent them to Washington, purportedly for purposes of identification. These are the kinds of actions that have evoked Crow Dog's searing hatred.

Although much of her narrative concentrates almost exclusively on racial concerns, Crow Dog's comments about Anna Mae Aquash and others establish the convergence of race and gender. She details the problems of being the wife of a holy man. While her husband concerns himself with other people's problems, she is left to attend to him and the rest of the family. According to Crow Dog, tribal women are burdened with hardships begotten of marginalization, yet they remain devoted to the native community and its continuity. Enumerating native women's frustrations and feelings of hopelessness throughout the work, she asserts, "It is not the big, dramatic things so much that get us down, but just being Indian, trying to hang on to our way of life, language, and values while being surrounded by an alien, more powerful culture. It is being an iyaska, a half-blood, being looked down upon by whites and full-bloods alike. . . . Most of all it is being a woman" (4). Despite these bleak statements, *Lakota Woman* bears a positive message, the possibility of renewal. The Lakota and other tribal nations can achieve a transformation not unlike her own by reconnecting to their traditions, rituals, and value systems. As Mary Crow Dog declares in the last sentence of her text, "Life goes on." Native women assure that perseverance; they also proclaim that continuity to America and the world.

Mankiller and *Lakota Woman* present powerful testaments in their own distinctive ways. When they are positioned side by side, the force of their messages is compounded. Readers of either text can learn about native histories and cultures, but exposure to both works exemplifies differences among native groups and the particularity of individual motivations, perceptions, and responses. Despite those differences, when Wilma Mankiller and Mary Crow Dog report the problems of poverty or describe the exhilaration they felt during the Red Power movement, their perceptions reverberate remarkably. Supplying viewpoints that have too long been absent in American culture, these autobiographies illustrate that native peoples have been individually and collectively besieged, even in the recent past. Together, the works confirm that the consensus of mythic texts has not advanced the whole story of America's peoples. Probably the most important common thread of the autobiographies is their authors' unwavering belief in renewal and continuity and the special role that native women play within their societies. Not surprisingly, both texts quote a traditional Cheyenne proverb: "A nation is not lost as long as the hearts of its women are not on the ground." Mary Crow Dog and Wilma Mankiller confirm that Lakota and Cherokee women's hearts are not on the ground. Nor are their nations lost.

Short stories, poetry, novels, autobiographies, and other texts created by indigenous people have begun to attract significant readership on the continent and around the world. According to reporter Michael Bezdek, recent offerings by native writers, texts such as *Love Medicine, Lakota Woman,* and *Mankiller,* have made headway in confronting Indian stereotyping. They impart information and understandings that Euro-America has previously overlooked or suppressed. While many tribal works do not focus on native women, acute awareness of indigenous cultures would undoubtedly undermine previous assumptions about Indian princesses and squaw/drudges. Interesting not only because they deny simplification and categorization of complex peoples and their cultures, texts written by Momaday, Silko, Welch, Erdrich, Crow Dog, Mankiller, and many others also illustrate native survival. Native artists affirm their existence and their endurance, for themselves and for outsiders.

Tying comments about native survival to the need for additional exposure, Abraham Chapman joins other scholars in calling for the inclusion of native texts in the American canon. Decrying the blindness of the Euro-American culture, he asserts: "The rich and unique mythic memories of the contemporary American Indian writers, and the qualities of enrichment and diversity they add to contemporary American literature, cannot be overestimated" (6). These works, most of which concentrate quite legitimately upon their own groups' self-definitions and contexts, in addition to their interactions with the dominant culture, can familiarize students with alternate voices within American society.

This contribution alone might suffice to convince educators to include such scripts in the curricula, but testimony of native realities would not be the sole benefit of their incorporation. Literatures created by native artists are essentially different from Euro-American literary traditions, according to Arnold Krupat. Polyvocal and dialogic, native texts embody difference, diversities that are not necessarily in opposition to any others. They reflect the heterodoxy of American culture, expressing collective selves within the nation. As Karl Kroeber insists, Erdrich's *Love Medicine* is among the best examples of truly American fiction because it provides "individual voicings" that reveal an "intensely American experience of encounters among diverse cultures" (2).

Krupat offers another reason that heteroglossic works written by native peoples are valuable for inclusion in the canon. As he argues, texts written by Euro-Americans have presumed their own orthodoxy. Positing their unquestionable authority and the right to speak for all, canonical works have constituted a monologue. They have offered one-sided portrayals of America. As observed in the Sacagawea legend, monologic texts have excluded other perspectives, defining a single, legitimate viewpoint for the population to embrace and emulate. Not only do native texts submit visions different from those of monovocal works, but they also urge a resistance to orthodoxy because they embody multiplicity.

If Americans acquired understandings of native peoples' histories, literatures, cultures, and meanings in formal educational settings and through individual reading and investigation, they would learn that traditional mythic narratives have never embraced heterodoxy. Such cultural decoders could discover that mythic texts have silenced certain voices and concealed the realities of marginalized peoples. Interpreters of multicultural and canonical works might begin to reevaluate America's western experiences and reassess tribal peoples. These are the very issues at stake in the Sacagawea legend. If the United States is dedicated to pluralism, if it is committed to the promise of difference, if diversity no longer implies subordination and marginalization, then the nation must embrace diverse texts and multicultural education. As Patricia Limerick argues in *The Chronicle of Higher Education,* we Americans must "explain ourselves to each other" (B2). That ambition can be realized only if we are allowed opportunities to listen to each other's stories. That process will entail taking risks and setting aside assumptions, activities that the academic community can foster.

The former director of Dartmouth's Native American Studies program, Michael Dorris argues, "The discovery of just one other way of being and becoming human puts to rest forever, for that discoverer, the destructive myth of a Euro-American monopoly on civilization, or language, or humanity" ("Native American Literature," 157). As Dorris's statement implies, multicultural education can encourage students of every ethnicity and race to learn about all American peoples, to engage the polyvocality of the continent.

CONCLUSION

D URING ITS MANY and varied commemorations of Sacagawea since the turn of the twentieth century, North Dakota has displayed little dissonance concerning her place in the history of the state, the region, or the nation. When I was growing up in Bismarck, I too joined the ranks as a celebrant of the legend.

Trips to the state capitol grounds and museum were among the most exciting events of the year. First, my friends, my brother, and I ventured to the top floor of the museum. That area illustrated North Dakota's past. Displaying stuffed bison, elk, and bears—all in threatening postures—archivists presented us with evidence of the not-so-distant savagery of the Great Plains. Tepees, native clothing, and crude cooking utensils were exhibited in other rooms on the same floor. Most compelling was a miniature Mandan village, the tiny clay-packed mounds set in the case in the middle of one room. As the displays reminded us, Indians had once lived on the plains.

These exhibits were fascinating, exotic, but most assuredly part of the state's past. They signified a vanished life that had been "rightly" vanquished by civilization. We viewed displays of an obviously "superior" culture in other parts of the museum. An oldtime dentist chair, silverware, and a train engine—these were signs of North Dakota's pioneer days. This collection signified our heritage, emblematic of the great, worthwhile struggle to settle a challenging wilderness.

At noon, we ate our sack lunches outside, gathered beneath Leonard Crunelle's *Bird Woman*. Frozen forever in time, the native woman gazed west, head high, her baby on her back. For us, she symbolized the possibilities of civilization. We had no doubt that she was one of us, if not by blood, then at least by volition and service to the cause. No one spoke of the irony that surrounded the statue. No one mentioned that this American heroine might more appropriately relate another past. No one said that her presence could point to a different narrative.

Since that time, North Dakota has erected a new Heritage Center, a structure that presents different versions of the region's histories. Events outside that building often document a changing approach to race and ethnicity as well. Unlike the 1911 ceremony to unveil Crunelle's monument, the 1989 state centennial celebrations included Chippewa, Mandan, Hidatsa, Dakota, Lakota, Arikara, and other tribal peoples who illustrated the existence and vibrance of their various cultures. Men and women in traditional ceremonial dress performed hoop and circle dances. Elders told stories. Native artists demonstrated their crafts and sold them in booths.

During my 1989 visit to Bismarck, I also noticed that a few statues have joined *Bird Woman* on the capitol grounds. One bronze piece depicts young pioneer children running hand in hand toward America's future. *Bird Woman* still faces west.

Neither the state nor the nation may ever forsake Sacagawea, but through education, children can learn to interrogate "received" ideas. They might come to understand that Crunelle's text points to Euro-American ideologies. As Americans read works written by Louise Erdrich, Mary Crow Dog, Wilma Mankiller, and others, their comprehensions will echo and reinforce other evidence that tribal peoples have been important to the nation, that they relate identities and meanings vital to the culture. Someday, North Dakota and other states may provide visual proof of their commitment to cultural pluralism and polyvocality, by erecting statues in celebration of a different native woman, a "tribal chairwoman in blue jeans."

NOTES

Introduction

1. One hotly contested issue concerning Sacagawea has been the "correct" spelling, translation, and pronunciation of her name. Because expedition diarists extend various spellings, no one, in all likelihood, will ever certify Sacagawea's "true" name. In spite of these problems, scholars seem compelled to promote either "Sacajawea," "Sacagawea," or "Sakakawea."

Once opinions are sorted out, however, it becomes apparent that a variety of factors, rather than the relative merits of specific evidence, have motivated scholarly choices. Such influences include the researcher's geographical region, his/her proximity to either the Shoshones or the Hidatsas, a desire to reach large audiences who recognize a particular spelling based on Euro-American historical tradition, and/or the need to employ the designation adopted by U.S. government agencies. Untangling the seemingly simple identification of Sacagawea's "real" name illustrates the challenge of any project focusing on this woman, a native whose story has become part of America's mythic experience.

Of the three common spellings, I have opted to use "Sacagawea." Only in cases of direct quotation will alternate spellings appear.

2. While some critics might argue that Sacagawea texts themselves constitute myth, most mythographers distinguish between myth and legend. As William Bascom writes in "The Forms of Folklore," myths and legends are true and vital narratives of a culture. Generally, however, the former are defined as sacred tales of a remote past while the latter feature cultural heroes operating in a more recent period. Although Martin S. Day notes in *The Many Meanings of Myth* that differentiations between the two categories are subject to exceptions and that definitional slippages are common, he and Bascom suggest that scholars accept these distinctions.

3. By emphasizing supernatural beings and transcendent times in *Myth and Reality*, Mircea Eliade seems to preclude the emergence of traditional narratives in American society. However, many other myth specialists, including Lauri Honko and G. S. Kirk, assert that pinpointing the precise attributes of myth is a singularly difficult task.

4. Historical and literary researchers, such as Robert Berkhofer in *The White Man's Indian: Images of the American Indian from Columbus to the Present*, have wrestled with applying appropriate designations to individuals and groups among the indigenous peoples of the North American continent. In *Shadows of the Indian: Stereotypes in American Culture*, Raymond Stedman adopts and justifies his use of the title "Indian(s)." Others, like Joe S. Sando in "White-

Created Myths about the Native American," reject that reference as mistaken at best and pejorative at worst, opting instead for "Native American(s)."

Because this study addresses the historical existence of tribal peoples as well as socially constructed and culturally approved images that have defined them on the continent, I differentiate the two characterizations. Only when high-lighting Euro-American ideological constructions do I employ such labels as "Indian," "Indian princess," "squaw," and "noble savage." In all other situa-tions, in an effort to underscore the difference between self-referential and ex-ternally ascribed designations, I use tribal identifications whenever possible. When it is necessary to refer to the collective by collapsing tribal distinctions, I employ "native(s)," "native peoples," "aboriginals," and "indigenous people(s)/groups."

1. Frontier Myths and "Indian" Images: Essential Elements for the Making of the Sacagawea Legend

1. Although various critics, such as Julius W. Pratt in "The Origins of Manifest Destiny," John S. Bowman in *The World Almanac of the American West,* and Frederick Merk in *Manifest Destiny and Mission in American History,* associate the phrase "manifest destiny" almost exclusively with expansionist at-titudes of the mid 1840s, Weinberg does not in *Manifest Destiny: A Study of Nationalist Expansion in American History.* Others sharing Weinberg's percep-tions are Howard Lamar in *The Reader's Encyclopedia of the American West* and Norman A. Graebner in *Manifest Destiny.*

2. Scholars investigating frontier traditions are Charles M. Segal and David C. Stineback in *Puritans, Indians, and Manifest Destiny,* Lucille Van Keuren in *American Indian Responses and Reactions to the Colonists as Recorded in Seven-teenth and Eighteenth-Century American Literature,* and Leslie Fiedler in *The Return of the Vanishing American.*

3. Those espousing the "epic" quality of the mission are Frederick Young, David Holloway, and Helen West in "The Higher Significance in the Lewis and Clark Expedition," *Lewis and Clark and the Crossing of North America,* and "The Lewis and Clark Expedition," respectively.

4. In agreement with Kolodny's and Steiner's assertions about the "mas-culinity" of the mythic West, Susan Armitage and Elizabeth Jameson write that frontier traditions have omitted more cultural truths than they relate. Identify-ing expurgations and offering new information about female histories as they intersect American frontiers in *The Women's West,* Armitage and Jameson hope to free the nation of the "all-pervasive masculinity of the popular image of the American West" (5).

5. Such texts include Gerald Snyder's *In the Footsteps of Lewis and Clark,* Howard Zahniser's "Towards the West," and Calvin Tomkins's *The Lewis and Clark Trail.*

6. Numerous studies have investigated "Indian" images in American liter-ary works, in textbooks, and in American media. Literary texts include Jeannette

Henry's *The American Indian Reader*, Philip Butcher's *The Minority Presence in American Literature, 1600–1900*, Ward Churchill, Mary Anne Hill, and Norbert Hill's "Examination of Stereotyping," Tim Shaughnessy's "White Stereotypes of Indians," Robert F. Berkhofer's *The White Man's Indian: Images of the American Indian from Columbus to the Present*, Nancy B. Black and Bette S. Weidman's *White on Red: Images of the American Indian*, D'Arcy McNickle's "American Indians Who Never Were," Wynette Hamilton's "The Correlation between Societal Attitudes and Those of American Authors in the Depiction of American Indians, 1607–1860," and Francis Haines's "Don't Stereotype Our Indians!"

Reviewing images presented in children's books and in textbooks are the American Indian Historical Society's *Textbooks and the American Indian*, Lee H. Bowker's "Red and Black in Contemporary American History Texts," Laura Herbst's "That's One Good Indian: Unacceptable Images in Children's Novels," Barbara D. Stoodt and Sandra Ignizio's "The American Indian in Children's Literature," Anne Troy's "The Indian in Adolescent Novels," and Arlene Hirschfelder's *American Indian Stereotypes in the World of Children*.

Researchers have also offered a profusion of studies evaluating film portrayals of America's native peoples. They include Michael Hilger's *The American Indian in Film*, Jenni Calder's *There Must Be a Lone Ranger*, Richard Brenzo's "American Indians vs American Writers," Donald Kaufmann's "The Indian as Media Hand-Me-Down," Sharon Murphy's "American Indians and the Media: Neglect and Stereotype," John C. Ewers's "The Static Images," Philip French's "The Indian in the Western Movie," Ralph and Natasha Friar's *The Only Good Indian . . . The Hollywood Gospel*, and James R. Richburg's "Media and the American Indian: Enthnographical, Historical, and Contemporary Issues."

7. While John A. Price contends in "The Stereotyping of North American Indians in Motion Pictures" that Indian stereotyping has recently declined, Gretchen Bataille and Charles Silet in *The Pretend Indians: Images of Native Americans in the Movies*, disagree. In "A Brief Review of the Native American in American Cinema," Hedy Hartman presents a list of complaints the American Indian Movement (AIM) has leveled against apparently pro-Indian movies. As she asserts, American films continue to adhere to old stereotypes.

8. Focusing on imagery of native women are Karen Elliott in "The Portrayal of the American Indian Woman in a Select Group of American Novels," Gretchen M. Bataille and Kathleen Mullen Sands in *American Indian Women: A Guide to Research*, Marla Powers in *Oglala Women: Myth, Ritual and Reality*, William Gerdts in "The Marble Savage," Katherine M. Weist in "Beasts of Burden and Menial Slaves: Nineteenth-Century Observations of Northern Plains Indian Women," and Rayna Green in "Review Essay: Native American Women" and "The Pocahontas Perplex."

9. The term "squaw" has not always carried pejorative connotations that modern readers now associate with its use. According to archaeologist Arthur C. Parker, "squaw" derives from the Narragansett word "squa," meaning "female," and was originally employed by early colonists to designate an Indian woman (Seaver 34; 329). As captivity narratives, dime novels, and other popular

texts burgeoned in America, the designation "squaw" inevitably came to imply specific negative qualities and behaviors.

10. These include Leslie Fiedler in *The Return of the Vanishing American,* J. Leitch Wright, Jr., in *The Only Land They Knew: The Tragic Story of the American Indians in the Old South,* and Albert Keizer in *The Indian in American Literature.*

11. Several recent works have begun to reassess images and meanings of Malinche legendry, including Norma Alarcon's "Chicana's Feminist Literature: A Re-Vision Through Malintzin/or Malintzin: Putting Flesh Back on the Object" and Cherrie Moraga's "From a Long Line of Vendidas: Chicanas and Feminism."

2. Original Expedition Journals and Earliest Editions: Raw Materials of Legend

1. Early editorial compilations of the original journals include the following: the 1811 M'Keehan edition of Patrick Gass's journal; the 1814 Biddle text; and the Coues edition, an 1893 reissue of Biddle, which presents additional annotations, chapter and subchapter headings, and selective quotations from the originals.

2. According to Paul Cutright in *A History of the Lewis and Clark Journals,* the Biddle edition did not sell well. One reason for poor sales might have been the seven-year lapse between the conclusion of the exploration and publication of the journals, possibly allowing popular enthusiasm for the mission to wane. Another problem might have been the $6 price for the two small volumes. Whatever the causes, sales of the first 2,000 sets did not warrant reprintings, in spite of positive reviews (64–67).

3. Euro-Americans interpreted all native economies as savage and inferior, based on a belief that native subsistence strategies consisted of a single type, that of hunting. Because this concept complemented other ways of thinking about indigenous peoples, the notion propagated in spite of evidence that many groups employed agriculture as the mainstay of their existence or as a supplement to hunting and gathering. For an analysis of native agriculture, refer to R. Douglas Hurt's *Indian Agriculture in America: Prehistory to the Present.*

4. Unlike many captivities, which were purportedly written by the redeemed captives themselves, some were published in the as-told-to format. Hanson, for example, related her experience to Samuel Bownas, who subsequently wrote and published the story.

5. Such works include James Hosmer's *History of the Expedition of Captains Lewis and Clark 1804–5–6;* Olin Wheeler's *The Trail of Lewis and Clark, 1804–1904: A Story of the Great Exploration across the Continent in 1803–06; with a Description of the Old Trail, Based upon Actual Travel over It, and of the Changes Found a Century Later;* and David Holloway's *Lewis and Clark and the Crossing of North America.*

6. Because Gass's original journal has never been recovered, the only extant version of his diary is the work edited by David M'Keehan, a little-known book

and stationery store owner from Pittsburgh who turns Gass's text into "resolutely correct, preceptorial prose of the early nineteenth-century schoolmaster" (Cutright 28).

7. The original journals contain numerous spelling, capitalization, and syntactical errors. To present as accurate a picture of the works as possible, I omit notations of such faults so as not to interfere with comprehension. Since Reuben Gold Thwaites was the first to publish the original journals of Lewis, Clark, and Whitehouse, all quotations and paraphrases taken from those works refer to the Thwaites edition. I note the volume and pages on which entries appear.

8. By the early nineteenth century, according to Barbara Welter in "The Cult of True Womanhood: 1820–1860," America had codified purity, piety, submissiveness, and domesticity as the cardinal virtues of "true womanhood." Neither the phrase nor the four traits, consequently, required definition or elaboration in works of the period.

9. According to Ronald L. Meek in *Social Science and the Ignoble Savage,* socioeconomic thought in Europe during the latter half of the nineteenth century hinged on meanings supplied by proponents of the four-stage theory. This "scientific" doctrine was primarily constructed on observations of a culture's mode of subsistence. Formulating their hypotheses based upon textual evidence portraying North American native cultures, theorists embraced a conflated conception of native cultures as exemplifying the first stage, that of a savage, hunting society. As Reginald Horsman writes in "Scientific Racism and the American Indian in the Mid-Nineteenth Century," popular works had long espoused the innate inferiority of natives, only later supporting their contentions by citing scientific "proofs."

10. In *Mythography,* Doty discusses the operational vitality of myths. According to his definition, frontier myths must have been in the "implicit" stage for the men of the Corps because certain concepts emerging from that tradition seem the only natural way of perceiving the world, as evidenced by their lack of awareness of contradictions they record.

11. Gass might also have included commentary about Sacagawea's illness, but the edited version of his text offers none.

12. Although the Biddle edition most often compresses incidents and eliminates detail, on certain occasions the editors provide more information than is available in the journals. Such additions are possible since Nicholas Biddle supplements his understanding of events through interviews with Clark and George Shannon, another of the expedition members.

3. The Birth and Proliferation of the Sacagawea Legend: The Progressive Era

1. Many scholars, such as Emily Rosenberg in *Spreading the American Dream* and Wynette Hamilton in "The Correlation between Societal Attitudes and Those of American Authors in the Depiction of American Indians, 1607–1860," have shown that after 1830, American writers employed images of natives

to illustrate differences between savagery and civilization. According to John Ewers, by the mid-nineteenth century, "Indian" images emerged from drawings and paintings of George Catlin, Karl Bodmer, and Felix O. C. Darley. Roger Nichols adds that dime novels, or "penny dreadfuls," were among the most significant cultural texts reflecting and popularizing ideas of savagery in nineteenth-century America.

2. According to J. W. Pratt's "The Origins of Manifest Destiny," John L. O'Sullivan first used the phrase in an editorial published in New York City's *Morning News* in 1845.

3. Critics commenting on cultural disruptions during the Progressive Era include Arthur Link and Richard McCormick in *Progressivism*, Richard Hofstadter in *The Age of Reform*, and Robert H. Wiebe in *The Search for Order: 1877–1920*.

4. Supporting this contention are D. S. Otis in *The Dawes Act and the Allotment of Indian Lands*, Frederick Hoxie in *A Final Promise: The Campaign to Assimilate the Indians, 1880–1920*, and Leonard Carlson in *Indians, Bureaucrats, and Land* and "Federal Policy and Indian Land: Economic Interests and the Sale of Indian Allotments, 1900–1934."

5. In "The Native American as Myth and Fact," Natalia Belting asserts that American works have long vilified Frenchmen who came to America because the French formed military and economic alliances with native groups to oppose English and American settlement.

French fur traders furthermore signified the antithesis of American values and beliefs and reiterated the dangers of the frontier. Also discussing this notion in *Regeneration through Violence*, Richard Slotkin explains that American heroes, unlike such marginal characters as French "squawmen," had to overcome the lure of the wilderness. Armed with newly acquired skills obtained through their initiation in the frontier, they employed violence to pave the way for civilization.

6. Such assertions were typical of suffragist strategies, according to Aileen Kraditor in *The Ideas of the Woman Suffrage Movement, 1890–1920*. In agreement with Kraditor, Blanche Glassman Hersh asserts that suffragists based many of their arguments on the special moral and domestic responsibilities that women supposedly maintained in American culture. Inverting previous conceptions of women's biological inferiority, leading suffragists employed such ideas to prove women's superiority and their fitness to vote.

7. As Eleanor Flexner argues in *Century of Struggle: The Women's Rights Movement in the United States* and Ida Husted Harper asserts in *The History of Woman Suffrage*, woman suffrage was not easily won. Success was not possible, according to these writers, without support from such women as Elizabeth Cady Stanton, Susan B. Anthony, Carrie Chapman Catt, and Anna Howard Shaw. Even those dynamic and devoted leaders could not accomplish their goal until American culture envisioned a legitimate role for women outside the confines of the domestic sphere.

8. In "Lust between the Bookends," a chapter offered in *Shadows of the Indian: Stereotypes in American Culture*, Raymond Stedman provides an excel-

lent overview of images associated with savage men. As Stedman claims in his text and Louise Barnett asserts in *The Ignoble Savage: American Literary Racism, 1790–1890* and "Nineteenth-Century Indian Hater Fiction: A Paradigm for Racism," such culturally approved ideas emerged from captivity narratives and other colonial texts.

9. Harrington cites Carl Bitter, Chief of the Department of Sculpture for the St. Louis Exposition. She also notes that the statue has since been lost.

10. Although 20,000 copies may not seem considerable, this number probably blanketed the state since the population of North Dakota was only 300,000 in 1900, rising to about 500,000 by 1910.

11. Other sources have repeated this claim, including the 1916 pamphlet, *Sakakawea—The Indian Girl Who Helped to Open an Empire* and a 1922 news article, "Sa-ka-ka-we'-a Trail. Named for the Indian Bird Woman."

4. Variation and Elaboration: The Sacagawea Legend from the 1940s through the 1960s

1. According to "Sacajawea: A Symposium," Hebard helped to draft and circulate a woman suffrage petition directed to the Constitutional Convention of Wyoming in 1889.

2. During the same decade, the federal government employed Dr. Charles Eastman, a Sioux who graduated from Dartmouth in 1887 and received his M.D. from Boston University in 1890, to investigate Sacagawea's burial site. Eastman conferred with some informants that Hebard interviewed and agreed with Hebard's conclusions.

3. Although she offers no evidence from written sources or eyewitnesses, Eva Emery Dye asserts that Sacagawea was as slight and slender as a Euro-American woman.

4. These researchers generally cite evidence from Luttig's and Brackenridge's diaries, as well as a journal entry written by Clark when he was governor of the Louisiana territory, to verify that Sacagawea died in her twenties.

5. As Kathleen Houts and Rosemary Bahr argue in "Stereotyping of Indians and Blacks in Magazine Cartoons," cartoons published in *Saturday Evening Post* from 1922 to 1931 and from 1958 to 1968 are almost exclusively oriented toward the past. The figure most frequently depicted is the warrior, "a primitive, historical bow-and-arrow type who has no place in the modern society" (113).

6. The phrase "melting pot" originates from Israel Zangwill's 1908 play, *The Melting Pot* (Sollors, *Beyond Ethnicity*, 66–68).

7. The image of the orchestra, according to Gleason, was first proposed by Horace Kallen in his 1915 essay, "Democracy vs the Melting Pot: A Study of American Nationality" (43).

8. According to Fixico, the first step toward termination was the establishment of the Indian Claims Commission in 1946. The commission codified procedures for native people to sue the federal government for land that they felt had been illegally expropriated. Although this might appear to have benefited

only natives, Leonard Carlson concludes in "What Was It Worth? Economic and Historical Aspects of Determining Awards in Indian Land Claims Cases" that gratuitous offsets and lack of accrued interest on the awards protected the U.S. treasury against large claims.

9. Brophy was the Commissioner of Indian Affairs during the Roosevelt and Truman administrations.

10. As Richard White reports in *"It's Your Misfortune and None of My Own": A History of the American West,* although Euro-American men were less likely than French Canadians or Anglo Canadians to marry native women during the early 1800s, at least 33 percent of American trappers and hunters entered into interracial marriages (46–47). In spite of these data, White asserts that most American hunters and trappers scorned native cultures as inferior and savage.

11. Among the films of the 1950s, *The Far Horizon* has been Hollywood's sole attempt to relate the narrative of the Lewis and Clark Expedition. Donna Reed becomes a nearly white Sacagawea who fixates on the dashing Clark, played by Charlton Heston. Faithful to the original novel, screenwriters and directors identify Charbonneau as the villain of the piece and legitimate Sacagawea's response to Clark. The text presents the familiar and popular plot of unrequited love of the Indian maiden for the "civilized" hero, but reviewers in *Time, Newsweek, Commonweal, America,* and *The New York Times* panned the film.

Although filmmakers' experimentations with stories of miscegenation have been common, creators of *The Far Horizon* omit the presence of Baptiste, Sacagawea's baby. Probably concerned that the presence of an infant, in a love story about its mother, would disturb viewers, writers and producers never venture beyond culturally acceptable visions of frontier traditions. American audiences may have been ready for another version of hopeless love of an Indian princess for a gallant captain in the wilderness, but producers never invite them to recognize that the man might return those emotions. Nor are they asked to consider that such a relationship might endure.

5. The Sacagawea Legend Since 1970: Proliferation of Popular Traditions and Dissenting Portrayals

1. Historians embrace a project that began in the mid 1960s. Penning "The Mystery of Sacagawea's Death" in 1967, Helen Howard reviews evidence and proclaims that Sacagawea was the interpreter and guide of the expedition. Two years earlier, in "Sacajawea—Inspiration Maid" Bernard DeVoto states that she was helpful during the journey, but denies that her translating was significant. He also contends that she did practically no guiding. Others concurring with Howard during this period have included Howard Lamar in *The Reader's Encyclopedia of the American West* and John Bowman in *The World Almanac of the American West.* Both declare that Sacagawea was a guide.

2. Lawsuits initiated by the Fort Berhold and Standing Rock tribes were not settled until December 1992, when the U.S. Congress authorized a $240,000,000 trust fund to be used for tribal economic development in ex-

change for the loss of 67,000 acres that the Garrison and Oahe Dams had caused (Olson).

3. Borden does not specify which edition he read, but it was, in all likelihood, the Thwaites text since that is now regarded as the most authoritative version of the expedition. He no doubt read Hebard's biography. The novel Borden is referring to is Anna Lee Waldo's *Sacajawea*.

4. Citations to *Sakakawea: The Woman with Many Names* refer to act and page numbers of the written script.

5. Ellipses are presented in Borden's script, to suggest overlapping songs.

6. The Sacagawea Legend: Past Images and Future Prospects

1. Two other *Sacagawea* monuments, identical to Jackson's original piece, are displayed at the University of Wyoming in Laramie and Central Wyoming College in Riverton.

2. As Green notes, most dissenting depictions have been perfunctory, and equally harmful, portraits of the squaw.

3. Among those emphasizing the importance of multicultural education are Gerald Pine and Asa Hilliard who present their arguments in "Schools Should Emphasize Ethnicity," and Todd Gitlin who offers his opinions in "The Classics Must Be Broadened to Include Multicultural Literature."

4. In addition to Stensland and Shoemaker, other critics suggesting that native texts ought to be presented in schools are Jarold Ramsey in "The Teacher of Modern American Indian Writing as Ethnographer and Critic," Michael Dorris in "Native American Literature in an Ethnohistorical Context," Gerald Haslam in *Forgotten Pages of American Literature,* and Francis Haines in "Don't Stereotype Our Indians!"

5. Texts based on non-native contexts are plentiful. George Catlin's *Letters and Notes on the Manners, Customs and Condition of the North American Indians,* for example, overflows with distortions borne of his conviction of his own cultural superiority. Many works written in the twentieth century, such as Gordon Macgregor's *Warriors without Weapons: A Study of the Society and Personality Development of the Pine Ridge Sioux,* continue to interpret native culture based upon a Euro-American world view and value systems. Fewer works, especially those concerned with native women, incorporate indigenous meanings. These include Marla Powers's *Oglala Women: Myth, Ritual, and Reality* and Judith Brown's "Iroquois Women: An Ethnohistoric Note."

6. Dexter Fisher's *The Third Woman: Minority Women Writers of the U.S.* does not feature native women's texts exclusively, but the anthology offers many important tribal contributions.

7. Mary Crow Dog's experiences at boarding school are reminiscent of emotions and meanings related in Louise Erdrich's poem "Indian Boarding School: The Runaways." This work portrays the intense anguish that thousands of native children suffered as a result of separation from their families and societies. Although selected to receive "civilized" education in segregated boarding schools, Erdrich's protagonists have attempted to flee their incarceration,

only to be recaptured. Employing mental and physical humiliation, administrators punish the children for their rejection of such a precious gift.

8. Mary Crow Dog is not the only native woman who honors Anna Mae Aquash and doubts the reported cause of death. Dedicating *A Gathering of Spirit: Writing and Art by North American Indian Women* to Aquash, Beth Brant writes that the Micmac woman was a "casualty of the war between the FBI and the Indian People."

WORKS CITED

Adams, James Truslow. "The Six Most Important American Women." *Good Housekeeping*, February 1941, 30.
———, ed. "Sacagawea." In *Who Was Who in America: A Companion Biographical Reference Work to Who's Who in America*. Vol. II, 531. Chicago: Marquis Who's Who, 1950.
Alarcon, Norma. "Chicana's Feminist Literature: A Re-Vision Through Malintzin/or Malintzin: Putting Flesh Back on the Object." In Moraga and Bambara, 182–90.
Albers, Patricia. "New Perspectives on Plains Indian Women." In Albers and Medicine, 1–26.
Albers, Patricia, and William R. James. "Illusion and Illumination: Visual Images of American Indian Women in the West." In Armitage and Jameson, 35–50.
Albers, Patricia, and Beatrice Medicine, eds. *The Hidden Half: Studies of Plains Indian Women*. New York: University Press of America, 1983.
Allen, Paula Gunn. "The One Who Skins Cats." In Brant, 19–24.
———. "Pocahontas To Her English Husband, John Rolfe." In *New Worlds of Literature*, ed. Jerome Beaty and J. Paul Hunter, 813–14. New York: W. W. Norton, 1989.
———. "The Sacred Hoop: A Contemporary Perspective." In *Studies in American Indian Literature: Critical Essays and Course Designs*, ed. Paula Gunn Allen, 3–22. New York: Modern Language Association, 1983.
———. *The Sacred Hoop: Recovering the Feminine in American Indian Traditions*. Boston: Beacon Press, 1986.
———. "Teaching American Indian Women's Literature." In *Studies in American Indian Literature: Critical Essays and Course Designs*, ed. Paula Gunn Allen, 133–44. New York: Modern Language Association, 1983.
———, ed. *American Indian Literature: Critical Essays and Course Designs*. New York: Modern Language Association, 1983.
———, ed. *Spider Woman's Granddaughters: Traditional Tales and Contemporary Writing by Native American Women*. Boston: Beacon Press, 1989.

American Indian College Fund Advertisement. *Country Living*, May 1993, 89.

American Indian Historical Society. *Textbooks and the American Indian.* San Francisco: Indian Historian Press, 1970.

Anderson, Irving W. "Probing the Riddle of the Bird Woman: How Long did Sacajawea Live? When and Where Did She Die?" *Montana, the Magazine of Western History* 23.4 (October 1973): 2–17.

———. "Profiles of the American West: A Charbonneau Family Portrait." *The American West* 17.2 (March–April 1980): 4–9, 58–61.

———. "Sacajawea, Sacagawea, Sakakawea?" *South Dakota History* 8.4 (Fall 1978): 305–11.

Andrist, Ralph K. *To the Pacific with Lewis and Clark.* New York: Harper and Row, 1967.

Anonymous. Review of *The Far Horizon. Time*, 6 June 1955, 56.

Armitage, Susan. "Through Women's Eyes: A New View of the West." In Armitage and Jameson, 9–18.

Armitage, Susan, and Elizabeth Jameson, eds. *The Women's West.* Norman: University of Oklahoma Press, 1987.

Bahr, Howard M., Bruce A. Chadwick, and Robert C. Day, eds. *Native Americans Today: Sociological Perspectives.* New York: Harper and Row, 1972.

Bakeless, John, ed. *The Journals of Lewis and Clark.* New York: Mentor Books, 1964.

———. *Lewis and Clark: Partners in Discovery.* New York: William Morrow and Co., 1947.

Banks, James. "Cultural Pluralism and the Schools." In *Ethnic America*, ed. Marjorie P. K. Weiser, 189–93. New York: H. W. Wilson, 1978.

Banta, S. E. *Buckelew: The Indian Captive or The Life Story of F. M. Buckelew While a Captive among the Lipan Indians in the Western Wilds of Frontier Texas, as Related by Himself.* 1911. Reprint. Vol. 107. Garland Library of North American Captivities. New York: Garland, 1977.

Barnett, Louise K. *The Ignoble Savage: American Literary Racism, 1790–1890.* London: Greenwood Press, 1975.

———. "Nineteenth-Century Indian Hater Fiction: A Paradigm for Racism." *South Atlantic Quarterly* 74 (Spring 1975): 224–36.

Barry, Nora, and Mary Prescott. "The Triumph of the Brave: *Love Medicine*'s Holistic Vision." *Critique* 30.2 (Winter 1989): 123–38.

Bascom, William. "The Forms of Folklore: Prose Narratives." In Dundes, 5–29.

Bataille, Gretchen M., and Kathleen M. Sands. *American Indian Women: A Guide to Research.* New York: Garland Publishing, 1991.

Bataille, Gretchen M., and Charles L. P. Silet, eds. *The Pretend Indians: Images of Native Americans in the Movies*. Ames: Iowa State University Press, 1980.

Beaty, Jerome, and J. Paul Hunter, eds. *New Worlds of Literature*. New York: W. W. Norton, 1989.

Bechtold, Carl. "Jackson's Statue Dedicated: nearly half-million in sales." *The Cody* [WY] *Enterprise*, 9 July 1980, A-11.

Beer, David F. "Anti-Indian Sentiment in Early Colonial Literature." In *The American Indian Reader: Literature*, ed. Jeannette Henry, 207–17. San Francisco: Indian Historian Press, 1973.

Bell, Catherine. *Ritual Theory, Ritual Practice*. New York: Oxford University Press, 1992.

Belting, Natalia Maree. "The Native American as Myth and Fact." *Journal of the Illinois State Historical Society* 69 (May 1976): 119–26.

Berger, Peter L., and Thomas Luckmann. *The Social Construction of Reality: A Treatise in the Sociology of Knowledge*. New York: Doubleday, 1966.

Berkhofer, Robert F. *The White Man's Indian: Images of the American Indian from Columbus to the Present*. New York: Alfred A. Knopf, 1978.

Berkovitch, Sacvan. Afterword. In Berkovitch and Jehlen, 418–42.

———. "The Problem of Ideology in American Literary History." *Critical Inquiry* 12 (Summer 1986): 631–53.

Berkovitch, Sacvan, and Myra Jehlen, eds. *Ideology and Classic American Literature*. New York: Cambridge University Press, 1986.

Bezdek, Michael. "Indian Writers Gaining Ground: Words Open Up Hearts, bury 'savage' mystiques." *Sunday* [Daytona Beach] *News-Journal*, 15 August 1993, 1, 5.

Billington, Ray Allen. *The Far Western Frontier, 1830–1860*. New York: Harper and Row, 1956.

———. *Westward Expansion: A History of the American Frontier*. New York: Macmillan, 1949.

Black, Nancy B., and Bette S. Weidman. *White on Red: Images of the American Indian*. Port Washington, NY: Kennikat Press, 1976.

Blassingame, Wyatt. *Sacagawea: Indian Guide*. Champaign, IL: Gerrard, 1965.

Borden, Bill. Libretto for *Sakakawea: The Woman with Many Names*. Grand Forks, ND: By the author, 1989.

Borden, Bill, and Thomas Peterson. *Sakakawea: The Woman with Many Names*. Video cassette. Grand Forks: University of North Dakota, 1989.

Bowker, Lee H. "Red and Black in Contemporary American History Texts: A Content Analysis." In Bahr, Chadwick, and Day, 101–10.

Bowman, John S., ed. *The World Almanac of the American West*. New York: Pharos Books, 1986.

Bownas, Samuel. *An Account of the Captivity of Elizabeth Hanson, Now or Late of Kachecky, in New England: Who, with Four of her Children and Servant-Maid, was taken captive by the **Indians**, and carried into **Canada***. 1760. Reprint. Vol. 6. Garland Library of Narratives of North American Captivities. New York: Garland Publishing, 1977.

Brackenridge, Henry M. *Views of Louisiana: Together with a Journal of a Voyage Up the Missouri River in 1811*. 1814. Reprint. Chicago: Quadrangle Books, 1962.

Brant, Beth, ed. *A Gathering of Spirit: Writing and Art by North American Indian Women*. n.p.: Sinister Wisdom Books, 1984.

Brenzo, Richard Allen. "American Indians vs American Writers." *Margins* 14 (October/November 1974): 40–45, 88.

Broker, Ignatia. *Night Flying Woman: An Ojibway Narrative*. St. Paul: Minnesota Historical Society Press, 1983.

"Bronze Tablet Placed on Sakakawea Statue." *Bismarck* [ND] *Tribune*, 20 October 1911, 4.

Brophy, William A., and Sophie D. Aberle. *The Indian: America's Unfinished Business—Report of the Commission on the Rights, Liberties, and Responsibilities of the American Indian*. Norman: University of Oklahoma Press, 1966.

Brown, Judith. "Iroquois Women: An Ethnohistoric Note." In *Toward an Anthropology of Women*, ed. Rayna R. Reiter, 235–51. New York: Monthly Review Press, 1975.

Buffalohead, Priscilla K. "Farmers Warriors Traders: A Fresh Look at Ojibway Women." *Minnesota History* 48.6 (Summer 1983): 236–44.

Buller, Galen. "New Interpretations of Native American Literature: A Survival Technique." *American Indian Culture and Research Journal* 4.1&2 (1980): 165–77.

Burt, Olive Wooley. *Sacajawea: A Visual Biography*. New York: Franklin Watts, 1978.

Butcher, Philip, ed. *The Minority Presence in American Literature, 1600–1900: A Reader and Course Guide*. Washington, DC: Howard University Press, 1977.

"By Land from the U. States in 1804 and 1805 with Meriwether Lewis and William Clark." *Time*, 10 October 1955, 66–73.

Cagidemetrio, Alide. "A Plea for Fictional Histories and Old-Time 'Jewesses.'" In *The Invention of Ethnicity*, ed. Werner Sollors, 14–43. New York: Oxford University Press, 1989.

Calder, Angus, and Jenni Calder. *Scott.* New York: Arco Press, 1971.

Calder, Jenni. *There Must Be a Lone Ranger: The American West in Film and in Reality.* New York: Taplinger, 1974.

Calloway, Colin. *New Directions in American Indian History.* Norman: University of Oklahoma Press, 1988.

Carleton, Phillips D. "The Indian Captivity." *American Literature* 15 (May 1943): 169–80.

Carlson, Leonard A. "Federal Policy and Indian Land: Economic Interests and the Sale of Indian Allotments, 1900–1934." *Agricultural History* 57.1 (January 1983): 33–45.

———. *Indians, Bureaucrats, and Land: The Dawes Act and the Decline of Indian Farming.* Westport, CT: Greenwood Press, 1981.

———. "What Was It Worth? Economic and Historical Aspects of Determining Awards in Indian Land Claims Cases." In *Irredeemable America: The Indians' Estate and Land Claims,* ed. Imre Sutton, 87–107. Albuquerque: University of New Mexico Press, 1985.

Catlin, George. *Letters and Notes on the Manners, Customs and Condition of the North American Indians: Written during Eight Years' Travel Amongst the Wildest Tribes of Indians in North America in 1832, 33, 34, 35, 36, 37, 38, and 39.* Vol. 1 of 2. London: Tilt and Bogue, 1842.

Chafe, William H. *The American Woman: Her Changing Social, Economic, and Political Roles, 1920–1970.* New York: Oxford University Press, 1972.

Chandler, Katherine. *The Bird-Woman of the Lewis and Clark Expedition: A Supplementary Reader for First and Second Graders.* New York: Silver, Burdett, 1905.

Chandler, Milford G. "Sidelights on Sacajawea." *The Masterkey for Indian Lore and History* 43 (1969): 58–66.

Chapman, Abraham, ed. *Literature of American Indians: Views and Interpretations.* New York: Meridian, 1975.

Chardon, Francis A. *Chardon's Journal at Fort Clark: 1834–1839: Description of Life on the Upper Missouri; of a Fur Trader's Experiences Among the Mandans, Gros Ventres, and Their Neighbors; of the Ravages of the Small-Pox Epidemic of 1837.* Ed. Annie Heloise Abel. Pierre: South Dakota State University, 1932.

Christenson, Wes. "State natives trade tales of world wide opera involvement of 'Sakakawea' premiere at UND [University of North Dakota]: Stuttgart, New York performers sang lead roles in work by UND English professor Bill Borden." *University of North Dakota Alumni Review* 72.2 (October/November 1989): 5.

Chuinard, E. G. "The Bird Woman: Purposeful Member of the Corps or Casual 'Tag-Along'?" *Montana, The Magazine of Western History* 26.3 (July 1976): 18–29.

Churchill, Claire Warner. *South of the Sunset: An Interpretation of Sacajawea, The Indian Girl That Accompanied Lewis and Clark.* New York: R. R. Wilson, 1936.

Churchill, Ward. *Fantasies of the Master Race: Literature, Cinema and the Colonization of American Indians.* Monroe, ME: Common Courage Press, 1992.

Churchill, Ward, Mary Anne Hill, and Norbert S. Hill. "Examination of Stereotyping: An Analytic Survey of Twentieth-Century Indian Entertainers." In Bataille and Silet, 35–48.

Churchill, Ward, and Norbert Hill. "Media Stereotyping and Native Response: An Historical Overview." *Indian Historian* 11 (December 1978): 45–56, 63.

Clark, Ella E. *Indian Legends from the Northern Rockies.* Norman: University of Oklahoma Press, 1966.

———. "Sacajawea Loyally Served Lewis and Clark: On the Expedition's Anniversary Here Is a Firsthand Account of Shoshoni Traditions About Her." *Spokesman Review,* 23 October 1955, 8–9.

———. "Sesquicentennial Remembrances: The Lewis and Clark Expedition as Seen Through the Eyes of the Indians in the Northern Rocky Mountains." *Montana: The Magazine of Western History* (April 1955): 31–39.

Clark, Ella, and Margot Edmonds. *Sacagawea of the Lewis and Clark Expedition.* Berkeley: University of California Press, 1979.

Clark, Helen. "Where Is the Grave of Sacajawea? Fort Washiakie, Wyoming or Fort Manuel, South Dakota? Which of these historic sites is the resting place of the Lewis and Clark guardian angel?" *Real West* 10.53 (May 1967): 21–23.

Clark, Robert. *History, Ideology, and Myth in American Fiction, 1823–52.* London: Macmillan, 1984.

Clarke, Charles G. *The Men of the Lewis and Clark Expedition: a biographical roster of the fifty one members and a composite diary of the activities from all known sources.* Glendale, CA: Arthur H. Clark, 1970.

Clift, Edith Connelly. "Sacajawea, Guide to the Lewis and Clark Expedition." *Prairie Lore* (April 1933): 194.

Cook, Liz. "American Indian Literatures in Servitude." *The Indian Historian* 10.1 (Winter 1977): 3–6.

Cooper, Alice. Unnamed Statue of Sacagawea. Sculpture in Bronze. 1905. Washington Park, Portland, Oregon.

Coues, Elliott, ed. *History of the Expedition under the Command of Lewis and Clark.* 3 vols. New York: Dover Publications, 1965. Originally published as *History of the Expedition under the Command of Lewis and Clark, To the Sources of the Missouri River, thence across the Rocky Mountains and down the Columbia River to the Pacific Ocean, performed during the Years 1804–5–6, by Order of the Government of the United States. A New Edition, Faithfully Reprinted from the Only Authorized Edition of 1814, with Copious Critical Commentary, Prepared upon Examination of Unpublished Official Archives and Many Other Sources of Information, Including a Diligent Study of the Original Manuscript Journals and Field Notebooks of the Explorers, together with a New Biographical and Bibliographical Introduction, New Maps, and Other Illustrations and a Complete Index.* 4 vols. 1893.

Crawford, Helen. "Sakakawea." *North Dakota Historical Quarterly* 1.3 (April 1927): 4–15.

Creel, George. "The Path of Empire." *Colliers, The National Weekly,* 17 April 1926, 7–8, 46.

Crow Dog, Mary, and Richard Erdoes. *Lakota Woman.* New York: Grove Weidenfeld, 1990.

Crunelle, Leonard. *Bird Woman.* Sculpture in Bronze. 1910. State Capitol Grounds, Bismarck, ND.

Cutright, Paul Russell. *A History of the Lewis and Clark Journals.* Norman: University of Oklahoma Press, 1976.

Day, Martin S. *The Many Meanings of Myth.* Lanham, MD: University Press of America, 1984.

Dearborn, Mary V. *Pocahontas's Daughters: Gender and Ethnicity in American Culture.* New York: Oxford University Press, 1986.

Defenbach, Byron. *Red Heroines of the Northwest.* Caldwell, ID: Caxton, 1929.

de Lauretis, Teresa, ed. *Feminist Studies/Critical Studies.* Bloomington: Indiana University Press, 1986.

Deloria, Ella C. *Waterlily.* Lincoln: University of Nebraska Press, 1988.

Deloria, Vine, Jr. *Custer Died for Your Sins.* New York: Avon, 1969.

———. "The Distinctive Status of Indian Rights." In Iverson, 237–48.

DeVoto, Bernard. *The Course of Empire.* Boston: Houghton Mifflin, 1952.

———. "Sacajawea—Inspirational Maid." In *The Red Man's West: True Stories of the Frontier Indians from Montana,* ed. Michael Kennedy, 119–20. New York: Hastings House, 1965.

———, ed. *The Journals of Lewis and Clark.* Boston: Houghton Mifflin, 1953.

Dillon, Richard. *Meriwether Lewis: A Biography.* New York: Coward-McCann, 1965.

Discover the Spirit! North Dakota '92–93 Vacation Guide. Bismarck: North Dakota Horizons, 1992.

Dorris, Michael. "The Grass Still Grows, The Rivers Still Flow: Contemporary Native Americans." *Daedalus* 110 (Spring 1981): 43–65.

———. "Native American Literature in an Ethnohistorical Context." *College English* 41.2 (October 1979): 147–62.

———. *A Yellow Raft in Blue Water.* New York: Henry Holt, 1987.

Doty, William G. *Mythography: The Study of Myths and Rituals.* Tuscaloosa: University of Alabama Press, 1986.

———. "Silent Myths Singing in the Blood: The Sites of Production and Consumption of Myths in a 'Mythless' Society." Unpublished paper, 1991.

Drake, Samuel G., ed. *Tragedies of the Wilderness; or, True and Authentic Narratives of Captives, Who Have Been Carried Away by the Indians from the Various Frontier Settlements of the United States, from the Earliest to the Present Times.* Boston: Antiquarian Bookstore and Institute, 1839.

Drury, Clifford. "Sacagawea's Death, 1812 or 1884?" *Oregon Historical Quarterly* 5 (1955): 211–25.

Dundes, Alan, ed. *Sacred Narrative: Readings in the Theory of Myth.* Berkeley: University of California Press, 1984.

Dye, Eva Emery. *The Conquest: The True Story of Lewis and Clark.* Chicago: A. C. McClurg, 1902.

Edge, Mary. "Sacajawea, A Wonderful Woman." *Indian School Journal: An Illustrated Monthly Magazine of the United States Indian Service* 19 (June 1919): 16–17.

Eidie, Ingvard Henry. *American Odyssey: The Journal of Lewis and Clark.* Chicago: Rand McNally, 1969.

Eliade, Mircea. "Cosmogonic Myth and 'Sacred History.' " In Dundes, 137–51.

———. *Myth and Reality.* Trans. Willard R. Trask. New York: Harper and Row, 1963.

Elliott, Karen Sue. "The Portrayal of American Indian Women in a Select Group of American Novels." Ph.D. diss., University of Minnesota, 1979.

Emmons, Della Gould. *Sacajawea of the Shoshones.* Portland: Binfords & Mort, 1943.

"Engineers to Sell Sakakawea Lots." *Grand Forks* [ND] *Herald,* 31 July 1971, 1.

Erdrich, Louise. "Captivity." *Jacklight*. New York: Henry Holt and Co., 1984.

———. "Indian Boarding School: The Runaways." In *Jacklight*. New York: Henry Holt and Co., 1984.

———. *Love Medicine*. New York: Bantam Books, 1984.

Ewers, John C. "The Static Images." In Bataille and Silet, 16–21.

"An Exclusive Presentation of the Hamilton Collection *Sacajawea* by David Wright: Premiere Issue in the *Noble American Indian Women Plate Collection*." Brochure advertisement. Jacksonville, FL: The Hamilton Collection, 1989.

"Exclusive! *Sacajawea* by Anna Lee Waldo." Brochure of New Releases from *Books on Tape, World's Largest Selection of Unabridged Audio Books*. May 1994, 2.

"Fair Warning." Review of *The Far Horizon*. *Newsweek*, 2 June 1955, 98.

Falkenhagen, Maria. "The Native American in Juvenile Fiction." *Natural History* 70 (November 1961): 4, 6–9.

The Far Horizon. 16mm., 108 min., B&W. Motion Picture. Paramount. 1955.

Farnsworth, Frances Joyce. *Winged Moccasins: The Story of Sacajawea*. New York: Julian Messner, 1954.

Ferguson, Mary Anne. *Images of Women in Literature*. 4th ed. Boston: Houghton Mifflin, 1986.

Fiedler, Leslie A. *The Return of the Vanishing American*. New York: Stein and Day, 1968.

Firth, Raymond. "The Plasticity of Myth: Cases from Tikopia." In Dundes, 207–24.

Fisher, Dexter, ed. *The Third Woman: Minority Women Writers of the U.S.* Boston: Houghton Mifflin, 1980.

Fisher, Philip. *Hard Facts: Setting and Form in the American Novel*. New York: Oxford University Press, 1987.

Fisher, Vardis. *Tale of Valor: A Novel of the Lewis and Clark Expedition*. Garden City, NY: Doubleday, 1958.

Fixico, Donald L. *Termination and Relocation: Federal Indian Policy, 1945–1960*. Albuquerque: University of New Mexico Press, 1986.

Fleming, E. McClung. "The American Image as Indian Princess, 1765–1783." *Winterthur Portfolio* 2 (1968): 65–81.

———. "Symbols of the United States: From Indian Queen to Uncle Sam." In *Frontiers of American Culture*, ed. Ray B. Browne et al., 1–22. Lafayette, ID: Purdue University Studies, 1968.

Fletcher, F. W. "Sacajawea." *Out West*, August 1905, 113–25.

Flexner, Eleanor. *Century of Struggle: The Women's Rights Movement in the United States*. Cambridge: Harvard University Press, 1959.

French, Philip. "The Indian in the Western Movie." In Bataille and Silet, 98–105.

Friar, Ralph E., and Natasha A. Friar. *The Only Good Indian . . . : The Hollywood Gospel.* New York: Drama Book Specialists, 1972.

Friedman, Albert B. "The Usable Myth: The Legends of Modern Mythmakers." In Hand, 37–46.

Fuller, George W. *A History of the Pacific Northwest with Special Emphasis on the Inland Empire.* New York: Alfred Knopf, 1938.

Fuller, Margaret. *Woman in the Nineteenth Century.* 1845. Reprint. Introduction by Bernard Rosenthal. New York: W. W. Norton, 1971.

———. *Summer on the Lakes in 1843.* Reprint. Chicago: University of Illinois Press, 1991.

Gardiner-Sharp, Abbie. *History of the Spirit Lake Massacre and Captivity of Miss Abbie Gardiner.* Des Moines: Iowa Printing, 1902.

Gass, Patrick. *Gass's Journal of the Lewis and Clark Expedition.* Edited by James Hosmer. Chicago: A. C. McClurg, 1904. Originally published as *Journal of the Voyage and Travels of A Corps of Discovery, Under the command of Captain Lewis and Captain Clarke of the army of the United States, from the Mouth of the River Missouri through the Interior Parts of North America to the Pacific Ocean, During the Years 1804, 1805, and 1806. Containing An authentic relation of the most interesting transactions during the expedition; a description of the country; and an account of its inhabitants, soil, climate, curiosities, and vegetable and animal productions.* Edited by David M'Keehan. 1811.

Geertz, Clifford. *The Interpretation of Cultures.* New York: Basic Books, 1973.

Georgi-Findlay, Brigitte. "The Frontiers of Native American Women's Writing: Sarah Winnemucca's *Life among the Piutes.*" In *New Voices in Native American Literary Criticism,* ed. Arnold Krupat, 222–52. Washington: Smithsonian Institution Press, 1993.

Gerdts, William H. "The Marble Savage." *Art in America* 62.4 (July–August 1974): 64–70.

Ghent, W. J. *The Early Far West: A Narrative Outline, 1540–1850.* New York: Longman's Green, 1931.

Giannetti, Louis. *Understanding Movies.* Englewood Cliffs: Prentice-Hall, 1972.

Giannetti, Louis, and Scott Eyman. *Flashback: A Brief History of Film.* Englewood Cliffs: Prentice-Hall, 1986.

Gitlin, Todd. "The Classics Must Be Broadened to Include Multicultural Literature." In *Culture War: Opposing Viewpoints,* ed. Fred Whitehead, 79–83. San Diego: Greenhaven Press, 1994.

Gleason, Philip. "American Identity and Americanization." In *Harvard Encyclopedia of American Ethnic Groups*, 31–57.

Goddard, Donald. "Shaped From Earth, Immortalized in Bronze: Sculptor Harry Jackson's *Sacagawea*." *The American West* 17.2 (March–April 1980): 14–15, 56.

Goddard, Donald, Larry Pointer, and Marjorie Spitz. *Monument in Bronze: Sacagawea by Harry Jackson*. Cody, WY: Buffalo Bill Historical Center, 1980.

Graebner, Norman A. *Manifest Destiny*. New York: Bobbs-Merrill, 1968.

Green, Rayna. *Native American Women: A Contextual Bibliography*. Bloomington: Indiana University Press, 1983.

———. "The Only Good Indian: The Image of the Indian in American Vernacular Culture." Ph.D. diss., Indiana University, 1973.

———. "The Pocahontas Perplex: The Image of Indian Women in American Culture." *Massachusetts Review* 16.4 (Autumn 1975): 698–714.

———. "Review Essay: Native American Women." *Journal of Women in Culture and Society: Studies in Change* 6.2 (Winter 1980): 248–67.

———. *That's What She Said: Contemporary Poetry and Fiction by Native American Women*. Bloomington: Indiana University Press, 1984.

———. *Women in American Indian Society*. New York: Chelsea House, 1992.

Gyles, John. *Memoirs of Odd Adventures, Strange Deliverances, Etc., in the Captivity of John Gyles, Esq., Commander of the Garrison on St. George River, in the District of Maine*. 1736. In *Tragedies of the Wilderness; or, True and Authentic Narratives of Captives, Who Have Been Carried Away by the Indians from the Various Frontier Settlements of the United States, from the Earliest to the Present Times*, ed. Samuel G. Drake. Boston: Antiquarian Bookstore and Institute, 1839.

Hagan, William. "Private Property: The Indian's Door to Civilization." *Ethno-history* 3.2 (Spring 1956): 126–35.

Haines, Francis. "Don't Stereotype Our Indians!" *Oregon Education Journal* 27 (February 1953): 11, 30.

Haines, Madge, and Leslie Morrill. *Lewis and Clark: Explorers to the West*. New York: Abingdon Press, 1959.

Hall, Charles Gilbert. *The Great Adventure*. New York: Thomas Nelson and Sons, 1935.

Hamilton, Wynette. "The Correlation between Societal Attitudes and Those of American Authors in the Depiction of American Indians, 1607–1860." *American Indian Quarterly* 1 (Spring 1974): 1–26.

Hand, Gail Stewart. "Play is clever, moving, riveting." Review of *Sakakawea: The Woman with Many Names,* by William Borden and Thomas Peterson. *Grand Forks* [ND] *Herald,* 16 September 1989, 1A.

Hand, Wayland D., ed. *American Folk Legend: A Symposium.* Berkeley: University of California Press, 1971.

Harper, Ida Husted, ed. *The History of Woman Suffrage.* Vol. 5: 1900–1920. New York: J. J. Little and Ives, 1922.

Harry Jackson: Thirty Works. Cody, WY: Harry Jackson Studios, 1990.

Hartman, Hedy. "A Brief Review of the Native American in American Cinema." *Indian Historian* 9.3 (Summer 1973): 27–29.

Hartung, Philip T. "The Screen." Review of *The Far Horizon. Commonweal* 62 (10 June 1955): 256.

Harvard Encyclopedia of American Ethnic Groups. Edited by Stephen Thernstrom, Ann Orlov, and Oscar Handlin. Cambridge: Harvard University Press, 1980.

Haslam, Gerald W. *Forgotten Pages of American Literature.* Boston: Houghton Mifflin, 1970.

Haupt, Carol Magdalene. "The Image of the American Indian Female in the Biographical Literature and Social Studies Textbooks of the Elementary Schools." Ph.D. diss., Rutgers University, 1984.

Hebard, Grace Raymond. *The Pathbreakers from River to Ocean: The Story of the Great West from the Time of Coronado to the Present.* Glendale, CA: Arthur H. Clark, 1932.

———. "Pilot of First White Men to Cross the American Continent: Identification of the Indian Girl who Led the Lewis and Clark Expedition over the Rocky Mountains in their Unparalleled Journey into the Mysteries of the Western World in Recognition of Sacajawea as the Woman Who Guided the Explorers to the New Golden Empire." *Journal of American History* 1 (1907): 467–84.

———. *Sacajawea: A guide and interpreter of the Lewis and Clark Expedition, with an account of the travels of Toussaint Charbonneau, and of Jean Baptiste, the expedition papoose.* 1932. Reprint. Glendale, CA: Arthur H. Clark, 1957.

Hennessy, Mary T. "Sakakawea, Bird Woman." *University of North Dakota Alumni Review* 72.2 (October/November 1989): 5.

Henry, Jeannette, ed. *The American Indian Reader: Literature.* San Francisco: Indian Historian Press, 1973.

Henry, Will. [Henry Wilson Allen]. *The Gates of the Mountains.* 1963. Reprint. Boston: Gregg Press, 1980.

Henry, William A. "Beyond the Melting Pot." *Time,* 9 April 1990, 28–31.

Herbst, Laura. "That's One Good Indian: Unacceptable Images in Children's Novels." *Top of the News* (January 1975): 192–98.

Hersh, Blanche Glassman. *The Slavery of Sex: Feminist Abolitionists in America.* Chicago: University of Illinois Press, 1978.

Hilger, Michael. *The American Indian in Film.* Metuchen, NJ: Scarecrow Press, 1986.

Hirschfelder, Arlene. *American Indian Stereotypes in the World of Children: A Reader and Bibliography.* Metuchen, NJ: Scarecrow Press, 1982.

Hobson, Geary. *The Remembered Earth: An Anthology of Contemporary Native American Literature.* Albuquerque: University of New Mexico Press, 1979.

Hodge, Frederick Webb. *Handbook of American Indians North of Mexico.* 2 vols. Washington, DC: Government Printing Office, 1910.

Hofstadter, Richard. *The Age of Reform: From Bryan to FDR.* New York: Alfred A. Knopf, 1965.

Holloway, David. *Lewis and Clark and the Crossing of North America.* New York: Saturday Review Press, 1974.

Holm, Tom. "Fighting a White Man's War: The Extent and Legacy of American Indians' Participation in World War II." In Iverson, 149–68.

Honko, Lauri. "The Problem of Defining Myth." In Dundes, 41–52.

Hopkins, Sarah Winnemucca. *Life among the Piutes: Their Wrongs and Claims.* Edited by Mrs. Horace Mann. 1883. Reprint. Bishop, CA: Sierra Media, 1969.

Horsman, Reginald. *Expansion and American Indian Policy: 1783–1812.* East Lansing: Michigan State University Press, 1967.

———. "Scientific Racism and the American Indian in the Mid-Nineteenth Century." *American Quarterly* 27.2 (May 1975): 152–68.

Hosmer, James K. *History of the Expedition of Captains Lewis and Clark 1804–5–6.* 2 vols. Chicago: A. C. McClurg, 1903.

———. *The History of the Louisiana Purchase.* New York: D. Appleton, 1902.

Hough, Emerson. *The Magnificent Adventure: This Being the Story of the World's Greatest Exploration, and the Romance of a very Gallant Gentleman: A Novel.* New York: D. Appleton, 1916.

Houts, Kathleen C., and Rosemary S. Bahr. "Stereotyping of Indians and Blacks in Magazine Cartoons." In Bahr, Chadwick, and Day, 110–14.

Howard, Harold P. *Sacajawea.* Norman: University of Oklahoma Press, 1971.

Howard, Helen. "The Mystery of Sacagawea's Death." *The Northwest Quarterly* 5 (January 1967): 1–11.

Hoxie, Frederick E. *A Final Promise: The Campaign to Assimilate the Indians, 1880–1920.* Lincoln: University of Nebraska Press, 1984.

Humphrey, Grace. *Women in American History.* Freeport, NY: Books for Libraries Press, 1919.

Hungry Wolf, Beverly. *The Ways of My Grandmothers.* New York: William Morrow and Co., 1980.

Hurt, R. Douglas. *Indian Agriculture in America: Prehistory to the Present.* Lawrence: University of Kansas Press, 1987.

"Indians Inspect Statue of Bird Woman." *Minot* [ND] *Optic,* 31 January 1910, 1.

Iseminger, Gordon L., and Mary Louise Defender Wilson. "Who Was Sakakawea?" *Sakakawea: The Woman with Many Names,* playnotes, 13–16.

Iverson, Peter, ed. *The Plains Indians of the Twentieth Century.* Norman: University of Oklahoma Press, 1985.

Jackson, Donald, ed. *Letters of the Lewis and Clark Expedition with Related Documents 1783–1854.* Urbana: University of Illinois Press, 1962.

Jackson, Harry. *Sacagawea.* Sculpture in Bronze, Polychrome. 1977. Buffalo Bill Historical Center, Cody, Wyoming.

Jahner, Elaine. "A Critical Approach to American Indian Literature." In *Studies in American Indian Literature: Critical Essays and Course Designs,* ed. Paula Gunn Allen, 211–24. New York: Modern Language Association, 1983.

James, Edward, ed. "Sacajawea." In *Notable American Women, 1607–1950: A Biographical Dictionary,* vol. 1, 218–19. Cambridge: Harvard University Press, 1971.

Jassem, Kate. *Sacajawea: Wilderness Guide.* Mahwah, NJ: Troll Associates, 1979.

Jehlen, Myra. "Introduction: Beyond Transcendence." In Berkovitch and Jehlen, 1–19.

Jennings, Francis. *The Invasion of America: Indians, Colonialism, and the Cant of Conquest.* New York: W. W. Norton, 1975.

Johnson, Larry. "Indians Seek Control of Lake Area." *Bismarck* [ND] *Tribune,* 7 February 1981, 1.

Johnston, Johanna. *The Indians and the Strangers.* New York: Dodd, Mead, 1972.

Jones, Maldwin. *American Immigration.* Chicago: University of Chicago Press, 1960.

Josephy, Alvin. *Now That the Buffalo's Gone: A Study of Today's American Indians.* New York: Alfred A. Knopf, 1982.

Judson, Katharine B. *Montana: The Land of Shining Mountains.* Chicago: A. C. McClurg, 1909.

Kammen, Michael. "The Problem of American Exceptionalism: A Reconsideration." *American Quarterly* 45.1 (March 1993): 1–33.

Kaufmann, Donald. "The Indian as Media Hand-Me-Down." In Bataille and Silet, 22–34.

Keizer, Albert. *The Indian in American Literature.* New York: Farrar, Straus, and Giroux, 1975.

Kelley, Jane Holden. *Yaqui Women: Contemporary Life Histories.* Lincoln: University of Nebraska Press, 1978.

Kelly, Fanny. *My Captivity Among the Sioux Indians.* New York: Corinth Books, 1962.

Kessler-Harris, Alice. *Out to Work: A History of Wage-Earning Women in the United States.* New York: Oxford University Press, 1982.

King, Tom. Review of *Love Medicine,* by Louise Erdrich. *Western American Literature* 21.1 (May 1986): 62–63.

Kingston, C. S. "Sacajawea as Guide: The Evaluation of a Legend." *Pacific North West Quarterly* 35 (1944): 3–18.

Kirk, G. S. "On Defining Myths." In Dundes, 53–61.

Klawans, Stuart. "The Greatest Story Ever Told, Or, When Worlds Collide." Review of *Native Roots: How the Indians Enriched America,* by Jack Weatherford. *Voice Literary Supplement* 100 (November 1991): 10–11.

Kolodny, Annette. *The Land Before Her: Fantasy and Experience of the American Frontiers, 1630–1860.* Chapel Hill: University of North Carolina Press, 1984.

———. *The Lay of the Land: Metaphor as Experience and History in American Life and Letters.* Chapel Hill: University of North Carolina Press, 1975.

Kraditor, Aileen. *The Ideas of the Woman Suffrage Movement, 1890–1920.* New York: Columbia University Press, 1965.

Kroeber, Karl, ed. *Studies in American Indian Literatures* 9.1 (Winter 1985): 1–28.

Krupat, Arnold. *The Voice in the Margin: Native American Literature and the Canon.* Berkeley: University of California Press, 1989.

Lakoff, George, and Mark Johnson. *Metaphors We Live By.* Chicago: University of Chicago Press, 1980.

Lamar, Howard, ed. *The Reader's Encyclopedia of the American West.* New York: Thomas Y. Crowell, 1977.

Larson, Charles R. *American Indian Fiction.* Albuquerque: University of New Mexico Press, 1978.

Laut, Agnes. "What the Portland Exposition Really Celebrates." *Review of Reviews* (April 1905): 428–32.

Lavender, David. *Land of Giants: The Drive to the Pacific Northwest, 1750–1950*. Garden City, NY: Doubleday, 1956.

Lawson, Michael L. "Federal Water Projects and Indian Lands: The Pick-Sloan Plan, a Case Study." In Iverson, 169–85.

Leechman, Douglas. "The Indian in Literature." *Queens Quarterly* 50 (May 1943): 155–63.

Lewis, Meriwether, and William Clark. *The Lewis and Clark Expedition*. 3 vols. Philadelphia: J. B. Lippincott, 1961. Originally published as *History of the Expedition under the Command of Captains Lewis and Clark to the Sources of the Missouri, Thence Across the Rocky Mountains and Down the Columbia River to the Pacific Ocean. Performed During the Years 1804–5–6. By Order of the Government of the United States*. 2 vols. 1814.

Lewis and Clark at the Great Divide. You Are There [Television] *Series*. CBS, 16mm., 21 min. 1971.

Limerick, Patricia Nelson. *The Legacy of Conquest: The Unbroken Past of the American West*. New York: W. W. Norton, 1987.

———. "Some Advice to Liberals on Coping with Their Conservative Critics." *Chronicle of Higher Education*, 4 May 1994, B1–2.

Link, Arthur S., and Richard L. McCormick. *Progressivism*. Arlington Heights, IL: Harlan Davidson, 1983.

Loos, John Louis. "A Biography of William Clark, 1770–1813." Ph.D. diss., Washington University, 1953.

Luttig, John C. *Journal of Fur-Trading Expedition on the Upper Missouri, 1812–13*. Ed. Stella M. Drum. New York: Argosy-Antiquarian, 1964.

Macgregor, Gordon. *Warriors without Weapons: A Study of the Society and Personality Development of the Pine Ridge Sioux*. Chicago: University of Chicago Press, 1946.

Madden, David. *A Primer of the Novel: For Readers and Writers*. Metuchen, NJ: Scarecrow Press, 1980.

Mankiller, Wilma, and Michael Wallis. *Mankiller: A Chief and Her People*. New York: St. Martin's Press, 1993.

Martin, James Kirby, et al. *America and Its People*. Glenview, IL: Scott, Foresman, 1989.

Matusow, Allen J. *The Unraveling of America: A History of Liberalism in the 1960s*. New York: Harper and Row, 1984.

McGuire, Amy Jane. *The Indian Girl Who Led Them: Sacajawea*. Portland: J. K. Gill, 1905.

McNickle, D'Arcy. "American Indians who Never Were." *Indian Historian* 3.3 (Summer 1970): 4–7.

McTaggart, Fred. "American Indian Literature: Contexts for Understanding." In *The Worlds between Two Rivers: Perspectives on American Indians in Iowa*, ed. Gretchen M. Bataille, David M. Gradwohl, and Charles L. P. Silet, 3–9. Ames: Iowa State University Press, 1978.

Medicine, Beatrice. "Indian Women and the Renaissance of Traditional Religion." In *Sioux Indian Religion: Tradition and Innovation*, ed. Raymond J. DeMallie and Douglas R. Parks, 159–72. Norman: University of Oklahoma Press, 1987.

———. "Indian Women: Tribal Identity as Status Quo." In *Women's Nature: Rationalizations of Inequality*, ed. Marian Lowe and Ruth Hubbard, 63–74. New York: Pergamon, 1983.

Meek, Ronald L. *Social Science and the Ignoble Savage*. Cambridge: Cambridge University Press, 1976.

Mehta, Naushad, Susan Tift, and Richard Woodbury. "Bigots in the Ivory Tower: An alarming rise in hatred roils U.S. campuses." *Time*, 7 May 1990, 104–6.

Mehta, Naushad, Sylvester Monroe, and Don Winbush. "Citizenship: Forging a New Identity." *Time*, 9 April 1990, 31.

Merk, Frederick. *Manifest Destiny and Mission in American History: A Reinterpretation*. New York: Alfred A. Knopf, 1963.

Meyer, Roy. *History of the Santee Sioux: United States Indian Policy on Trial*. Lincoln: University of Nebraska Press, 1967.

Milkman, Ruth. *Gender at Work: The Dynamic of Job Segregation by Sex during World War II*. Chicago: University of Illinois Press, 1987.

Minton, Lynn. "Lynn Minton Reports: Fresh Voices." *Parade*, 3 July 1994, 12.

Momaday, N. Scott. *House Made of Dawn*. New York: Harper and Row, 1966.

Moraga, Cherrie. "From a Long Line of Vendidas: Chicanas and Feminism." In de Lauretis, 173–90.

Moraga, Cherrie, and Toni Cade Bambara, eds. *This Bridge Called My Back: Writings by Radical Women of Color*. New York: Kitchen Table/Women of Color Press, 1983.

Morison, Samuel Eliot, Henry Steele Commager, and William E. Leuchtenburg, eds. *A Concise History of the American Republic*. 1971. Reprint. Oxford: Oxford University Press, 1983.

Mossiker, Frances. *Pocahontas: The Life and the Legend*. New York: Alfred A. Knopf, 1976.

Munves, James. *We Were There with Lewis and Clark*. New York: Grosset and Dunlap, 1959.

Murphy, Sharon. "American Indians and the Media: Neglect and Stereotype." *Journalism History* 6.2 (Summer 1979): 39–43.

Nash, Jeffrey, et al., eds. *The American People: Creating a Nation and a Society.* New York: Harper and Row, 1986.

"Newsmen Tour State's Biggest Lake." *Bismarck* [ND] *Tribune,* 16 July 1955, 1.

The New York Times Films Reviews, 1913–1968. Review of *Far Horizon.* Vol. 4: *1949–58.* New York: Arno Press, 1970.

Nichols, Roger L. "The Indian in the Dime Novel." *Journal of American Culture* 5 (Summer 1982): 49–55.

"North Dakota Wants Land for Tourism, Recreation." *Bismarck* [ND] *Tribune,* 15 October 1982, 1.

Olivia, Leo E. "The American Indian in Recent Historical Fiction: A Review Essay." *Prairie Scout* 1 (1973): 95–120.

Olson, Jeff. "Resorts Likely to Stay Private." *Bismarck* [ND] *Tribune,* 26 December 1992, 1, 14a.

"1 of every 50 marriages is interracial." *The Orlando* [FL] *Sentinel,* 12 February 1993, 8.

Ortiz, Simon J. *Earth Power Coming: Short Fiction in Native American Literature.* Tsaile, AZ: Navajo Community College Press, 1983.

Ortner, Sherry B. "Is Female to Male as Nature Is to Culture?" In *Women, Culture, and Society,* ed. Michelle Zimbalist Rosaldo and Louise Lamphere, 67–87. Stanford: Stanford University Press, 1974.

Osborne, Kelsie Ramey. *Peaceful Conquest: Story of the Lewis and Clark Expedition.* Portland: Beattie and Co., 1955.

Osgood, Ernest Staples, ed. *The Field Notes of Captain William Clark, 1803–5.* New Haven: Yale University Press, 1964.

Otis, D. S. *The Dawes Act and the Allotment of Indian Lands.* 1934. Reprint. Norman: University of Oklahoma Press, 1973.

Palmer, Bertha R. "Sakakawea Statue Recalls Early History." *Little Chronicle* [North Dakota Federation of Women's Clubs Newsletter]. Reprint. *The* [Fargo, ND] *Forum,* 15 December 1925, 1.

Paredes, Americo, ed. and trans. *Folktales of Mexico.* Chicago: University of Chicago Press, 1970.

Patterson, G. W. "Trail of Sakakawea Memorials Pursued." *Minot* [ND] *Daily News,* 8 April 1967, 11.

Pearce, Roy Harvey. *Savagism and Civilization: A Study of the Indian and the American Mind.* Berkeley: University of California Press, 1988. Originally published as *The Savages of America.* 1953.

———. "The Significances of the Captivity Narrative." *American Literature* 19 (March 1947): 1–20.

Peattie, Donald Culross. *Forward the Nation.* New York: G. P. Putnam's Sons, 1942.

Pine, Gerald J., and Asa G. Hilliard III. "Schools Should Emphasize Ethnicity." In *Racism in America: Opposing Viewpoints,* ed. William Dudley, 193–200. San Diego: Greenhaven Press, 1991.

Plumb, J. H. "America: Illusion and Reality." *American Heritage: The Magazine of History* 27.5 (August 1976): 16–22.

Polenberg, Richard. *One Nation Divisible: Class, Race, and Ethnicity in the United States Since 1938.* New York: Viking Press, 1980.

Portales, Marco. "People With Holes in Their Lives." Review of *Love Medicine,* by Louise Erdrich. *New York Times Book Review,* 23 December 1984, 6.

Powers, Alfred. *History of Oregon Literature.* Portland: Metropolitan Press, 1935.

Powers, Marla N. *Oglala Women: Myth, Ritual, and Reality.* Chicago: University of Chicago Press, 1986.

"Prairie Flower." The Princesses of the Plains Series. Advertisement for The Hamilton Collection Limited Edition Plate. Illustration in *Country Living,* May 1993, inset.

Pratt, Julius W. "The Origins of Manifest Destiny." *American Historical Review* (July 1927): 795–98.

Price, John A. "The Stereotyping of North American Indians in Motion Pictures." *Ethnohistory* 20.2 (Spring 1973): 153–71.

Pringle, Louise A. "Saccajawea of the Shoshones." *American Mercury* 81 (July 1955): 147–50.

Prucha, Francis Paul. *The Great Father: The United States Government and the American Indians.* 2 vols. Lincoln: University of Nebraska Press, 1984.

Quaife, Milo M., ed. *The Journals of Captain Meriwether Lewis and Sergeant John Ordway: Kept on the Expedition of Western Exploration, 1803–1806.* Madison: State Historical Society of Wisconsin, 1916.

Radway, Janice A. *Reading the Romance: Women, Patriarchy, and Popular Literature.* Chapel Hill: University of North Carolina Press, 1984.

Ramsey, Jarold. *Reading the Fire: Essays in the Traditional Indian Literatures of the Far West.* Lincoln: University of Nebraska Press, 1983.

———. "The Teacher of Modern American Indian Writing as Ethnographer and Critic." *College English* 41.2 (October 1979): 163–69.

Rees, John E. "Madame Charbonneau: The Indian Woman Who Accompanied the Lewis and Clark Expedition. 1804–1806. How she received her Indian Name and what became of her." Salmon, ID: Lemhi County Historical Society, 1970.

———. "The Shoshoni Contribution to Lewis and Clark." *Idaho Yesterdays* 2.2 (Summer 1958): 2–13.

Reid, Russell, ed. *Lewis and Clark in North Dakota: The original manuscript journals and the text of the Biddle edition during the time the expedition remained in North Dakota.* Bismarck: State Historical Society of North Dakota, 1947.

———. *Sakakawea: The Bird Woman.* Bismarck: State Historical Society of North Dakota, 1950.

———. "Sakakawea—The Bird Woman." *The Museum Review of The State Historical Society of North Dakota* 1.2 (February 1946): 1–4.

Remley, David. "Sacajawea of Myth and History." In *Women and Western American Literature,* ed. Helen Winter Stauffer and Susan J. Rosowski, 70–89. Troy, NY: Whitston, 1982.

"Reservoir's 'Sakakawea' But Dam Still Garrison." *Bismarck* [ND] *Tribune,* 5 July 1967, 1.

"Revenge of the Chippewa Witch." Review of *Tracks,* by Louise Erdrich. *Commonweal,* 4 November 1988, 596–97.

Richburg, James R. "Media and the American Indian: Ethnographical, Historical, and Contemporary Issues." *Social Education* 36 (May 1972): 526–33.

Riley, Patricia. "Adventures of an Indian Princess." In *Earth Song, Sky Spirit: Short Stories of the Contemporary Native American Experience,* intro. Clifford E. Trafzer, 135–40. New York: Doubleday, 1993.

Robinson, William G. "Sakakawea-Sacajawea: When and Where Did the Indian Bird Woman Die and Where Was She Buried?" *The Wi-iyohi: Bulletin of the South Dakota Historical Society* 10.6 (September 1956): 1–8.

Ronda, James P. *Lewis and Clark among the Indians.* Lincoln: University of Nebraska Press, 1984.

Rosenberg, Emily. *Spreading the American Dream: American Economic and Cultural Expansion, 1890–1945.* New York: Farrar, Straus, Giroux, 1982.

Ross, Nancy Wilson. "Heroine in Buckskin." *Readers' Digest* 44 (February 1944): 118–20.

Rowland, Della. *The Story of Sacajawea, Guide to Lewis and Clark: A Yearling Book.* New York: Dell, 1989.

Rowlandson, Mary. *A True Story of the Captivity and Restoration of Mrs. Mary Rowlandson, A Minister's Wife in New England: Wherein is Set Forth, The Cruel and Inhumane Usage she Underwent amongst the Heathens, for Eleven Weeks time: And her Deliverance from them.* 1632. Reprint. Vol. 1. Garland Library of Narratives of North American Captivities. New York: Garland, 1977.

Ruoff, A. LaVonne Brown. "Alienation and the Female Principle in *Winter in the Blood.*" *American Indian Quarterly* 4 (1978): 107–21.

———. "American Indian Authors, 1774–1889." In *Critical Essays of*

Native American Literature, ed. Andrew Wiget, 191–201. Boston: G. K. Hall, 1985.

———. *American Indian Literatures: An Introduction, Bibliographic Review, and Selected Bibliography.* New York: Modern Language Association, 1990.

———. *Literatures of the American Indian.* New York: Chelsea House Publishers, 1991.

———. "Old Traditions and New Forms." In *Studies in American Indian Literature: Critical Essays and Course Designs,* ed. Paula Gunn Allen, 147–67. New York: Modern Language Association, 1983.

"Sacajawea: A Brave and Noble American Heroine." Advertisement for The Hamilton Collection Limited Edition Plate. Illustration in *Parade,* 22 October 1989, 15.

"Sacajawea: A Fine Art Tribute to a Bold and Brave American Indian Heroine." Advertisement for The Hamilton Collection Limited Edition Sculpture. Illustration in *Parade,* 16 May 1993, 13.

"Sacajawea: A Symposium." *Annals of Wyoming* 13 (July 1941): 162–94.

"Sakakawea." *Evening Times* [Portland], 18 January 1907, 3.

Sakakawea (Bird Woman) Statue Notes. Fargo, ND: Porte Company, 1906.

Sakakawea—The Indian Girl Who Helped to Open an Empire. Bismarck: State Library Commission, 1916.

Sakakawea: The Woman with Many Names. Playnotes. Grand Forks: University of North Dakota Press, 1989.

"Sa-ka-ka-we'-a Trail. Named for the Indian Bird Woman. Halliday First Town after Crossing the Little Missouri." *Halliday* [ND] *Promoter,* 16 June 1922, 1.

Sanders, Ronald. "Literature of the Indian: A Critique." In Jeannette Henry, 219–44.

Sando, Joe S. "White-Created Myths about the Native American." *Indian Historian* 4.4 (Winter 1970): 10–11.

Savage, William W., Jr. *Indian Life: Transforming an American Myth.* Norman: University of Oklahoma Press, 1977.

Schlissel, Lillian. *Women's Diaries of the Westward Journey.* New York: Schocken Press, 1982.

Scholes, Robert. "An Approach through Genre." In *Towards a Poetics of Fiction,* ed. Mark Spilka, 41–51. Bloomington: Indiana University Press, 1977.

———. *Protocols of Reading.* New Haven: Yale University Press, 1989.

———. *Semiotics and Interpretation.* New Haven: Yale University Press, 1982.

Schultz, James Willard. *Bird Woman (Sacajawea): The Guide of Lewis and Clark: Her Own Story Now First Given to the World.* Boston: Houghton Mifflin, 1918.

Scott, L. T. *Sacajawea (The Bird Woman): The Unsung Heroine of Montana: 1805–1806.* Dillon, MT: The Montana Federation of Women's Clubs, 1915.

Seaver, James Everett. *A Narrative of the Life of Mrs. Mary Jemison, Who was taken by the Indians in the year 1755, when only about twelve years of age, and has continued to reside amongst them to the present time.* Cananadeigua: J. D. Bemis, 1824.

Segal, Charles M., and David C. Stineback. *Puritans, Indians, and Manifest Destiny.* New York: G. P. Putnam's, 1977.

Seibert, Jerry. *Sacajawea: Guide to Lewis and Clark.* Boston: Houghton Mifflin, 1960.

Seymour, Flora Warren. *Sacagawea: Bird Girl.* New York: Howard W. Sams, 1945.

———. *Women of Trail and Wigwam.* New York: Women's Press, 1930.

Shaughnessy, Tim. "White Stereotypes of Indians." *Journal of American Indian Education* 19.2 (January 1978): 20–24.

Shaul, David L. "The Meaning of the Name Sacajawea." *Annals of Wyoming* 44 (Fall 1972): 237–40.

Sheehan, Bernard. *Seeds of Extinction: Jefferson, Philanthropy, and the American Indian.* Chapel Hill: University of North Carolina Press, 1973.

Sheppard, R. Z. "Bloodlines." Review of *Tracks,* by Louise Erdrich. *Time,* 12 September 1988, 80, 82.

Shoemaker, Nancy. "Point of View: Teaching the Truth About the History of the American West." *Chronicle of Higher Education,* 27 October 1993, A48.

Silberman, Robert. "Opening the Text: *Love Medicine* and the Return of the Native American Woman." In *Narrative Chance,* ed. Gerald Vizenor, 101–20. Norman: University of Oklahoma Press, 1993.

Silko, Leslie Marmon. *Ceremony.* New York: Penguin Books, 1977.

Skold, Betty W. *Sacajawea: The Story of an American Indian.* Minneapolis: Dillon Press, 1977.

Slotkin, Richard. "Myth and Literature in a New World." In Bataille and Silet, 5–8.

———. "Myth and the Production of History." In Berkovitch and Jehlen, 70–90.

———. *Regeneration through Violence: The Mythology of the American Frontier, 1600–1860.* Middletown, CT: Wesleyan University Press, 1973.

Smith, Dwight L. "Shawnee Captivity Ethnography." *Ethnohistory* 2 (1955): 29–41.

Smith, Helen Krebs, ed. *With Her Own Wings: Historical Sketches, Reminiscences, and Anecdotes of Pioneer Women.* Portland: Beattie and Co., 1948.

Smith, Henry Nash. *Virgin Land: The American West as Symbol and Myth.* Cambridge: Harvard University Press, 1950.

———. "Symbol and Idea in *Virgin Land.*" In Berkovitch and Jehlen, 21–35.

Smith, James. *An Account of the Remarkable Occurrences in the Life and Travels of Colonel James Smith, (Late a Citizen of Bourbon County, Kentucky,) during his Captivity with the Indians, in the Years 1755, '56, '57, '58 and '59.* In Drake, 178–234.

Smith, Sherry L. "Beyond Princess and Squaw: Army Officers' Perceptions of Indian Women." In Armitage and Jameson, 63–75.

Snyder, Gerald S. *In the Footsteps of Lewis and Clark.* Washington, DC: National Geographical Society, 1970.

———. "Westways Women: The Girl of History Who Became a Woman of Fable." *Westways* 66.3 (March 1974): 36–39, 71, 73.

Sollors, Werner. *Beyond Ethnicity: Consent and Descent in American Culture.* New York: Oxford University Press, 1986.

———. *The Invention of Ethnicity.* New York: Oxford University Press, 1989.

Sprague, William F. *Women and the West: A Short Social History.* Boston: Christopher Publishing, 1940.

"Statue of Sakakawea May Be Put in Hall of Fame." *Bismarck* [ND] *Tribune,* 30 October 1945, 3.

"Statue Unveiling at State Capitol Is Unique Event." *Bismarck* [ND] *Tribune,* 14 October 1910, 1, 6, 8, 12.

Stedman, Raymond William. *Shadows of the Indian: Stereotypes in American Culture.* Norman: University of Oklahoma Press, 1982.

Steiner, Stan. *The Vanishing White Man.* New York: Harper and Row, 1976.

Stensland, Anna Lee. "The Indian Presence in American Literature." *English Journal* 66 (March 1977): 37–41.

Stensland, Anna Lee, and Aune M. Fadum, eds. *Literature by and about the American Indian: An Annotated Bibliography for Junior and Senior High School Students.* Duluth, MN: National Council of Teachers of English, 1979.

Stevens, William Oliver. *Famous Women of America.* New York: Dodd, Mead, 1950.

Stoodt, Barbara D., and Sandra Ignizio. "The American Indian in Children's Literature." *Language Arts* 53 (January 1976): 17–21.

"The Story of the 'Bird Woman.'" *The* [Portland] *Oregonian,* 9 April 1916, 5.

Strouse, Jean. "In the Heart of the Heartland: *Tracks.*" Review of *Tracks,* by Louise Erdrich. *The New York Times Book Review,* 2 October 1988, 1, 41–42.

Sundquist, Asebrit. *Pocahontas & Co.: The Fictional American Indian Woman in Nineteenth-Century Literature: A Study of Method.* Atlantic Highlands, NJ: Humanities Press International, 1987.

Sweney, Kathryn. "She speaks for Sakakawea: Oral Tradition tells her story." *Grand Forks* [ND] *Herald,* 14 September 1989, A1.

Taber, Ronald W. "Sacajawea and the Suffragettes: An Interpretation of a Myth." *Pacific Northwest Quarterly* 58.1 (January 1967): 7–13.

Takaki, Ronald T. *Iron Cages: Race and Culture in Nineteenth-Century America.* New York: Alfred A. Knopf, 1979.

Taylor, Graham D. *The New Deal and American Indian Tribalism: The Administration of the Indian Reorganization Act, 1934–45.* Lincoln: University of Nebraska Press, 1980.

Thwaites, Reuben Gold, ed. *Original Journals of the Lewis and Clark Expedition, 1804–1806.* 8 vols. New York: Dodd Mead, 1904–1906.

Tomkins, Calvin. *The Lewis and Clark Trail.* New York: Harper and Row, 1965.

Tompkins, Jane. "'Indians': Textuality, Morality, and the Problem of History." *Critical Inquiry* 13 (Autumn 1986): 101–19.

———. *Sensational Designs: The Cultural Work of American Fiction 1790–1860.* New York: Oxford University Press, 1985.

———. *West of Everything: The Inner Life of Westerns.* New York: Oxford University Press, 1992.

Towers, Robert. "Roughing It." Review of *Tracks,* by Louise Erdrich. *New York Review of Books,* 10 November 1988, 10.

———. "Uprooted." Review of *Love Medicine,* by Louise Erdrich. *New York Review of Books,* 11 April 1985, 36.

Trennert, Robert A. "Popular Imagery and the American Indian: A Centennial View." *New Mexico Historical Review* 51.3 (July 1976): 215–32.

Trosper, Ronald L. "American Indian Relative Ranching Efficiency." *American Economic Review* 68 (1978): 503–14.

Troy, Anne. "The Indian in Adolescent Novels." *The Indian Historian* 8.4 (Winter 1975): 32–35.

Turner, Frederick Jackson. *The Frontier in American History.* Malabar, FL: Robert E. Kreiger, 1920.

———. *Reuben Gold Thwaites: A Memorial Address.* Madison: State Historical Society of Wisconsin, 1914.

————. *The Significance of Frontier in American History.* Edited by Harold P. Simonson. New York: Frederick Ungar Press, 1963.

Turner, Victor. *Dramas, Fields, and Metaphors: Symbolic Action in Human Society.* Ithaca: Cornell University Press, 1974.

Van Baaren, Th. P. "The Flexibility of Myth." In Dundes, 217–24.

VanDerBeets, Richard. *The Indian Captivity: An American Genre.* New York: University Press of America, 1984.

————. "The Indian Captivity Narrative as Ritual." *American Literature* 43 (1972): 548–62.

————. "A Surfeit of Style: The Indian Captivity Narrative as Penny Dreadful." *Washington State Research Studies* 39.4 (December 1971): 297–306.

————. " 'A Thirst for Empire': The Indian Captivity Narrative as Propaganda." *Washington State Research Studies* 4.3 (September 1972): 207–15.

Van Keuren, M. Lucille. *American Indian Responses and Reactions to the Colonists as Recorded in Seventeenth- and Eighteenth-Century American Literature.* Ann Arbor: University Microfilms International, 1981.

Viorst, Milton. *Fire in the Streets: America in the 1960s.* New York: Simon and Schuster, 1979.

Voices from Wounded Knee, 1973: In the Words of the Participants. Multi-Media Communications Group of the Mohawk Nation. Rooseveltown, NY: Akwesasne Notes, 1975.

Voight, Francis. *Sacajawea: A See and Read Beginning to Read Biography.* New York: G. P. Putnam's, 1967.

Waldo, Anna Lee. *Sacajawea.* 1979. New York: Avon Books, 1984.

Walsh, Moira. "Films." Review of *The Far Horizon. America* 93 (25 June 1955): 339.

Waltrip, Lela, and Rufus Waltrip. *Indian Women: Thirteen Who Played a Part in the History of America from Earliest Days to Now.* New York: David MacKay, 1964.

Warner, Marina. *Alone of All Her Sex: The Myth and Cult of the Virgin Mary.* New York: Random House, 1983.

Watson, George. *The Story of the Novel.* New York: Harper and Row, 1979.

Weatherford, Jack. *Native Roots: How the Indians Enriched America.* New York: Fawcett Columbine, 1991.

Weinberg, Albert. *Manifest Destiny: A Study of Nationalist Expansion in American History.* Baltimore: Johns Hopkins Press, 1935.

Weist, Katherine M. "Beasts of Burden and Menial Slaves: Nineteenth Century Observations of Northern Plains Indian Women." In Albers and Medicine, 29–52.

Welch, James. *Fools Crow.* New York: Viking, 1986.

——. *Winter in the Blood.* New York: Penguin Books, 1974.

Welter, Barbara. "The Cult of True Womanhood: 1820–1860." *American Quarterly* 18 (Summer 1966): 151–75.

Wessel, Thomas R. "Agent of Acculturation: Farming on the Northern Plains Reservations, 1880–1910." *Agricultural History* 60.2 (Spring 1983): 233–40.

West, Helen B. "The Lewis and Clark Expedition: Our National Epic." *Montana, The Magazine of Western History* 16.3 (July 1966): 2–5.

Wheeler, Olin D. *The Trail of Lewis and Clark, 1804–1904: A Story of the Great Exploration across the Continent in 1803–06; with a Description of the Old Trail, Based upon Actual Travel over It, and of the Changes Found a Century Later.* 1870. 2 vols. Reprint. New York: G. P. Putnam's Sons, 1926.

White, Richard. *"It's Your Misfortune and None of My Own": A History of the American West.* Norman: University of Oklahoma Press, 1991.

——. *The Roots of Dependency: Subsistence, Environment, and Social Change among the Choctaws, Pawnees, and Navajos.* Lincoln: University of Nebraska Press, 1983.

Wiebe, Robert H. *The Search for Order: 1877–1920.* New York: Farrar, Straus, and Giroux, 1967.

Wiget, Andrew, ed. *Native American Literature.* Boston: Twayne, 1985.

Williams, John. *The Redeemed Captive Returning to Zion or the Captivity and Deliverance of Rev. John Williams of Deerfield.* 1795. Reprint. Indian Captivities Series. Springfield: H. R. Hunting, 1969.

Wissler, Clark. *Indians of the United States.* 1940. Reprint. Garden City, NY: Doubleday, 1966.

——. *Red Man Reservations.* New York: Macmillan, 1971. Originally published as *Indian Cavalcade or Life on the Old-Time Indian Reservations.* 1938.

Wolfrom, Anna. *Sacajawea, The Indian Princess: The Indian Girl Who Piloted the Lewis and Clark Expedition across the Rocky Mountains. A Play in Three Acts.* Kansas City: Burton, 1918.

Wright, J. Leitch, Jr. *The Only Land They Knew: The Tragic Story of the American Indians in the Old South.* New York: Free Press, 1981.

Young, Frederick George. "The Higher Significance in the Lewis and Clark Expedition." *Oregon Historical Quarterly* 6.1 (March 1905): 1–25.

Young, Philip. "The Mother of Us All: Pocahontas Reconsidered." *Kenyon Review* 24.3 (Summer 1962): 391–414.

Zahniser, Howard. "Towards the West." *Nature Magazine* 48 (December 1955): 508–9.

Zimm, Bruno. Unnamed Statue of Sacagawea. Sculpture in Bronze. 1904. Displayed during the Louisiana Purchase Exposition in St. Louis, current whereabouts unknown.

Zitkala-Sa. "Impressions of an Indian Childhood." *Atlantic Monthly* 85 (January 1900): 37–47.

———. "An Indian Teacher Among Indians." *Atlantic Monthly* 85 (January 1900): 381–86.

———. "The School Days of an Indian Girl." *Atlantic Monthly* 85 (January 1900): 185–94.

INDEX

Acculturation, 6, 101, 105, 109, 113–14, 124–25, 126, 137, 189. *See also* Assimilation; Cultural diversity/pluralism; Melting pot

Affirmative action programs: cultural responses to, 143–44

Allen, Paul, 32–33, 49, 76

Allen, Paula Gunn, 194, 198, 203; "Pocahontas To Her English Husband," 194, 195, 196; "The One Who Skins Cats," 194–96, 197

American canon, 206

American Indian Movement (AIM), 144–45, 146, 204, 205, 213 (n. 7). *See also* Red Power movement; Trail of Broken Treaties; Wounded Knee Occupation of 1973

American myths. *See* Euro-American myths

American Revolution, 35

American West, 1, 6, 13, 16, 168, 188; images associated with, 13, 16, 38, 68, 179–80; masculinity of, 116, 180, 212 (n. 4). *See also* Frontier; Frontier myths; Manifest destiny

Anthologies of native texts, 198–99, 219 (n. 6)

Anthony, Susan B., 66, 216 (n. 7)

Apaches, 73, 101

Aquash, Anna Mae, 204–205, 220 (n. 8)

Arikaras, 46, 93, 115, 210

Army Corps of Engineers, 111–12, 114, 144–45. *See also* Dam projects

Assimilation, 21, 24, 93–94, 101, 105, 109, 111–14, 115, 124–25, 137, 172, 177. *See also* Acculturation; Cultural diversity/pluralism; Melting pot

Autobiographies by native peoples, 201, 206

Banks, Dennis, 146, 204

Bataille, Gretchen: and Charles Silet, 147, 213 (n. 7); and Kathleen Sands, 184, 213 (n. 8)

Berger, Peter, and Thomas Luckmann, 67, 174

Biddle, Nicholas, 32, 49, 76, 215 (n. 12). *See also* Biddle edition of the Lewis and Clark journals

Biddle edition of the Lewis and Clark journals, 32–33, 46, 49, 63–64, 76, 81, 98, 115, 214 (nn. 1, 2), 215 (n. 12); as composite narrative, 32, 64; as mythic text, 51, 58, 63; on captains' heroism, 58; on female subordination, 46; on native childbirth, 47; on savagery and civilization, 47; Sacagawea's illness, 58; Sacagawea's role in the mission, 50, 55, 62

Biographies by native peoples, 201–202

Bird Woman by Leonard Crunelle, 10, 67, 90, 97, 209; as mythic text, 90, 92, 94–96, 209; dedication ceremony, 92–94; memorabilia associated with, 9–10; native attendance at dedication, 92–94; on Sacagawea's heroism, 96, 210; promotional campaign, 90–92; unveiling, 94. *See also* Crunelle, Leonard

Blackfeet, 197–98

Boarding schools for native children, 93, 168, 204, 219–20 (n. 7)

Borden, William, 140, 161–62, 170,

ABOUT THE AUTHOR

DONNA J. KESSLER is a Professor of Humanities, Embry-Riddle Aeronautical University, Daytona Beach, Florida. She received her bachelor's degree from Mary University in Bismarck, North Dakota, her master's from North Dakota State University in Fargo, North Dakota, and her doctorate from Emory University in Atlanta, Georgia.